UNSUSTAINABLE

Unsustainable

*Measurement, Reporting, and the
Limits of Corporate Sustainability*

Matthew Archer

NEW YORK UNIVERSITY PRESS
New York

NEW YORK UNIVERSITY PRESS
New York
www.nyupress.org

Please contact the Library of Congress for Cataloging-in-Publication data.
ISBN: 9781479822003 (hardback)
ISBN: 9781479822010 (paperback)
ISBN: 9781479822034 (library ebook)
ISBN: 9781479822027 (consumer ebook)

This book is printed on acid-free paper, and its binding materials are chosen for strength
and durability. We strive to use environmentally responsible suppliers and materials to the
greatest extent possible in publishing our books.

Manufactured in the United States of America

10 9 8 7 6 5 4 3 2 1

Also available as an ebook

To my parents, to my sister, and to Jan

CONTENTS

Introduction

Calculating Corporations

On October 1, 2015, the International Trade Center (ITC) launched a new initiative called the "Blue Number" at its annual Trade for Sustainable Development (T4SD) Forum. The theme of the forum was "Building Sustainable Supply Chains," meant to highlight the way supply chain transparency and traceability schemes could impact small farmers and other marginalized producers. In the opening speech, ITC executive director Arancha González confidently assured the audience that her organization's new initiative would promote sustainability in global supply chains by giving farmers in the Global South a unique "geolocation number" and setting up an "online networking platform" they could use to share information about their sustainability practices. The initiative had been developed in collaboration with the United Nations Global Compact, a voluntary corporate sustainability initiative led, in principle at least, by the CEOs and other senior executives of several thousand companies around the world. Farmers who chose to participate in the scheme would be assigned a Blue Number—named in homage to the United Nations and its bright-blue logo—linking them to a database containing information about their location, contact details, gender, and the products they sold. The idea behind the Blue Number initiative was that it would not only allow Southern farmers to share and access information about sustainability "best practices" but also allow Northern buyers to source their products from producers who fit their sustainability criteria; the hypothetical example that González offered during her remarks was a company that could use the Blue Number platform to source ingredients from women-owned farms, thus generating a measurable social impact. For González, the Blue Number was a potentially revolutionary tool that, through the proliferation of data about farmers' lives and livelihoods, would enhance the social, environmental, and economic sustainability of the global supply chains that entrain these farmers and their products.

The next day, the T4SD Forum moved across the street, from the World Trade Organization's sprawling campus on Geneva's *rive droite* to the offices of the World Meteorological Organization, where speakers on four different panels reinforced the data-driven approach to sustainability typified by the Blue Number initiative. In the day's opening session, panelists talked about the need for more concrete standards and more consistent indicators for measuring progress against the T4SD program's set of four "core principles," which included sustainability, transparency, harmonization, and alignment with the now-ubiquitous Sustainable Development Goals (SDGs). The SDGs had been formally adopted a week earlier at the UN Sustainable Development Summit in New York City, and like many sustainability initiatives since then, the Blue Number was explicitly linked to these vague and seemingly all-encompassing goals. A later session reiterated the need to harmonize the definition of different sustainability indicators and developing new, more rigorous measurement and reporting mechanisms, while another session that afternoon focused on the need to create metrics that would allow different actors in global supply chains to track their "continual improvement" over time. The conclusion of the forum was clear: building sustainable supply chains requires data about sustainability, and lots of it.

This lesson was repeated a few weeks later at the United Nations Forum on Business and Human Rights, where there were sessions on topics like "measuring and tracking businesses' implementation of the UN Guiding Principles on Business and Human Rights" and "measuring states' implementation" of these same guiding principles. A session on the role of corporate reporting featured speakers from companies in the private sector like Statoil and Ericsson alongside representatives from government bodies such as Chile's Ministry of Foreign Affairs and nongovernmental organizations (NGOs) like the Global Reporting Initiative. In an attempt to move "beyond reporting," the ambition of one group of speakers was to figure out a way to shift away from annual or even quarterly reporting toward the production of a more continuous and accessible stream of data about companies' impacts on human rights. The key takeaway from a pair of sessions that presented different examples of multistakeholder initiatives to implement the guiding prin-

ciples was that we need to develop new ways of measuring corporations'
progress on human rights in contexts ranging from industrial tomato
farms in Florida to textile factories in Cambodia that supply companies
like H&M and Zara.

In my field notes from these conferences, the quality and consistency
of indicators emerged as the primary concern for sustainability professionals working in contexts ranging from government ministries and
NGOs to global investment banks and oil companies. They believed that
measuring and reporting sustainability performance would invariably
improve sustainability performance. Conversations that were grounded
in concerns about the welfare of marginalized communities or the protection of endangered species invariably shifted to a discussion of the
challenge of measuring the impacts of specific interventions on these
problems. Defining, measuring, and reporting indicators of social and
environmental impact became a first step toward sustainability, which
my informants consistently told me was a journey rather than a destination. Indeed, this concern with metrics has become ubiquitous in
sustainability discourse, often following the "but" that is invariably ap-
pended to the announcement of an ambitious goal or target. During my
fieldwork, business leaders often claimed that they were deeply committed to enhancing the sustainability of their operations but that they were
waiting for regulators or other nonprofit actors to develop and enforce
industry standards. Investors claimed that they believed in the business
case for sustainability at a theoretical level but that they needed more
data on the environmental, social, and governance (or ESG) aspects of
invested companies before they could make a strong case to their clients.
Even informants working for NGOs and in research institutions insisted
that defining and measuring key performance indicators (KPIs) should
be the first task of global sustainability efforts, prompting a wave of both
nonprofit and for-profit initiatives and services aimed at improving sustainability data.

In nearly all the panels I attended, someone made a point about a
collective need to refine the definition of various sustainability indicators and to develop platforms for reporting and disseminating the data
that companies collect about these indicators. If the panelists failed to
address the topic of sustainability indicators on their own, a member
of the audience would usually ask a question about it. Although these

conferences were advertised as opportunities to discuss solutions to issues ranging from child slavery to illegal dumping of toxic waste, they
inevitably concluded with a call for better measurement and reporting
as a way of promoting transparency and accountability in global supply chains. Conversations about gender-based violence or biodiversity
loss smoothly evolved into conversations about the paucity of reliable
and consistent data about the scope of these problems, the difficulty of
measuring the extent to which specific actors are responsible for these
problems, and the necessity of developing more rigorous methods for
collecting, analyzing, and reporting data about these problems. Calls
for better data were typically followed by calls for more advanced technologies for collecting, analyzing, and disseminating data. At these conferences, sustainability professionals from corporations and financial
institutions sat beside academics and policy makers on panels about
topics like deforestation and human rights and greenhouse gas emissions, and they all seemed to agree that better metrics were the key to
solving these diverse problems.

The idea that better data about sustainability would lead to better sustainability outcomes was ubiquitous throughout the fieldwork I did following these conferences. Since starting my research in this area in the
fall of 2015, the cultivation of new and improved sources of data alongside more advanced ways of defining and measuring the diverse social
and environmental impacts of multinational corporations has remained
a constant theme in different field sites, from ESG analysts and impact
investors interested in improving the sustainability performance of their
portfolios to NGOs committed to mitigating the social and environmental impacts of products, companies, or entire sectors. Often, as in the
case of one organization's attempt to develop a framework for measuring
and reporting social capital, it was what drove their work, a necessary
first step—often pithily summarized by the managerialist maxim, "You
can't manage what you can't measure"—that seemed to become the final
step for many of my informants. At other times, it was used as a justification for more intense regimes of monitoring and surveillance of the people whom sustainability initiatives were supposed to help. And in other
instances, the growing obsession with measurement, reporting, and the
data that these activities generate led to a surprising ethical stance, as
in the case of financial analysts who see the profitable proliferation of

ESG data not only as a professional responsibility but as a key part of their moral responsibility as well. In this context, "the market" becomes ethicalized as a key part of sustainability professionals' ethical intersubjectivity.[1] In the years since I started this research, blockchain-enabled transparency and traceability schemes have emerged as a common feature of proposed sustainability initiatives, reflecting not only an embrace of the kinds of technological fixes that characterize eco-modernism but also a strong commitment to a particular form of sustainability that revolves around the measurement and reporting of diverse indicators of sustainability performance.[2] Data-driven sustainability, after all, only works if there is enough data to drive it.

Data, Data, Everywhere

This book examines the growing preoccupation with sustainability metrics, indicators, and data across distinct but related contexts. Based on extensive ethnographic research among people responsible for designing and implementing corporate sustainability projects in different contexts, it identifies the discourse around defining, measuring, and reporting sustainability impacts as a key feature of contemporary sustainability. And it also shows how this focus on measurement is a key impediment to the kinds of political action necessary to effectively mitigate and prepare for the inevitable impacts of the Earth's changing climate. Drawing on this research, it argues that the seemingly endless debates about the definitions and measurements of sustainability have obscured the extent to which businesses and their investors are able to shirk responsibility for social and environmental problems while profiting from the solutions they propose and support. At corporate sustainability and sustainable finance conferences, in interviews with sustainability professionals, and in the ever-increasing flurry of sustainability reports that their employers disseminate, my informants pay close attention to the way indicators are defined, measured, and reported. From sustainability managers at multinational food companies to investment analysts at Swiss private banks to people working at NGOs who are critical of industry-led sustainability initiatives, the most important task for my informants was to identify KPIs that are then used to establish clear baselines and track progress against well-defined, data-driven goals. This approach to sustainability is grounded in an ideology that the media theorist José van Dijck describes as "dataism," a belief in the objectivity of quantitative indicators and metrics that motivates the idea that things like human social and ecological relations can—and should—be understood through data.[3] I use the word "data" here like my informants do, denoting large amounts of ideally quantitative or at least quantifiable information, something that can be entered into a spreadsheet and transformed into an "objective" indicator of social, environmental, or economic performance. In one interview, I described a photography exhibition I had visited in London, which had been sponsored by the tea brand Twinings to showcase the impacts of its in-house sustainability initiative, called "Sourced with Care." My informant, who worked for a standards development organization, scoffed, "Anecdotes aren't data." On the basis of what he perceived as a lack of reliable, verifiable data, he dismissed the "Sourced with Care" campaign as greenwashing. Without the kind of "objective data" collected through surveys, audits, and various forms of monitoring, my informants insisted that it was impossible to know if they were really making an impact.

On the surface, the idea that sustainability solutions should be "data driven" and "evidence based" seems unproblematic, as do calls for greater transparency, traceability, and accountability in global supply chains and financial networks. Yet the perverse "seductions" of this kind of quantified approach to sustainability, as the anthropologist Sally Engle Merry has shown us, are myriad.[4] Numerical indicators of things like gender equality and human rights abuses offer knowledge about problems that are so complex that they might otherwise be intractable, helping people set goals and understand whether they are making progress toward achieving them. But within this sociotechnical imaginary of sustainability, the diverse narratives and experiences of unsustainability that defy quantification get excluded and overlooked, as do alternative approaches to sustainability that rely on other ways of seeing the world.[5] Quantitative indicators, according to Merry, rely on numerical knowledge that is often "decontextualized, homogenized, and remote from local systems of meaning."[6] My informants' commitment to measuring and reporting sustainability indicators as a necessary "first step" both reflects and reinforces an incrementalist approach to sustainability that precludes more stringent rules- and rights-based approaches. Rather than banning investments in new hydrocarbon developments, for instance, financial institutions use ESG and financial data to make investment decisions that take a more "balanced" approach to social, environmental, and economic concerns; rather than refusing to allow corporations to purloin and pollute Indigenous lands, we accept (or are forced to accept) corporate calculations of relative costs and benefits, which, in most cases, seem to favor economic growth and "development." The analysis of quantitative sustainability indicators can lead to rather baffling conclusions, with important political repercussions. Through the types of metrics that my informants develop and promote, countries like Denmark, which produces more waste per capita than almost any other nation, and Norway, a petrostate, are consistently ranked among the world's most sustainable countries, while countries like Bhutan, which has resisted neoliberal efforts to commoditize its old-growth forests for decades, and Ecuador, which in 2008 enshrined the rights of nature (Pachamama) in its constitution, are ranked much farther down the list.[7] By relying on these kinds of indicators and the rankings they facilitate, places like Scandinavia become a model for sustainability, reinscribing the wastefulness, consumerism, and numerous inequities on which the ostensible success of Scandinavian societies is built. Although the focus of this book is on corporate sustainability, the fact that many people are so comfortable ranking countries in terms of their sustainability, typically with little regard for the colonial histories that led to their current levels of relative "sustainability," shows how pervasive—and how powerful—this quantified, data-driven approach to sustainability is.

These quantitative indicators have other insidious effects that warrant critical scholarly attention.[8] They lend an air of objectivity and rationality to the political decisions that are based on them, making these decisions difficult to contest and portraying those who resist them as ignorant and backward.[9] The "trust in numbers" inherent in this kind of policy making obscures the extent to which the production of these numbers is as contested and negotiated as other forms of knowledge production, just as it hides the power of technical experts and the organizations that employ them.[10] In the past, these experts often worked for the state, and there is a huge body of scholarship that shows how different accounting systems—from the development of scientific forestry to colonial census records to impact assessments in contemporary universities—is intimately and inextricably linked to the state's exercise and enforcement of power.[11] As businesses and financial institutions have come to play an increasingly prominent role in determining the outcomes of sustainability negotiations, their power is also enhanced—and obscured—by this preoccupation with quantitative metrics, subjugating social and environmental sustainability to the logic of financial markets by rendering social and environmental impacts *commensurable*—that is, able to be compared using a common metric—with readily available measures of financial performance such as gross domestic product (GDP) or stock prices (themselves only apparently "objective").[12] Similar to the development industry's embrace of management consultants and its reorientation toward quantified targets, we now look to the experts and analysts working in the private sector for cutting-edge information on sustainability, at places like RobecoSAM and Dow Jones, which produce well-known sustainability indexes and conduct market research on sustainable investing.[13] Corporations and their investors have moved to the center of debates about sustainable development, not as targets of these debates but as active participants in the so-called multistakeholder initiatives that produce guidelines and standards for measuring and reporting their social and environmental impacts.

Within the "metrological regimes" or "metrological systems" that these initiatives generate, human and nonhuman actors alike have to follow the rules of measurement and accounting. Society and the environment are reimagined in terms of quantitative data about impacts, paving the way for their subsequent enrollment in the logic of the market and circuits of capital. Human geographers like Andrew Barry, Mark Cooper, and Susanne Freidberg have shown how these metrological regimes are exceedingly fragile, a house of cards easily toppled by claims that the indicators they generate were not rigorously defined and measured or by the emergence of updated reporting and verification standards.[14] And yet, the fragility of a specific metrological regime does little to challenge the notion that there should be a metrological regime in the first place. Instead, every time corporations, banks, and international organizations respond to the perceived fragility of these systems by trying to improve them, they reinforce the idea that these metrological regimes are in fact necessary. By constantly debating the way we should define sustainability indicators, the methods we should use to measure them, and the guidelines we should adopt to govern their dissemination, more fundamental debates about the political and ethical repercussions of theorizing sustainability as a measurable phenomenon get pushed aside. The assumption that we *should* be measuring these indicators comes to be deeply embedded in the notion of sustainability itself.

The logic underlying the focus on recording and disclosing a company's social and environmental impacts is that the market, equipped with accurate data about social and environmental impacts, will lead to the efficient and optimal distribution of these impacts, both positive and negative, such as offsetting pollution at one point in time or space with investments in pollution mitigation elsewhere (or even more dubiously, offsetting those emissions with positive social outcomes like poverty reduction).[15] Companies come to be seen as sustainable if they are reporting data about their impacts, because these reports help the market work more efficiently. Industry publications like *Corporate Knights* and investment research firms like RobecoSAM confer awards like "World's Most Sustainable Company" and give gold medals for sustainability performance on the basis of the amount of data companies disclose and how faithfully their disclosures comply with standardized reporting protocols like those published by the Global Reporting Initiative and similar organizations. Meanwhile, financial institutions like hedge funds and insurance companies have almost all adopted some kind of ESG strategy, leading to dubious but widely circulated claims that there are now trillions of dollars of sustainably managed assets and generating a narrative that the financial industry's sustainability performance is rapidly improving. Although the past few years have witnessed a growing number of journalists, regulators, and even industry representatives who are critical of ESG's role in "greenwashing," the solutions they propose invariably rely on further standardizing and expanding both the scale and scope of ESG measurement and reporting. NGOs like the Rainforest Alliance might seem like different animals, but their annual impact reports also increasingly focus more on disclosing data about their operations and providing technical accounts of their "impact pathways" rather than on offering grounded, context-specific accounts of whether and how they are making a difference.

Put differently, banks, corporations, and NGOs come to be celebrated for disclosing quantitative data about their sustainability performance, no matter what the data actually say, because there is an implicit assumption that by virtue of disclosing these data, the market will use them to generate the most sustainable outcomes. Producing these data, in turn, becomes one of these institutions' main sustainability goals. The crux of the problem is that efforts to buttress sustainability's admittedly fragile metrological regimes by figuring out more rigorous and "objective" ways to measure sustainability impacts end up facilitating the expansion of oppressive market logics into (previously) nonmarket domains.[16] One informant who works for an organization that develops standards that help other organizations demonstrate their social and environmental impacts described her day-to-day work as focused almost exclusively on figuring out ways to make the data the organization collects more accurate and reliable, telling me about the rules it has around reporting and especially auditing. While she "appreciate[s] advocacy organizations" that organize protests and target specific companies, she personally prefers "working for an organization that uses the market to achieve its aims." By contributing to the development and enforcement of standards that lead to the production and dissemination of accurate, verifiable data about impacts, this informant believed that she was enabling markets to efficiently manage everything from gender inequality to biodiversity threats. As we will see, "the market" in this imaginary is faceless and amorphous, sometimes a convenient scapegoat but more often an entity that sustainability professionals imagine themselves collaborating with to achieve their sustainability objectives, a kind of engagement that helps obscure this power of the multinational corporations and banks that control this ostensibly "free" market. If the propensity to quantify and measure impacts contributes to market rule, as Mark Cooper has argued, it also further empowers those market actors who are already very powerful.[17]

Broken Promises

We hear a lot these days about companies trying to be more sustainable and the leading role they are supposed to play in what is often referred to as "green" or "sustainable" transitions. They set targets for reducing their emissions. They support organizations that are committed to rainforest conservation and join multistakeholder roundtables to negotiate new standards for chopping down those rain forests and replacing them with industrial farms. They sponsor local sports teams and set up small community development funds. Their CEOs sit on panels in university lecture halls munching on vegan snacks served with biodegradable cutlery while talking about the business case for sustainability. Hedge fund managers write public investor relations letters promising that they will take charge in achieving global sustainability, not just because it is the right thing to do but because it is also the most profitable thing to do. They emphasize all the money they spend to develop clean energy technologies and all the time their workers spend in sustainability training modules. They establish incubators to support sustainability entrepreneurs. Nearly every large corporation is a member or signatory of one of the dozens of sustainability schemes that have proliferated over the past few decades—the World Business Council for Sustainable Development (WBCSD), the United Nations Principles for Responsible Investing (PRI), the Global Reporting Initiative (GRI), the United Nations Global Compact (UNGC), B-Corp, the Roundtable for Sustainable Palm Oil (RSPO), and so on. As ESG indicators come to play an increasingly prominent role in narratives around environmentally sustainable and socially responsible finance, banks and asset managers gleefully tout the tens of trillions of dollars they have invested "sustainably," a number that has grown exponentially over the past few years. Business newspapers like the *Wall Street Journal* and the *Financial Times* celebrate these investments, waxing poetic about the visionary sustainability leadership of the companies and banks that stand sentry at the ever-expanding frontiers of green capitalism. Even as these outlets grow increasingly critical of the way nonstandardized ESG reports can facilitate greenwashing, their critiques typically end up reinforcing the idea that sustainability needs to be quantified and measured, calling for more rigorous measurement and reporting guidelines rather than questioning the logic of market-driven sustainability governance.

At the same time, greenhouse gas emissions are growing rather than subsiding, old-growth forests are being cleared for monocrop plantations and meat production, storms and droughts and wildfires are increasing in both frequency and severity, average temperatures are soaring, plant and animal species are blinking out of existing, and sea levels are rising unabated.[18] Of all the market-oriented initiatives developed and promoted by banks and corporations in collaboration with the political elites of industrialized countries to mitigate their negative social and environmental impacts and channel money toward adaptation efforts, few have delivered any noticeable results. In the face of all this, the legal scholar David Whyte theorizes the modern corporation as an ecocidal force without parallel in human history, a form mobilized by detached stakeholders to increase profits no matter the social or environmental cost. "The corporation," he argues, "is a major threat to us, yet it is a threat that we are not taking seriously enough. If the threats to our environment are left under the control of CEOs and capitalist investors, acting through corporations, all we will be able to do is appeal to their better judgement. The tactic of asking politely is doomed to fail."[19] The paradox of corporate sustainability is systemic. As Murray Bookchin writes, "One might more easily persuade a green plant to desist from photosynthesis than to ask the bourgeois economy to desist from capital accumulation," an economy in which "the plunder of nature" is foundational.[20]

This book shows how the tools and techniques of corporate sustainability and sustainable finance do little, if anything, to address the immense problems we are facing. By rendering society, the environment, and the economy commensurate through the common metric of quantified and often monetized sustainability indicators, corporate sustainability, sustainable finance, and sustainable development practitioners contribute to the subjugation of these diverse domains to a regime of neoliberal governance, a mode of governance in which "the market" obscures the power and privilege of large corporations and their investors. This approach to managing the relationship between society, the environment, and the economy is both rooted in and reproduces moral and political ecologies of extraction, dispossession, and domination.

Understanding this pervasive and increasingly hegemonic definition of sustainability as something that can be calculated and then left to the market to achieve is key to understanding why contemporary sustainability keeps failing to deliver on its promises.

In general, I think most people intrinsically have a much more complex understanding of the relationships that sustainability requires us to navigate than the metrological regimes of corporate sustainability and sustainable finance can account for and manage, and I think most people are skeptical of relying on corporations to save the world from intersecting crises that those same corporations, embedded in a globalized capitalist political economy, originated. And yet, the dominant approach to sustainability, one that is defined by market-oriented measurement and reporting protocols, leaves very little room for the kind of imagining and organizing needed to resist the logic of profit-driven corporations and the increasingly intense regimes of extraction, consumption, and waste on which they rely. In describing the ways in which the contemporary sustainability industry reinforces itself and thinking about the kinds of futures this industry forecloses, this book offers a useful tool in the ongoing struggle against the market's outsize influence over our lives and livelihoods.[21]

Neoliberal Sustainability

The relationship between my informants' blinkered focus on the measurement of sustainability impacts and the rule of markets turns on the relationship between commensuration and neoliberalism. To make sense of this, it is necessary to explain what I mean by "neoliberal sustainability," since it is a phrase I will use rather frequently throughout the remainder of the book. Neoliberalism, according to the geographer David Harvey, reflects an assumption that markets not only are able to solve problems but are the best tool for solving problems. It is "a theory of political economic practices that . . . holds that the social good will be maximized by maximizing the reach and frequency of market transactions, and it seeks to bring all human action into the domain of the market."[22] Within this neoliberal worldview, the problems that markets are supposedly able to solve extend far beyond economic problems, encompassing social and environmental problems as well. If we theorize the social and environmental problems related to corporate activities as externalities caused by imperfect markets, then the solution seems obvious: internalize them by putting a price on them and let the market work its magic, yielding efficient distributions of goods and bads, of costs and benefits.[23] Internalizing these costs and benefits so the market can manage them involves making them legible to the market, rendering them commensurable by giving them a value—sometimes explicitly monetary but almost always numerical (which makes statistical correlations relatively simple)—that the market can interpret and act on. Thus, the solutions that gain the most traction in global climate negotiations tend to be programs like payments for ecosystem services and carbon markets, which reinforce, rather than challenge, the growth-focused neoliberal logic of contemporary capitalism.

The answer, then, to the question of why my informants care so deeply about measuring and reporting impacts is that they believe that once these impacts are measured and reported, market dynamics will lead to sustainable outcomes. For them, sustainability cannot happen without sustainability indicators. In advocating an approach to sustainability that relies on the market to take the outputs of their work (sustainability reports) and use those outputs to generate more sustainable outcomes, they offer a perfect case of the mechanics of neoliberal sustainability. Neoliberal sustainability, as we will see, manifests itself in many different ways, transgressing the divides of ethical, epistemological, and even ontological inquiry. It goes to the heart of our understandings about what is right and wrong; it shifts what we accept as evidence of good or bad sustainability performance; and it sits rather incongruously with the reality of the modern corporation and its role in a global capitalist political economy.

With that in mind, I understand neoliberal sustainability as more of an orientation to a problem rather than a particular solution, even if several purported solutions—payments for ecosystem services, carbon markets, sustainability certification schemes, and so on—epitomize neoliberal sustainability. From the perspective of neoliberal sustainability, unsustainability is seen as problem that is best attributed to imperfect markets rather than something that is systemic in capitalist socioecological relations of extraction, exploitation, and accumulation. What this means is that much of the work of sustainability—work that is performed in large part by my informants—involves doing things that sustainability professionals think will make it more likely that the market will yield more sustainable outcomes. This includes things like defining and redefining certain indicators, trying to increase the uptake of these particular definitions, and promoting the standardization of more rigorous methods for measuring these indicators and more transparent modes of reporting these measurements. If, on the one hand, Harvey is correct in asserting that, within the context of neoliberalism, the state's primary role is to facilitate the expansion of markets, and if, on the other hand, the so-called retreat of the state has indeed left a vacuum wherein multinational corporations are able to concentrate their power, then it makes sense that corporations themselves (alongside investors and business-friendly NGOs) are now responsible for facilitating this expansion.[24] They do this by promoting a mode of socioecological accountability that implicitly relies on "the market" to achieve its sustainability goals, conveniently obscuring corporate and investor power, even as that power grows.

The seemingly pedantic debates about what to measure and how to measure are a defining feature of neoliberal sustainability, transforming immanently political discussions about accountability and responsibility into technical squabbles about calculative methods. Corporations and banks rely on the ostensible rigor and objectivity of standardized measurement and reporting protocols to demonstrate both their commitment to sustainability (in widely circulated corporate sustainability reports) and to shirk responsibility for the negative impacts they generate through their operations and through their investments. As Susanne Freidberg reminds us, companies are not merely interested in measuring as a means of management but also "seek to manage the measures" in order to ensure that sustainability's "still-malleable metrics . . . come to serve their own business models."[25] Even when they attempt to account for public concerns through structured protocols for stakeholder engagement, the kinds of technical reports these organizations regularly publish, according to the environmental anthropologist Karen Hébert, tend to "[reinscribe] the validity of some forms of authority over others and [limit] the political possibilities of certain spokespersons." Through an ethnographic analysis of the production of a report on the potential social and environmental effects of mineral development in Bristol Bay,

Alaska, Hébert shows how technical approaches to both past harms and future risks "prematurely [foreclose] the possible futures that might be envisioned through participatory activities."[26] These kinds of reports also foreclose the more radical or transformative actions that are increasingly necessary to both mitigate and adapt to the worst effects of climate change, leaving these effects to manifest themselves unchecked while elites nitpick about methods for measuring and evaluating risks. As the environmental scientists James Dyke, Wolfgang Knorr, and Robert Watson pithily observe, "The path to disastrous climate change is paved with feasibility studies and impact assessments."[27]

Ethnographies of Neoliberal Sustainability

The arguments in this book draw on qualitative data collected through participant observation, interviews, and document analysis conducted between 2015 and 2021. For over a decade, there has been a growing interest among ethnographers in the topic of corporate sustainability and corporate social responsibility, typically from the perspective of the people and communities who find themselves on the receiving end of corporate efforts to mitigate some harm or clean up some mess, from polluted mining sites in South Africa and Indonesia to polluted towns in upstate New York and southern Louisiana.[28] Whereas much of this research has focused on the interface between unsustainable multinational corporations and affected communities, my work goes behind the scenes to the conference centers and board rooms where corporate sustainability initiatives are designed and negotiated.[29] In an effort to achieve what Laura Nader has called "studying up," ethnographers interested in the inner workings of banks, corporations, and other typically walled-off organizations often have to get creative, foregoing the traditional year or two of detailed, site-specific participant observation for a more "patchwork" or mosaic approach, taking advantage of public industry conferences and corporate receptions to meet people who can help negotiate access to their colleagues.[30] As the anthropologist of finance Daniel Souleles argues, even if luck plays some role in the success of these kinds of projects, planning, persistence, and flexibility are even more important.[31]

The fieldwork for this book was conducted as part of three separate but connected research projects that rarely went to plan but nevertheless yielded interesting results. Although my informants worked in different contexts, from sustainable development to sustainable finance, they were mostly united in their embodiment of what I call the "sustainability ethic," an orientation toward social and environmental problems that has two main elements: the first is a genuine commitment to solving these diverse problems; the second is a belief that only market-based solutions can solve them and a subsequent commitment to developing and promoting market-based solutions.[32] The sustainability ethic is where value and values meet, and in my informants' attempts to act on their sustainability ethic, much of their work ended up revolving around a collective effort to render the diverse values of sustainability commensurable through the definition and measurement of different kinds of quantitative indicators.

Sustainability Professionals in Switzerland

Between September 2015 and August 2016, I conducted a year of fieldwork in Geneva, Switzerland, among a group of people I started to refer to as "sustainability professionals." By that term, I mean people who work on sustainability in professional settings, either as the main part of their job (as, say, the global head of sustainability at a private bank) or for an organization that is focused on sustainability (like most of the people working at the World Business Council for Sustainable Development). The category "sustainability professional" also highlights the professionalization of sustainability, in which a specific set of practices and orientations has emerged over the past few decades that is characterized by a commitment to market-based sustainability solutions and work that revolves around attempts to define and measure sustainability impacts. In Geneva, I conducted participant observation and more than a hundred informal and semistructured interviews at different organizations that promote corporate sustainability, sustainable finance, and market-based sustainable development, often exchanging my unpaid labor (e.g., as a research assistant) for access to staff meetings, conference fee waivers, and so on. This helped me gain access to the day-to-day work of these organizations, which in turn legitimized my participation at workshops and conferences on corporate sustainability and sustainable finance. Many of my informants worked for large companies or banks, but the majority of them worked *with* those companies, either as sustainability consultants in the private sector or as employees of the numerous NGOs and international organizations in Geneva that work to promote corporate sustainability and sustainable finance.

Sustainability Certifications in the Kenyan Tea Supply Chain

More recently, between 2018 and 2020, I conducted research as part of a team of anthropologists working on a project at Copenhagen Business School that was designed to better understand the role of voluntary sustainability standards in the governance of the Kenyan tea supply chain. My role on the project focused on the design, marketing, and enforcement of these standards, and while my colleagues' work was grounded in sites of Kenyan tea production and exchange, my work took a more global view due to the nature of the standards (and standards organizations) I was studying, which rarely focused on a single commodity (like tea) or a single production area (like Kenya). Between 2018 and 2020, I conducted more than sixty interviews with people working in standards development organizations, major tea brands, international organizations, and independent tea shops. I also spent nearly two months in London, Amsterdam, Rotterdam, Hamburg, New York, and Washington, DC, where I conducted interviews, site visits, and participant observation with these informants. Alongside these interviews and observations, I cultivated a large archive of documents pertaining to sustainability in the tea supply chain, such as Unilever webpages, Rainforest Alliance press releases, and research reports from organizations like the Food and Agriculture Organization (FAO); previous, current, and draft versions of popular sustainability standards; and guidelines and training materials that sustainability organizations publish to help farmers comply with their standards more effectively. Although many of my informants worked for large tea companies and tea traders, most of them worked for various standards developers and sustainability organizations.

ESG at Norebank

Finally, the book draws on research conducted in 2018 and 2019 that examined a bank's efforts to integrate ESG considerations into its investment process. A member of the sustainability team at the bank, which I call Norebank, helped me set up interviews with his colleagues on the sustainability team, as well as with approximately twenty investment managers, for a total of around thirty interviews. More than anything, these interviews helped show how investors think about the sustainability of their investments vis-à-vis the sustainability of the companies in which they are invested, establishing a clear link between corporate sustainability, sustainable finance, and sustainable development.

A Note on Access

A few things facilitated the kind of access necessary to conduct ethnographic research on corporate sustainability and sustainable finance: First, as a White person from the United States studying at an elite university, my efforts to make contact with people working in the Geneva sustainability scene were enhanced by a level of cultural capital that many people do not have. I became acutely aware of this fact when I lost some of that cultural capital, after moving to Europe to take up an academic position at a university that did not have the same cachet as an Ivy League university, where it was noticeably harder to access companies like Unilever and Tata Global Beverages. During my dissertation research, when my informants introduced me to other people who they thought were relevant to my project—what qualitative researchers refer to as "snowball" sampling—they often introduced me as a PhD student at Yale studying corporate sustainability, which added to their own credibility and made networking relatively easy. As a student, moreover, I was less of a threat than if I had been a well-known critical researcher with a big platform.

Second, I did my PhD research at the School of Forestry and Environmental Studies (now the Yale School of the Environment), which, due to its intimacy with the Yale School of Management and its many alumni who have gone on to have successful careers in the fields I was studying, afforded me access that a different department at a different university (e.g., anthropology or human geography) might have impeded, given these disciplines' more openly critical stance toward corporate sustainability. At conferences, I met people who were more willing to talk to me because they or their colleagues had studied in the same department or because they had read a book by one of the school's more public-facing professors, whose practitioner-focused books on corporate sustainability and sustainable finance are popular references among aspiring sustainability professionals.

To put it simply, my informants were able to recognize me as one of their own. This certainly affected the kinds of insights I was able to glean through interviews and participant observation, and yet it is an important perspective precisely because these are the people who shape global sustainability debates and determine which sustainability initiatives get funded and promoted. Like me, they were mostly White and middle or upper-middle class, although many of them were actually quite wealthy. Although most of my informants were Europeans, they all spoke English fluently and comfortably, having pursued international careers after studying at elite universities in the United States and the United Kingdom, often after earning their high school diplomas from private international schools (they regularly talked about their "IB," or international baccalaureate, experience). It is probably not surprising that most of the people working in corporate sustainability in places like Switzerland and Scandinavia are White, and the few people of color I encountered during my fieldwork were often from very privileged backgrounds, members of elite families in Asia and, less often, Africa. Among my informants, women seemed to outnumber men in corporate sustainability and especially in sustainability-focused NGOs, although the managers in these organizations were still predominantly men; finance, on the other hand, remains a thoroughly male-dominated field. Although I interviewed several women working in sustainable finance (on the sustainability team at Norebank and as sustainability managers of private banks in Switzerland), I interviewed only one woman working in finance who was working in "conventional" investing rather than on her employer's sustainability team.

Pluralizing Sustainability

In focusing on the elite spaces in which sustainability professionals define and enforce a particular approach to sustainability, I am not trying to caricature sustainability as the invention of a monolithic West that is imposed on the rest of the world. Nor am I trying to suggest that all sustainability professionals working today will agree with each other or even necessarily see themselves in the people I describe in this book. In practice, sustainability is necessarily as diverse as the countless unsustainabilities to which it responds, leading scholars across disciplines to approach sustainability as a pluralized phenomenon.[33] As the feminist anthropologist Debarati Sen shows in her ethnography of Darjeeling tea plantations, sustainability is just one of innumerable points in the swirling constellation of social, environmental, and economic concerns that constitute people's everyday lives, and it is different in each permutation.[34] At the same time, through a focus on standardizing the measurement and reporting of impacts, corporate sustainability—rooted in an assumption that the social, the environmental, and the economic are distinct but commensurable domains—undermines and attempts to curb that plurality. As Julie Sze and colleagues write, "Sustainability depends on context," and yet banks and corporations peddle a market-driven approach to sustainability that they insist is applicable in every context.[35] The spread of neoliberal sustainability precludes versions of sustainability that might actually make the world a better place to live for more than just the lucky few in places where climate change and its socioecological effects will be relatively manageable.[36] It leaves little room for the kinds of everyday sustainabilities and everyday environmentalisms that people design in response their pluriversal (as opposed to universal) experiences of changing socioecologies.[37] It aggressively undermines the "bad environmentalism" of the poor and working class, enhancing the power of profit-seeking actors to impose their own language of valuation and inhibiting the proliferation of more diverse sustainabilities that prioritize social, ecological, and economic justice.[38] Through its prioritization of quantitative indicators as the only valid form of knowledge about social and environmental impacts, alternative forms of accounting for sustainability—fiction, poetry, artwork, and so on—come to be seen as ornamental embellishments to the corporation's more rational, more technical, more *serious* epistemological approach.[39] So while this book is an ethnography of the work that sustainability professionals do to reconcile incommensurate values, and while it necessarily describes a narrow—albeit exceedingly influential— perspective on the question of sustainability, it is also a rumination on the broader effects of my informants' work and their beliefs, an effort to take account of the structures and strictures left in the wake of neoliberal sustainability and the innumerable worlds and worldviews that get pushed aside and obscured.[40]

A pluralized approach to sustainability rejects the idea that there is a one-size-fits-all solution to unsustainability, even if we can ultimately identify capitalist extraction and accumulation as a main source of many contemporary socioecological crises.[41] It recognizes that different sustainabilities are rooted in different histories, and they correspond to different futures. These sustainabilities draw on different ideas about what counts as knowledge and how to produce it, they reflect different assumptions about the world and how it works, and they respond to different ethical frameworks and moral obligations. The triple-bottom-line model of sustainability that is so pervasive and so dominant among my informants represents sustainability as the intersection of three distinct but overlapping dimensions: society, the environment, and the economy. This representation has become hegemonic, but it is only one model of sustainability. Other models also exist, and although these models are rooted in the specific histories and experiences of the communities that developed them, their production can serve as a model for others to develop their own theories and practices of sustainability. One such model, developed at the College of Menominee Nation's Sustainable Development Institute (SDI), identifies six (as opposed to three) dimensions of sustainable development: land and sovereignty; natural environment; institutions; technology; economics; and human perception, activity, and behavior. Rather than trying to resolve the tensions among these dimensions by rendering them commensurable, however, the SDI model "recognizes that there will always be tensions within and among model dimensions" and that "as tensions among model dimensions are relieved new tensions will arise." From the perspective of this model, sustainability is necessarily a "continual, and sometimes iterative, process."[42]

This understanding of sustainable development speaks to one of the overarching goals of this book, which is to mobilize alternative, often marginalized theories of sustainability in order to better understand the dominant approach to sustainability that is rooted in an impulse to quantify and measure sustainability indicators in a way that leaves the management of corporations' social and environmental impacts up to the whims of the market and the powerful actors—those same corporations and their investors—who control it. Refracting neoliberal sustainability through the multifaceted lens of Indigenous, Black, queer, and working-class theories of sustainability is a step toward what David Gegeo and Karen Watson-Gegeo have described as dehegemonizing the intersecting logics of capitalism and colonialism that contribute to the marginalization of "the other" while also facilitating its exploitation.[43]

Sustainability at the End of the World

In many ways, we seem to have reached the end of the world, with few viable ideas to postpone it and a socioeconomic system that prevents the few good ideas we do have from taking shape.[44] The blasted landscapes of the capitalocene are proliferating at an ever-increasing rate.[45] Social media has become an onslaught of bad news, with stories about wildfires and floods and droughts merging into one another. Every few months, the United Nations or some other international organization publishes a report frantically warning us that we are hurtling toward an uninhabitable future. And yet, the "solutions" that these warnings provoke—investments in renewable energy, carbon capture and storage schemes, net zero initiatives, and so on—end up creating new problems and fortifying old ones.[46] The multiple and interconnected crises that structure contemporary life are rooted in the violent colonial ambitions of European powers, which manifest themselves today in the neocolonial ambitions of multinational corporations and their investors, all of which sought and continue to seek the rapacious extraction of profits from people and planet, with little if any regard for their social and environmental costs. Now, the language of the *mission civilisatrice* has been replaced by the language of sustainability, contributing, through conspicuously similar mechanisms, to the domination of marginalized communities by powerful state and corporate actors.[47]

This book aims to make sense of the politics of sustainability. It focuses on an increasingly hegemonic approach to sustainability embraced by corporations, financial institutions, and large international organizations, one in which sustainability is understood primarily through quantitative data. This approach is exemplified by the dedicated efforts of sustainability professionals to improve their methods of defining, measuring, and reporting sustainability metrics and indicators. These efforts are motivated by the idea that, once sustainability has been measured and once these measurements have been reported, "the market" will lead to improved sustainability outcomes. It is an idea that epitomizes the performativity of environmental economics, a discipline that, for the most part, projects the calculative agency of the selfish "rational" actor onto questions pertaining to the future of the planet and its inhabitants, while at the same time calling our attention to the labor that goes into making these performances felicitous.[48] For decades, environmental economists have been largely committed to figuring out ways to quantitatively account for things like carbon emissions and land use change, with the explicit assumption that better information about those dynamics will enable the market to allocate social, natural, and economic capitals more efficiently, leading to the implicit claim that infinite growth is possible, even on a finite planet.[49] In this worldview, the correct response to imperfect markets is not to abandon the singularizing logic of the market for a pluralizing logic of relationality and reciprocity but rather to create the conditions of possibility for those markets to become perfect.[50] What this means in practice, at least from the perspective of my informants working in the relatively elite spaces of corporate sustainability and sustainable finance, is that the problem of unsustainability stems from a lack of information that inhibits the market from functioning like it is supposed to, rather than what we might otherwise interpret through the conceptual lenses of sovereignty, abolition, degrowth, or any number of other radical alternatives.[51] Although the work they do is certainly part of the problem, it is important to remember that the problem of neoliberal sustainability is also structural. As Bookchin observes, "It is not the perversity of the bourgeois that creates production for the sake of production, but the very market nexus over which he presides and to which he succumbs."[52]

So, one strand of the book focuses on this aspect of sustainability—its hegemonic prioritization of data-driven initiatives, its enforcement of new metrological regimes, and the ways in which these trends reproduce and reinforce a neoliberal political ecology, one in which the different dimensions of our diverse global socioecologies are rendered commensurable through quantified and often monetized sustainability indicators. As noted earlier, I call this "neoliberal sustainability," and I argue that commensuration is key to understanding its interrelated ontological, epistemological, and ethical aspects, an interrelatedness that is fundamental to many Indigenous philosophies that approach being, knowing, doing, and accounting as inextricably linked.[53] This means that the ontological questions of corporate sustainability—what the corporation *is*, what it means to *be* sustainable—are inseparable from the questions of how we know whether something is sustainable or not, how we act in response to this knowledge, whose knowledge counts as legitimate, how we determine whether we are making a difference, and how we decide whether the difference we are making is right or wrong. Recognizing the interdependency of these questions exposes the shortcomings of contemporary approaches to sustainability that are premised on measuring and reporting the social, environmental, and economic impacts of corporations and investors. If the Indigenous philosopher and activist Ailton Krenak is right in asserting that "no company on this earth is sustainable, no matter what they say," then squabbling over KPIs and accounting standards as a way of holding companies accountable is pointless, and the notion of "corporate sustainability" is revealed as yet another corporate oxymoron.[54]

A second strand focuses on the kinds of worlds neoliberal sustainability instigates and, crucially, the worlds it forecloses. This kind of counterfactual thinking is necessarily speculative. Nevertheless, it is a way to think through the "otherwise possibilities of relationality" between the world as it is and the worlds that might be, without the pressure of coming up with an answer or a solution.[55] Perhaps the biggest difference between what neoliberal sustainability offers and what we need in order to actually sustain ourselves within current and future socioecologies is the orientation toward incommensurability: advocates of neoliberal sustainability approach incommensurability as something in need of redress, as a problem that can be and must be solved through the creation of universally applicable indicators of social, environmental, and economic impacts. Resisting neoliberal sustainability means resisting the compulsion to render these dimensions of our collective well-being commensurable; it means taking away one of the conditions of possibility for neoliberal governance so that other, fairer modes of governance might be able to flourish.

Faced with the end of the world, simply accounting for sustainability seems to have become the raison d'être for many of the people and organizations interested in the problems of unsustainability. The allure of this kind of data-driven sustainability is obvious: it imbues a process that is inherently emotional and political and subjective with a veneer of rationality and objectivity. And yet, while the kinds of quantitative data and indicators that sustainability professionals pursue are certainly helpful in setting goals and tracking progress, we also need to be wary of the politics of measurement and reporting. Specifically, we need to ask what this increasingly pervasive and powerful discourse about data-driven sustainability obscures, what kinds of relations it reinforces, what kinds of futures it instigates, and what kinds of alternatives it precludes.

The Rest of the Book

Chapter 1 describes the meaning of sustainability as my informants understand it, theorizing their preoccupation with quantitatively accounting for social and environmental impacts as a process of commensuration that facilitates the establishment and enforcement of specific regimes of comparison and causality. I draw an explicit connection between neoliberal governance and the measurement and reporting of various sustainability indicators as a form of commensuration, focusing on the way my informants' commensuration of social, environmental, and economic factors reinforces the rule of markets and its attendant power relations.

Chapters 2 through 4 critically examine efforts to account for sustainability in several different contexts. They focus, respectively, on an international organization's attempts to integrate social capital in corporate reporting practices, the development and revision of sustainability certifications that govern global supply chains, and ESG integration in a bank's investment decision-making process. Chapters 5 and 6 focus on the relative sustainability of different lifestyles and livelihoods and the role of quantitative data in corporate future-making, drawing on a more diverse range of sources, including several pieces of speculative fiction that have helped me think through—and against—neoliberal sustainability.

There is a shift in tone and approach between these two sets of chapters, as chapters 2 through 4 draw on ethnographic research among sustainability professionals to show what the processes and practices of neoliberal sustainability look like. Chapters 5 and 6, on the other hand, turn to the question of what these processes and practices foreclose. Part of the challenge of writing these latter chapters was that they became a very personal attempt to make sense of something that, like many people interested in questions around sustainability, I found frankly quite terrifying (in addition to feeling quite hopeless). In the conclusion, I speculate about some of the consequences of the calculating corporation, and I outline a vision of sustainability that is more plural, more subjective, more collective, and hopefully more socially and ecologically just.

It may be apparent to people reading this book that we should not leave it to companies and banks to solve problems that they are in many ways responsible for. But it may be less obvious that many of the "solutions" we encounter in the prevailing discourse of global sustainability derive from a way of framing the problems of unsustainability that has been largely conditioned by those same organizations. Even if we accept that the ecocidal corporation is a threat that requires careful management, we must also not lose sight of the extent to which the corporation's obsession with quantitative data and indicators prefigures many of the initiatives that noncorporate and even anticorporate organizations develop and promote as solutions to socioecological crises. As we will see, a myopic focus on measurement and reporting as a strategy for holding companies and other unsustainable actors accountable for their actions neither challenges the status quo nor helps us mitigate and adapt to the harsh realities of rapidly changing socioecologies. Through an obsession with quantitatively accounting for these impacts, corporate sustainability transforms complex webs

of social, environmental, economic, ethical, and political relationships into sets of numerical indicators and data sets that are easily
commensurable with the financial performance of companies, investments, and products, engendering a mode of governance that places
the market and its corporate-financial avatars at the center of power.
Alternatives are desperately needed, as are spaces where these alternatives can flourish.

1

The Meaning of Sustainability

The connection between words and what they signified had
been broken.
—John Berger, "The Production of the World," in *Steps
towards a Small Theory of the Visible*

"Sustainability" is notoriously difficult to define, or so we are told. One
of the goals of my research in Geneva in 2015 and 2016 was to figure out
what sustainability meant from the perspective of the people working
in powerful organizations like banks and corporations, which play an
increasingly important role in global sustainability negotiations. Through
my participant observation in organizations engaged with different
aspects of corporate sustainability and sustainable finance and interviews with people working in these organizations, a definition emerged
that has three related components: first, sustainability is understood as
the integration of social, environmental, and economic dimensions; second, sustainability is a "journey," rather than a "destination," something
that can always be improved; and third, sustainability is seen as causally
related to the profitability of companies, investors, and local communities, even if the nature of that causal relationship remains unclear or
contested. As this chapter shows, the quantification and measurement of
social and environmental impacts underlies each of these components,
engendering a particular mode of neoliberal governance through interrelated processes of commensuration, comparison, and causation.

Professionalizing Sustainability

Geneva is arguably the global hub for the group of people I call "sustainability professionals," people whose jobs are concerned explicitly, at
least to some extent, with promoting sustainability both within and outside their organizations. They work in the sustainability departments of

investment banks, multinational corporations, family-owned businesses, international organizations, pension funds, insurance companies, and consulting firms. They have job titles like "sustainability analyst" or "global head of sustainability" or "corporate social responsibility manager" or "ESG director." Sometimes they work for organizations like the World Business Council for Sustainable Development (WBCSD) or the International Council for Trade and Sustainable Development (ICTSD) or the World Economic Forum (WEF), which bring together economic and political elites to chart business-friendly paths toward global sustainability, but more often than not, they work on sustainability from inside companies and banks like Nestlé and Credit Suisse and Archer-Daniels-Midland. Although it is difficult to provide a reliable estimate, one sustainable careers consultant I spoke to in 2016 estimated that there are over 100,000 sustainability professionals working today, a number that she claimed was growing rapidly. She was right: a LinkedIn group for "sustainability professionals" that I joined during my fieldwork had around 160,000 members in 2017, but by early 2022, its membership had increased to more than 280,000. During a Skype interview in 2016, the consultant told me that a person might be considered a sustainability professional if at least 50 percent of their work is devoted to some aspect of sustainability. So, regardless of the veracity of one executive's exasperated claim that "everyone has to think about sustainability nowadays," not everyone is (or should be) considered a sustainability professional.

I think of sustainability professionals as people who are responsible in a professional capacity for some aspect of their organization's sustainability or are tasked with promoting, developing, maintaining, improving, and/or enforcing the sustainability of some other organization. That means anyone who has the word "sustainability" in their job title (e.g., sustainability manager, sustainable supply chain manager, sustainability consultant, director of corporate sustainability, vice president of sustainable investing); anyone who works for a company or organization that promotes or relies on sustainability as its primary purpose or as a main source of revenue (e.g., the United Nations Environment Programme Finance Initiative, Sustainalytics, SustainAbility); people working in traditional financial institutions (e.g., banks, insurance companies, mutual funds) whose jobs require the active consideration of sustainability indicators (e.g., impact investors, "green alpha" fund managers,

ESG analysts); and people whose work at various levels of government (mostly city and regional but some national) involves crafting or negotiating sustainability regulations, designing sustainability frameworks, or overseeing sustainability initiatives. Some of the sustainability professionals I met during my fieldwork might more accurately be called sustainability nearly-professionals; that is, they are training to be (or hope to become) sustainability professionals but are still in school or in some cases "stuck" in jobs where they do not feel like they have a real impact, hoping and waiting for an opportunity to present itself.

Sustainability professionals perform much of the labor of corporate sustainability and sustainable finance, including the mundane work of data collection and analysis but also the more immaterial and affective labor of defining and negotiating these indicators as legible and legitimate social objects, of convincing "the rest of us" that we should take the measures and values of sustainability seriously. As a group of "traveling technocrats," sustainability professionals contribute to the reproduction and reinforcement of a specific definition of sustainability, enhancing its "portability" or the facility with which it can be applied in contexts often far beyond the sites where it was produced and refined.[1] Studying this process helps us understand how sustainability and its practices of measurement and reporting become such important technologies of neoliberal governance and how the values of for-profit organizations like corporations and their investors somehow get reproduced and reinforced as desirable social and environmental values.[2]

In the process of my studying sustainability professionals, which eventually led to my teaching "critical sustainability" courses at a business school and being invited to give talks about sustainability to several groups of interested practitioners, it was easy for me to slip into the fallacy that sustainability had become a ubiquitous concern among corporate and financial elites. Although uncomfortable, it was important, then, to be regularly reminded by friends and family working for large companies and banks that sustainability is almost completely off their radar, that as much as these organizations might talk about sustainability and responsibility for the sake of their external "stakeholders," it is actually a rather marginal part of their operations, often—if not typically—relegated to the marketing or public relations (PR) teams. That raises the question of why there are so many "sustainability professionals" in the world and what role they play in the larger socioeconomic structures of corporate and financial capitalism. Through their very public engagement with issues like biodiversity loss and human rights abuses and sea-level rise, sustainability professionals' main role seems to be spreading the message that the relationship between society, the environment, and the economy must be understood in a particular way that facilitates particular solutions, that is, as quantifiable impacts that the market can manage on our behalf. When *unsustainability* is framed as something that is understood through metrics and indicators, the only viable solutions are those that are also understood through metrics and indicators. To understand the way markets mediate the relationship between society and the environment, we have to understand what the market's powerful avatars—organizations like banks and corporations, in particular, but also the organizations and institutions that these actors rely on for their legitimacy—mean when they talk about sustainability.

What Does Sustainability Mean to You?

When I interviewed a sustainability professional for the first time, I usually began our conversation by asking them to tell me what sustainability means for them—how they define it in the context of their own work. I quickly learned that this was a contentious question, that they felt put on the spot. What I imagined as an easy icebreaker seemed to make them anxious, and they typically prefaced their answer with a disclaimer, insisting that it was a really difficult question or joking that if they knew the answer, they would be rich and famous. One informant, who had studied anthropology as an undergraduate, told me that it was like asking an anthropologist to define culture. Eventually, I started prefacing the question with a disclaimer of my own, telling them I did not expect an objective answer and promising not to hold them to whatever answer they provided. Admittedly, sustainability professionals are in an unenviable position, tasked with the impossible job of trying to mitigate the social and environmental degradation caused by profiteering corporations in a way that does not diminish those corporations' profits. They must navigate a complex sustainability landscape littered with obstacles: recalcitrant investors and executives, limited funding, short time horizons, unsupportive colleagues, and so on.[3] More fundamentally, as

Ailton Krenak puts it, "corporate sustainability managers have become the sacerdotes of a new planetary order, self-righteously preaching something their employers, by their very nature, can't practice."⁴ During interviews with my informants, especially those that were more informal and unstructured, I could tell that they liked having a chance to think out loud about the paradox of corporate sustainability, to philosophize a bit about problems they spent much of their time working on, and to explain why they had decided to devote a big chunk of their lives to solving these problems.

According to my informants, sustainability does not have a strict definition, and they insisted it was better that way. How, they asked rhetorically, could a company like ExxonMobil, a company like Google, and a company like Nestlé be judged by the same sustainability criteria when they offer such different products and services, to say nothing of what my informants often referred to as "mom-and-pop stores" and other so-called small and medium enterprises (SMEs)?⁵ Even if they could come up with a concrete definition of sustainability, my informants wondered, what would be the point? Talking to sustainability professionals, it seemed like anything can be evaluated along a dimension of sustainability—not just companies and the stuff they make but also types of products (organic food), tokens of those types of products (the organic oatmeal I had this morning for breakfast), people (the former CEO of Unilever Paul Polman), institutions (the British monarchy under its new, environmentally conscious king), cities and countries (like Copenhagen or Denmark), governments (those that govern relatively sustainable cities and countries), the policies that those governments enact (public transportation investments and clean energy incentives), and so on. These are the kinds of examples my informants provided, suggesting that behind the purported elusiveness of a concrete definition of sustainability lie numerous examples of sustainable things that are, in fact, quite concrete.

This commitment to "flexibility" is a form of strategic ambiguity that leads to a hollowing out of the concept of sustainability, creating what the critical accounting theorists Markus Milne and Rob Gray have famously referred to as an "empty signifier."⁶ And yet, if sustainability really is an empty signifier, that only means there is more space for companies to stuff it full of their own interests and ideologies. Thus, despite my informants' insistence not only that sustainability is impossible to define but also that it would be imprudent to even try to produce a clear definition, they actually seemed to have a definition of sustainability that was both very stable and widely shared. Without fail, when they finally got around to saying what sustainability meant to them, they elaborated some version of the so-called triple-bottom-line or three-pillars approach to sustainability, defining sustainability as the consideration of measurable social, environmental, and economic indicators. There are several variations on this theme. Some call it the three Ps (people, planet, and profit, a cheeky appropriation of the derisive characterization of the triple-bottom-line as a greenwashing strategy), while others call it the three Es (ecology, economy, and equity). My informants often talked about these distinct dimensions in terms of natural capital, social capital, and financial capital or alternatively in terms of social, environmental, and economic impacts, reflecting the pressure they face to come up with a way of thinking about these radically different dimensions using a common language, of figuring out a way to express social, environmental, and economic values through a shared metric such as "impacts" or "capital." This pressure manifests itself as an obsession with producing quantitative data about social and environmental impacts that they then attempt to correlate with indicators of financial performance. Conveniently enough, these financial indicators tend to be quantified (and of course monetized) from the outset. Measuring nonfinancial impacts is a key dimension of the work of sustainability professionals, who conceptualize the sustainability of a product, investment, or organization in terms of its component parts, which they further decompose into a panoply of measurable and manageable indicators. Thus, the first and most fundamental part of their definition of sustainability is the idea that sustainability is, at a general level, the consideration of something's social and environmental performance alongside its financial performance and that indicators of these performances can be quantified and measured, compared and correlated.

The relationship between these domains is typically visualized as either a set of three pillars (society, environment, and economy) holding up a pediment (sustainability) or as a Venn diagram with three circles (society, environment, and economy) whose zone of overlap is denoted as sustainability. Several variations of these figures exist, popping up everywhere from PowerPoint slides at sustainable development conferences to undergraduate corporate sustainability textbooks, but the basic form remains quite similar across the different media in which they appear. These images correspond to an imaginary that has become hegemonic in the sustainability discourse, leading to ad hoc sustainability assessments that are sometimes counterintuitive.[7]

One of my informants, Chet, the head of sustainability at a pan-African bank, visited Geneva in late 2015 for a workshop with one of the organizations I was observing. This provided a good opportunity to invite him for an interview about his work on financial inclusion in rural Africa, a widely publicized social responsibility initiative for many banks that operate in developing countries. Chet had a hard time enunciating why increasing rural banking services was an example of corporate social responsibility. For him, it was just obvious that people's lives were improved by access to things like loans and savings accounts, rather than relying on what he described as the communal "pots of money" that many rural communities maintain for emergencies like health issues and natural disasters. The conversation shifted to a discussion about the difference between sustainable investing, which Chet understood as the integration of social and environmental considerations in a way that increased (or at least maintained) return on investment (ROI), and philanthropy, which aims to achieve social and environmental goals without a concern for investment returns.[8] He gave a stereotypical example of the kind of project someone might consider "sustainable development," an investment to provide easier access to clean water for rural villagers. Chet insisted that this would not be truly sustainable from a financial point of view, despite its obvious social and environmental impacts, because it did not have a clear economic rationale and was not "scalable," which meant it would not attract continued investment. Further reflections led Chet to conclude that there *might* be an economic argument based on the increased productivity of sufficiently hydrated people who were no longer forced to walk miles and miles for clean water. Without considering all three dimensions of sustainability, these kinds of solutions are not really in the zone of sustainability; without attending to all three pillars, from the perspective of someone like Chet, the pediment crumbles.

For my informants, sustainability must be flexible enough to accommodate these different kinds of entities at the many different stages of what many informants referred to as their companies' "sustainability journeys." As it were, this idea that sustainability is "a journey rather than a destination" emerged as the second key component of my informants' definition of sustainability. They insisted that sustainability is not a quality that companies, investments, and products either have or lack but is a continuum they move along—never a matter of sustainable or unsustainable but rather more or less sustainable, a gradient. Sustainability, in other words, is not something an organization can achieve but is something that must be constantly pursued and improved on, an idea that resonates with classic theories of management that see quality management as a process of continuous improvement. My informants assured me that "you can always be more sustainable," that you can always make incremental, strategic improvements. In some ways, this belief reflects their training at the professional schools of elite universities, where they encounter ideas by management researchers and strategy consultants like R. Edward Freeman and Michael Porter, whose theories of stakeholder management and creating shared value (CSV) have migrated from business-school classrooms to corporate boardrooms.[9] In these settings, sustainability professionals approach sustainability through the lens of neoclassical economics, and they learn to understand efficiency and optimality not just as subjective or political or ethical goals but as objective and technical facts. Sustainability's quest for limitless improvements—understood through the notion of "impact"— mirrors capitalism's imperative for limitless growth; neither, in the world of sustainability professionals, is easily contested.

The third and final part of my informants' definition of sustainability deals explicitly with sustainability's economic dimension, specifically profitability, and its relationship with the other two dimensions. Sustainability, my informants insisted, helps companies and banks be more financially successful because it reveals new opportunities, exposes unforeseen risks, or some combination of the two. Sustainability's seemingly inevitable profitability, which my informants regularly refer to as the "business case for sustainability" and pithily describe as "doing well by doing good," is couched in the objectifying vocabulary of efficiency, optimization, and enhanced productivity. Like sustainability itself, the profitability of these organizations becomes something wholly depoliticized; the causal relationship between a company being more sustainable and more profitable starts to feel natural, as does the direction of that causality from more sustainable to more profitable.[10] The goal shifts from having a positive social or environmental impact to making sure those impacts are creating financial value for investors, and this new goal becomes interchangeable with social and environmental goals, especially when it comes to determining whether a company is sustainable or not (or, more accurately, how a company is progressing on its sustainability journey). Sustainability initiatives that fail to consider profits (understood in this worldview as a positive economic impact, since companies and investors are also "stakeholders") come to be seen as failing to adequately consider the triple-bottom-line, and they are assessed as patently unsustainable, no matter their social and environmental benefits. What this means in practice is that discussions about sustainability often start from the premise that the profitability of a company or an investor should not be diminished by a sustainability initiative.

The fact that my informants worked in such diverse contexts, from sustainable development NGOs to elite Swiss private banks, suggests that the definition of sustainability just described is not only stable but also relatively portable, able to be applied across diverse contexts. They imagine the sustainability performance of a company as something they can know through quantitative metrics and indicators, and they commit themselves to developing and implementing standardized protocols of social and environmental impact measurement and reporting. Through this specific mode of knowing whether a company is performing sustainably relative to both its peers in one moment and itself over time, the practices of measurement and reporting that my informants design and promote become a central but understudied feature of sustainability governance.

The meaning of sustainability matters. Meanings are not objective, immutable descriptions of some external reality but are inherently social, political, and ethical. The power to define sustainability corresponds to the power to define who or what is sustainable, which corresponds in turn to the power to determine who has access to and control over the increasingly vast amounts of human, natural, and financial resources that are being mobilized to promote, support, and achieve "global sustainability." N. J. Enfield contends that even if the meaning of a word is often unstable, meanings remain *useful* and that understanding the "historical utility" of a word in facilitating communication helps demonstrate the inherently subjective nature of these meanings.[11] The utility of the meaning of sustainability as my informants use it is that it allows them to continue with business as usual while reframing their profit-seeking activities as sustainable rather than unsustainable. As linguistic anthropologists in particular have shown in multiple contexts, understanding what a word like "sustainability" indexes—and how that indexicality is cultivated, proliferated, and reinforced—is key to understanding the formation and crucially the circumscription of social and political groups, as well as the establishment and governance of interdiscursive relationships.[12] From disciplines like anthropology and geography to feminist and Indigenous philosophies to popular works of fantasy and science fiction, there is a profound power associated with being able to name things, to establish definitions and classifications, and to create and enforce categories.[13] When corporations and their allies make claims about sustainability, they are not merely making a descriptive claim about a state of affairs; they are making a claim about what sustainability is, how we should understand it, and how we should enact it. They are reproducing a definition of sustainability that suits their interests, and they are reinforcing a "politics of unsustainability" that embraces incrementalism at the expense of the radicalism that these crises require, a politics that buoys the status quo, however momentarily, as the storm of progress inundates the rest of us in its ever-growing pile of debris.[14] The rest of this chapter brings the three elements of my informants' definition of sustainability into a coherent conceptual framing that turns on the relationship between commensuration, comparison, and causality.[15] In doing so, it theorizes sustainability as a key technology of neoliberal governance, one "invented by corporations to justify their theft of our idea of nature" and to reaffirm their powerful role in global political ecologies.[16]

Sustainability and the Politics of Commensuration

To recap, despite the ubiquitous claim that sustainability is difficult or impossible to define, asking sustainability professionals how they define sustainability actually yields a definition that is both relatively stable (they all define it in basically the same way) and relatively portable (they define it that way in very different contexts). This definition has three main parts: the first part is that sustainability is the explicit integration of three distinct domains—the social, the environmental, and the economic—in decision-making processes; the second part is that sustainability is a journey rather than a destination, that we have to think of sustainability as "more or less" rather than "either-or"; and the third part is that sustainability is causally related to profitability, encapsulated by the phrase "doing well by doing good."

Each part of this definition requires the commensuration of social, environmental, and economic impacts. In the first part, this is rather obvious in the sense that in order to integrate such diverse dimensions, there has to be a common metric for comparing them, which is the definition of commensuration. The second part, that sustainability is a journey rather than a destination, implies that organizations can be compared in terms of their sustainability over time while also implying that sustainability is a gradient rather than a binary. This kind of comparison—indeed any kind of comparison—presupposes some degree of commensuration, as I discuss in more detail shortly. Finally, the third part of the definition, the causal relationship between sustainability and profitability, not only presupposes comparison and thus also presupposes commensuration but is ultimately what makes the comparative grounds of sustainability so important. Taking these aspects of sustainability together, we can start to rethink the politics of sustainability through the politics of commensuration, which helps us make sense of the obsession with metrics and the role these metrics play in neoliberal governance.

Commensurating Society, the Environment, and the Economy

Chet's evaluation of development projects that fail to account for financial impacts as inherently unsustainable may seem callous, an overly economistic approach to questions of environmental degradation and human suffering. But the logic that underlies his worldview is pervasive. Thinking about access to clean water in financial terms allows Chet to determine whether investing in clean water infrastructure is worth it financially but also ethically; it lets him justify spending money on that project instead of some other project that his bank or any other organization might have funded with what he imagines as a limited pool of money. The same logic is at play when researchers try to assign a monetary value to social impacts of the COVID-19 pandemic or when governments determine what fee to impose on a polluting corporation to offset its environmental impacts or when consultants put a price on carbon emissions, all examples of "weak sustainability" that turn on an impulse to *commensurate* the financial (the price tag) with the nonfinancial (human suffering, biodiversity loss, etc.) so that they can be more easily compared. "Commensuration" here refers to "the expression or measurement of characteristics normally represented by different units according to a common metric. . . . Commensuration transforms qualities into quantities, difference into magnitude. It is a way to reduce and simplify disparate information into numbers that can easily be compared. This transformation allows people to quickly grasp, represent, and compare differences." According to the sociologists Wendy Espeland and Mitchell Stevens, "Most quantification can be understood as commensuration because quantification creates relations between different entities through a common metric. Commensuration is noticed most when it creates relations among things that seem fundamentally different."[17]

Consider the Brundtland Report's famous definition of "sustainable development" as development that meets the needs of people today without preventing future generations from meeting their own needs. The commensurability of indicators of welfare that will probably change quite dramatically over the course of even a few generations is fundamental to this definition. What makes the quantification of social and environmental impacts so important is that it facilitates comparison across different dimensions according to a common metric; in practice, the common metric that sustainability professionals tend to pursue is money, which is conveniently already quantified.

Commensuration is key to contemporary discourses of sustainability, especially to the extent that the triple-bottom-line or three-pillars approach has become a "hegemonic trio" within this discourse.[18] The idea that sustainability involves the consideration of social, environmental, and economic factors brings these distinct domains into a relationship with each other and requires a common way of thinking about them. Quantitative indicators offer the easiest way to represent and understand this relationship, and several metrological systems have emerged to generate these indicators. Metaphors of distinct "capitals" (social capital, natural capital, and financial capital) and measurable "impacts" (social impacts, environmental impacts, and economic impacts) are two of the most common approaches, often overlapping with each other, as we will see in chapter 2, on attempts to define and measure natural capital and social capital. Although the actual indicators used to communicate impacts are often fraught and almost always contested, the focus on improving measurement methods and reporting protocols circumscribes the discourse around sustainability to its technical dimensions, leaving little room to critique the commensurative impulse at a more fundamental level and naturalizing the kinds of reductive measurements that impact assessments or social and natural capital indicators tend to generate. More important, as critics of this triple-bottom-line thinking have shown, in attempting to quantify social and environmental impacts, the economic or financial impacts, which we already tend to understand in quantitative terms, usually emerge as the most important dimension, the dimension toward which the other two are oriented. Surely one of the reasons that "economic considerations overwhelm all else" is because the "all else" that sustainability deals with is so easily reframed as an economic consideration.[19] Indeed, the monetization of natural capital, social capital, and, more recently, cultural capital is often an explicit goal of the measurement and reporting exercises that people working in sustainability undertake.

The commensuration of sustainability's social, environmental, and economic dimensions is a condition of possibility for their substitutability, or what Fabiana Li has called a "logic of equivalence." Examples of this logic of equivalence in action include payments for ecosystem services, willingness-to-pay methods in environmental economics, and the increasingly popular notion of "net zero" approaches to greenhouse gas emissions, which illuminates the logic of equivalence at work in the much broader—and often implicit—discussions about "offsets" and the extent to which establishing these kinds of equivalencies is "the first step to potential commodification."[20] Especially in the case of net zero approaches to sustainability, we see emissions produced in one place rendered equivalent to emissions produced in another place, which might be unproblematic from a purely theoretical perspective but in practice depoliticizes the crucial questions of who generated the emissions (a corporation or a group of swidden agriculturalists) and to what ends (to produce cheap plastic widgets or to grow food for a community). Central to Li's argument is the idea that a particular "way of a framing a problem facilitates commensuration."[21] In her ethnographic research on a Chilean goldmine where Indigenous activists were protesting the depletion of local groundwater reserves, there were at least two ways to frame the problem: for people who rely on water for their lives and livelihoods, it was an existential problem whose only solution was to stop the degradation of the watershed; for the mining company, on the other hand, it was a technical problem, since technical alternatives such as desalination exist, even if they are expensive. In framing the problem as technical, engineers and consultants were able to "separate" their data-driven cost-benefit analyses from the broader—that is, existential—social and environmental issues raised by Indigenous activists. Similarly, in framing sustainability as a problem of measurement and reporting, my informants set the stage for the commensuration of people, planet, and profit through the language of impacts and capitals, shaping—rather than merely describing—the world they are trying to make more sustainable.[22]

The measurement and reporting of social and environmental impacts, as it were, has become the raison d'être for many of my informants, and during my fieldwork, their commitment to defining and measuring social and environmental impacts verged on fanatical. They seemed convinced that sustainability would just happen, if only they could accurately define and measure impacts and if only they could widely publicize the indicators that these measurements produced. Organizations like the Global Reporting Initiative (GRI), the Sustainable Accounting Standards Board (SASB), and the Climate Disclosure Standards Board (CDSB) have proliferated over the past few decades, creating an alphabet soup of competing standards and methods for measuring and reporting so-called nonfinancial impacts. The lack of standardized social and environmental impact metrics is one of the first things skeptics raise in their critiques of sustainability, especially in the financial sector, where environmental, social, and governance—now more commonly referred to as ESG—indicators are increasingly mainstream. Different approaches compete to attract subscribers and clients. Within the financial industry, for example, there are several options, including the Task Force on Climate-Related Financial Disclosures (TCFD), chaired by the billionaire Michael Bloomberg, and the Taskforce on Nature-Related Financial Disclosures (TNFD), cochaired by a consulting firm CEO and the general secretary of a UN agency. The fact that social and environmental impact reporting guidelines are modeled after traditional financial accounting principles is no accident, and one of the most important and insidious effects of these endless discussions about social and environmental impact reporting is that *financial* reporting comes to be implicitly seen as the gold standard for *nonfinancial* reporting, wherein the ideal sustainability report is simply a spreadsheet of easily comparable social, environmental, and financial data.

Commensurability is socially produced at the intersection of different epistemological frameworks; rarely is its social production smooth or complete, and incommensurability is persistent, despite the best efforts of experts.[23] As Jacqueline Gilbert, Tamra Gilbertson, and Line Jakobsen argue in a compelling analysis of corporate compensation schemes around Colombian coal mines, compensation agreements between powerful multinational mining companies and local Indigenous communities exemplify the incommensurability of the damages caused by mineral extraction with monetary payouts. Despite this glaring incommensurability, these schemes continue to be implemented and embraced by diverse actors, from the corporations themselves to states and large NGOs. Gilbert, Gilbertson, and Jakobsen argue that "the promise of compensation is a key component of corporate social technologies and works as a strategy of inclusionary control. The real purpose of such efforts is to discourage opposition from challenging institutional inequalities and damages from extractive practices. Even when hailed as a success by some, compensations act as a silencing mechanism masking the broader and more structural socioenvironmental damage done to local communities."[24] This helps explain why sustainability professionals are so committed to measurement, why they exhibit such a strong *commensurative impulse*. Like a company that distributes financial compensation for environmental pollution or social unrest, even though money is an imperfect metric for comparing these different impacts, the proliferation of impact reports helps placate regulators and NGOs that might otherwise be more antagonistic toward banks and corporations. It gives a sense that something is being done, and it creates a basis for "objective" decision-making.

In the face of such overwhelming incommensurability—that is, when faced with what I believe is a rather innate understanding that it is impossible to put a price on social and ecological relations—one of the clearest and most effective ways to exercise power in global political ecologies is to control not only the metrological regimes of sustainability but also the narrative about the legitimacy of those measurements, the narrative that connects measurements and the processes that generate them to "real world" impacts.[25] Corporations do not—and indeed cannot—do this alone. Rather, they work closely with partners, allies, and even rivals to establish and support initiatives that serve their own interests. Freidberg observes an interesting paradox regarding the commitment among large food companies to measuring and reporting a huge number of KPIs, even though there is no real benefit for their bottom line. Most consumers, as it were, could not care less whether one brand of coffee generated less carbon dioxide across its supply chain than a competing brand did, prompting many companies to shift their sustainability strategies from a consumer focus to a business-to-business focus. She argues that companies invest in these multistakeholder data-collection initiatives as a way of enhancing their "knowledge and expertise" about the sustainability performance of their own operations as well as their suppliers', since even the most skilled PR experts "cannot by themselves compensate for too little data."[26] And yet, there is something else going on in companies' widely publicized commitments to this data-driven approach to sustainability management. They have embraced this approach, I argue, not because it always yields some clear or immediate financial benefit or helps them improve their sustainability performance, even if these are also important and desirable potential outcomes, but because it reinforces an imaginary of sustainability in which companies are seen as contributing to global sustainability without being responsible for it, an imaginary that relies on the commensurability of society, the environment, and the economy.

Comparing Sustainability across Time and Space

For Espeland and Stevens, the expression or measurement of different domains as numbers allows those differences to be *compared* by transforming differences into magnitudes. Comparison across domains thus presupposes commensuration. There are several ways corporate sustainability relies on commensuration to compare different processes and entities. One is exemplified by my informants' insistence that sustainability is a journey, which implies that a company's sustainability performance is comparable over time. When companies like Unilever and Nestlé say that their sustainability performance is improving or that they are on track to meet their sustainability targets, what they are actually saying is that they defined a set of indicators at some point in the past, measured them at least once (benchmarking), and then measured them again at a different time, where the second set of calculations is different from the first (hopefully improved). Tracking these improvements has led sustainability organizations like the Rainforest Alliance to pursue strategies of "continuous improvement" that rely on increasingly intense regimes of measuring and evaluating the social and environmental impacts of industrial agriculture. Although these improvements are certainly welcome, decontextualized statistics like reduced water consumption per production unit or number of farmers complying with a particular sustainability standard often get reframed as ambitious narratives of global sustainability impacts, obscuring and understating the persistent structural challenges of global capitalist development. These easy-to-measure impacts are often accompanied by labels indicating which of the seventeen Sustainable Development Goals they are contributing to, suggesting that improved corporate sustainability performance is helping end problems like hunger and poverty and gender discrimination.

Even more interesting is when a company has improved in one dimension but failed to make progress (or even gotten worse) in another. Research on renewable energy companies has highlighted this paradox, in which companies like Vestas, which produces and installs wind turbines, emphasizes its environmental impacts, discursively offsetting (i.e., obscuring) the violence it inflicts on Indigenous communities through wind-farm development in places like Oaxaca.[27] Comparing the performance of these companies over time by "tracking" their performance across different areas of sustainability using stylized sustainability metrics not only relies on commensuration but also reinforces the idea that the different dimensions of sustainability can be commensurated and compared in the first place, thus reproducing a logic of equivalence while conveniently eliding dimensions of sustainability that are difficult or impossible to measure or simply uncomfortable—and potentially unprofitable—to disclose.

A second mode of comparison is between different companies at the same time, exemplified by corporate sustainability ratings and rankings like the Global 100 Index of the world's most sustainable companies published each year by the Canadian business magazine *Corporate Knights*, which has become rather influential. During my fieldwork in Geneva, for example, the list was announced at the invitation-only World Economic Forum's annual meeting in Davos, giving it the legitimacy that this sort of elitist setting tends to miraculously confer. Companies found to be among the world's most sustainable according to *Corporate Knights'* unique methodology, which includes a proprietary industry classification system and a weighting scheme that determines the relative importance of different indicators for different kinds of companies, are able to incorporate this "objective" assessment into their sustainability marketing materials. (For companies interested in a more detailed comparison of their sustainability performance relative to their peers, *Corporate Knights* also provides this analysis, for a fee.) Ratings like the Swiss investment firm RobecoSAM's ESG scorecard and ESG indexes provided by companies like Morningstar and MSCI perform a similar function, quantifying the sustainability performance of companies in a way that allows investors to more easily consider sustainability alongside more familiar financial indicators like profitability ratios or "earnings before interest, taxes, depreciation, and amortization" (EBITDA).[28]

Volkswagen offers a good example of comparison of the same company's sustainability performance over time and comparison of different companies at the same time. When I was conducting fieldwork in Geneva in 2015 and 2016, Volkswagen was embroiled in a scandal often referred to in the media as "Dieselgate." Researchers in the US had discovered that Volkswagen's "clean diesel" cars were equipped with software that helped them trick regulators during emissions tests by sensing whether it was on a test track or in the real world. Compared with laboratory tests, Volkswagen's diesel-powered vehicles emitted several times more nitrous oxide (NOx) in real-world driving conditions, a pollutant that is associated with several chronic respiratory illnesses and premature death.[29] It was a horrible crime, with significant knock-on effects. Many European governments, misled by Volkswagen's claims about its clean diesel technology, had incentivized diesel vehicles through various tax mechanisms for both individuals and employers, unknowingly generating high levels of pollutants that are particularly dangerous in cities. (Diesel-powered engines are more efficient than gasoline-powered engines from a greenhouse gas perspective, but they produce more toxic, local pollution, a problem that "clean diesel" promised to solve.) The effects of Dieselgate are still unfolding. The embrace of electric vehicles, which has already prompted massive investments in new extraction projects for lithium and other so-called rare earth minerals, is often explicitly connected to the Volkswagen scandal.

During my fieldwork, Dieselgate was a good example of what I viewed as the inherent tendency of for-profit corporations to cut corners when they thought they could get away with it, and it was a good opportunity to probe the limits of my informants' faith in the market's ability to yield sustainable outcomes. When I asked them about it, however, they thought Volkswagen actually proved their point about the business case for sustainability, a claim that turned on comparing Volkswagen's performance to other companies and comparing Volkswagen's performance over time. Regarding the first kind of comparison, my informants often compared Volkswagen to Nestlé, which around the same time in the fall of 2015 was being sued in US courts for hiding the fact that there were several documented cases of slavery in its seafood supply chains originating in East Asia. (Nestlé was also being sued in the US by former child slaves from Ivorian cocoa farms.) In response, Nestlé commissioned a report on slavery by the independent research firm Verité, which demonstrated that Nestlé did, in fact, have slaves in its seafood supply chain.[30] Ultimately, Nestlé decided to release and publicize the report, which several informants working in different sustainability roles in Geneva presented as evidence of the company's profound commitment to transparency.[31] They compared Nestlé favorably to Volkswagen, whose senior managers had lied about their role in the installation of the "default devices."

The second kind of comparison was between Volkswagen in 2015 and Volkswagen at other points in its history. During a small meeting of sustainable finance practitioners that took place in early 2016, one informant claimed that few people in the industry had been surprised at such shady dealings by Volkswagen's senior management. Since its founding, the company had been a close collaborator with the Nazi regime, which this informant evoked in her criticism of Volkswagen's corporate governance, noting that its governance failed to meet her bank's basic ESG criteria and claiming that such a scandal was "inevitable."[32] In fact, throughout the Dieselgate scandal and its aftermath, Volkswagen's historical ties to Nazism were regularly invoked, especially by political cartoonists. Compare this with an informant who helps manage the European "large cap" (that is, companies with large market capitalizations traded on European stock exchanges) portfolio at Norebank, who, in the fall of 2019, told me that Volkswagen had learned a "hard lesson" during the scandal and had really committed to sustainability over the past few years. Even today, coverage of Volkswagen in the financial press has continued to compare the Volkswagen of today—with its growing focus on electric cars and especially its early commitment to sourcing battery metals from supposedly conflict-free mines—with the Volkswagen of 2015.

Causal Relations between Sustainability and Profitability

Underlying claims about the difference between Volkswagen's and Nestlé's embodiment of corporate transparency or claims about the difference between Volkswagen today and Volkswagen in 2015 was an implicit comparison along another dimension: financial performance. I had expected the Volkswagen scandal to leave a few large cracks in the edifice of corporate sustainability, but in the end, it simply reinforced it. My informants insisted that this was the market doing what it was supposed to do. For them, the so-called business case for sustainability— "doing well by doing good"—was proved by the fact that the market not only rewards good, sustainable companies (like Nestlé) but also punishes bad, unsustainable companies (like Volkswagen). In the court of sustainability, the market is both judge and jury.

During my fieldwork in Geneva, I was involved with a consortium of private banks interested in sustainable finance, where I was asked to conduct a literature review on the relationship between the social and environmental performance and the financial performance of both companies and funds (especially exchange-traded funds, or ETFs, that are managed with some level of ESG integration). Underlying the idea that there might be a causal relationship between sustainability performance and financial performance is an implicit assumption that companies and funds can be compared in terms of their financial value and their sustainability impacts. Comparing financial values is relatively easy thanks to readily available information about share prices, whereas comparing sustainability impacts is relatively difficult due to the different indicators that companies use to communicate their impacts, giving rise to my informants' obsession with standardizing and quantifying sustainability indicators. The measurement of social and environmental impacts is inseparable from the "ecologies of comparison" that corporate sustainability relies on and engenders.[33] For the informants who made up this consortium, the task of sustainability analysts was to establish the comparative grounds of sustainability (through metrics and ratings and rankings) and link those comparisons to the more established comparative grounds of financial performance. Put differently, the task was to establish a causal link between a difference in sustainability performance, on the one hand, and a difference in financial performance, on the other hand, which they could then use and manipulate to make more money.

Discussions about the Volkswagen scandal made the causal relationship between sustainability performance and financial performance clear. Volkswagen's share price crashed in 2015, according to my informants, *because* the market was made aware of Volkswagen's unsustainability. Similarly, Volkswagen's later efforts to become more sustainable were reflected in the market's appreciation of these efforts, the market's forgiveness of the company's earlier transgressions. Growth in Nestlé's market value remained stable, in part, because its decision to publish the results of the slavery report reinforced its position as a leader in corporate sustainability through its commitment to transparency. In interviews and at conferences, sustainability professionals consistently praised Nestlé's foresight and proactiveness. One interviewee told me that Nestlé had gone "above and beyond" what most companies would do by publicly admitting that it had slavery in its supply chain by releasing a report that it had originally commissioned for internal use. By doing so, he told me, the company would enjoy a first-mover advantage that would allow it to determine the appropriate response to similar situations for other companies.

Measuring Sustainability Performance

Underlying these discussions about the value of sustainability is an obsession with measuring the sustainability performance of companies, products, investments, and so on. A widely cited essay in management studies offers a "systematic overview" of research on the relationship between corporate environmental performance and corporate financial performance, asking whether it "pay[s] to be green."[34] It highlights several positive links between the environmental and economic performance of firms, including opportunities for increasing revenue (such as selling their pollution-control technologies) and opportunities for decreasing costs (such as lowered costs of energy, materials, labor, and capital). Among the biggest challenges in establishing this relationship was finding convincing indicators of environmental performance, a problem exacerbated by the integration of social performance to try to achieve a true "triple-bottom-line" approach. The section on implications for future research focuses almost exclusively on the need for curating new data sets and developing new measurement techniques.

Indeed, the challenge of measuring these impacts has been at the center of discussions about the business case for sustainability since it was formulated. It has been nearly three decades since the economists Michael Porter and Claas van der Linde proposed that investing in sustainability was not necessarily costly but could actually create new "competitive advantages" for early movers.[35] The introductory essay of an influential edited volume called *Managing the Business Case for Sustainability* highlights the importance of measurement right in the title, which expands to "Measuring and Managing the Business Case for Sustainability." According to these authors, "In a business company, successful management of sustainability performance is achieved only if the management of environmental and social issues is in line with increased competitiveness and economic performance. As a consequence, sustainability management requires an integration of environmental, social, and economic management and thus covers all the links between non-market and economic issues."[36] Competitiveness here is seen as a function of corporate social performance, corporate environmental performance, and corporate financial performance. Regardless of whether managers interested in sustainability are motivated purely by the desire to "do well" or whether they also feel some ethical obligation to "do good," for these authors, the central task of research in corporate sustainability is to come up with quantitative indicators of social and environmental performance that are comparable to the much-better-established indicators of corporate financial performance. Even attempts to move "beyond the business case" for corporate sustainability by developing a "natural case" and a "societal case" maintain a commitment to metaphors of natural and social capital, and they do little more than define new indicators that need to be measured—not just socio-efficiency and eco-efficiency (which are essentially synonymous with corporate social performance and corporate environmental performance when they are defined as the economically efficient use of social and natural capital) but also eco-effectiveness, socio-effectiveness, ecological equity, and sufficiency.[37] This overarching preoccupation with defining and measuring sustainability indicators in the context of corporate sustainability's theory and practice reflects a commensurative impulse that is fundamental to contemporary sustainability and is crucial to understanding its politics.

Commensuration and Neoliberal Sustainability

To bring the three elements of commensuration, comparison, and causation into relation with each other, we turn to the theory of gradients and grading. For the anthropologist Paul Kockelman, gradients are "the way qualities vary in their intensity over space and time, and the way such variations relate to causal processes," while grading is "the ways agents assess and alter such intensities, and experience and intervene in causal processes."[38] Kockelman's concern with the variable intensity of qualities recalls Espeland and Stevens's definition of "commensuration" as the transformation of qualities into quantities and the transformation of differences into magnitudes. It highlights the extent to which grading presupposes commensuration and is presupposed by both comparison and causation, and the important bit of this theory for us is how these latter three components are related. As Kockelman argues, causal and comparative grounds are often inextricably intertwined. Comparative grounds are important *because* causal grounds are important: the kinds of differences that commensuration transforms into magnitudes and the qualities that commensuration transforms into comparable quantities "become salient precisely because they are posited to correlate with [some] important effect."[39] A dimension of comparison like sustainability is "highly mediate," which means it "consist[s] of an aggregated set of relatively immediate, concrete, and easy-to-quantify dimensions."[40] As we saw earlier, sustainability as a dimension of comparison disaggregates into social, environmental, and economic subdimensions. Each of these subdimensions disaggregates even further, into sub-subdimensions that grow increasingly easy to measure: "the social" comes to be understood as an aggregate of things like instances of gender-based violence or investments in education or volunteer hours among employees, while "the environmental" comes to be understood as an aggregate of things like tons of CO_2 emissions and cubic meters of water and hectares of deforested landscapes; other indicators cross these (sub-)subdimensions, such as a company's transparency about its social and environmental impacts as evidenced by its participation in one or another multistakeholder reporting initiatives or the extent to which its annual sustainability report has been sufficiently standardized. Conveniently—and this is crucial—"the economic" is understood through the exceedingly familiar metric of money.

As the drama around Dieselgate unfolded during my fieldwork, from my perspective, Volkswagen's stock price was lower in 2016 than it was in 2014 *because* of its scandal in 2015, while from my informant's perspective, Volkswagen's value was always lower than it could have been *because* it was inherently unsustainable according to her bank's ESG ratings, a legacy of bad governance extending back at least a century. Nestlé's stock price remained relatively stable while Volkswagen's stock price plummeted *because* Nestlé showed itself to be more sustainable than Volkswagen, even in the face of a scandal. Even if my informants' understanding of the causal direction between sustainability and profitability is not always clear, the fact that they believe there is a causal relationship one way or the other implies that they conceptualize both sustainability and profitability as calculable gradients.

Without belaboring the point, I think there are two interesting and important parallels between my informants' definition of sustainability and the relationship between commensuration, comparison, and causality. First, in the same way that both comparison and causality presuppose commensuration, the "sustainability as a journey" and the "business case for sustainability" both presuppose a triple-bottom-line approach to sustainability. Second, comparing companies in terms of their sustainability, whether it is the changing sustainability performance of one company over time or the relative sustainability performance of two different companies, really only becomes salient from the perspective of my informants when the company or companies can also be compared in terms of their financial performance and, crucially, when a link between these two comparisons can be established. Viewing sustainability through the lens of commensuration, comparison, and causation helps reveal the multifaceted role that sustainability plays in neoliberal governance. It allows us to better understand how seemingly mundane discussions about quantitative indicators and technical debates about methods for measuring and evaluating those impacts are actually central to the private sector's increasingly prominent position in global and local political ecologies. For Kockelman, "commensuration is the art of governance proper to neoliberalism," where governance refers to "a process whereby the possible actions of formally free individuals are enabled and constrained" and where neoliberalism is "a worldview that fosters market-based behavior as the pervasive mode of social conduct." In the context of neoliberalism, he argues, "freedom is the freedom to choose; and coercion is the enabling and constraining of possible choices. And insofar as choice (between two or more options) depends on comparability (of those options), and insofar as comparability depends on commensurability (if options are to be judged different in degree, not just different in kind), there is a deep resonance between neoliberalism and commensuration."[41] In fostering market-based behavior as the pervasive mode of social (and environmental) conduct, neoliberalism depends not just on comparison but on assumptions about causal relationships as well. In addition to presupposing a quite radical degree of comparability (and by extension commensurability), we know from Harvey's definition earlier that neoliberalism also advances an explicit claim about the causal relationship between "maximizing the reach and frequency of market transactions," on the one hand, and maximizing "the social good," on the other. From the outset, there is a need to quantify things like "the social good" or environmental well-being or at the very least to conceptualize them as quantifiable, so that they can be compared over time and correlated to the ever-expanding influence of the market and the financial performance of its corporate avatars. As the philosopher John O'Neill has argued at length, the insistence on the commensurability of incommensurate, plural values is fundamental to arguments in favor of market-based solutions but is also a way to undermine those who advocate nonmarket approaches.[42]

Neoliberal sustainability reflects the belief that enrolling social and environmental concerns in the logic of ever-expanding markets is the best way to address those concerns. But this begs the question of what "the market" is in the context of neoliberal sustainability and, specifically, how my informants working in sustainability imagine their relationship with the market. Sustainability professionals' understanding of the market comes, in part, from their training at universities where sustainability is often taught from the perspective of neoclassical economics. From this perspective, the market yields the most efficient and optimal social and environmental outcomes as long as it has enough information about things like costs, benefits, supply, and demand; one of the easiest ways to correct market failures is by providing the market with more information that it is able to interpret and act on. Subsequent policy proposals to address issues like underdevelopment or environmental pollution tend to focus on making sure markets are able to deliver these results by getting rid of undue political influence on markets (regulations), requiring the disclosure of the kinds of information markets need to yield efficient outcomes, and so on.[43] In the context of corporate sustainability, this inherent faith in the market's ability to yield optimal outcomes is enacted through efforts to create social and environmental indicators that the market can use to generate positive social and environmental impacts alongside positive financial impacts. The solution to the problems generated by market failures is to make sure markets are less likely to fail, and one of the main tasks of sustainability professionals becomes the provision of data that the market can use to yield better outcomes. The notion of neoliberal sustainability captures this orientation toward the market.[44] It is an orientation that is inseparable from efforts to calculate the impacts that companies and other organizations have on society and the environment, and it is an orientation that is inseparable from a worldview in which society and the environment are distinct domains that can be quantified and measured in the first place.

2

Measuring Sustainability

How to engineer an answer:
select what to measure, where.
Hire the experts.
Guide them in their work.
—Elise Marcella Godfrey, "How to Precipitate Yellowcake"

No Value without Measurement

I spent much of my time in Geneva conducting participant observation at international organizations that focused on promoting corporate sustainability. At one organization, I was embedded as a volunteer research consultant in a small team whose role was to develop a way for companies to measure and report what they were trying to conceptualize as "social capital." What my informants meant by "social capital" was a bit amorphous, referring to the ways in which companies both impacted and depended on society. In this way, they theorized the business-society relationship as a kind of feedback loop, recognizing that a business's negative effects on society could undermine its profitability, and not only through a diminished "social license to operate"—failing to invest in local education initiatives, for example, might make it difficult to hire skilled workers later; agreeing to pay a small bribe to an official for preferential treatment could balloon into exorbitant fees later on. The social, in this view of "social capital," is something to invest in with the expectation of future returns.

A few months into the project, four of us were sitting around a clean, white table on ergonomic office chairs in a sunny room, surrounded by floor-to-ceiling plate-glass walls and windows. The building, according to one of its junior architects, whom I met wandering around the building one day, was designed as an architectural nod to the supposed transparency of doing business in Switzerland. (This has become a common trope in contemporary architecture.) Colorful ethernet and HDMI cables sprouted from the center of the table like a bouquet of wilted plastic flowers. A wide LCD screen buzzed to life in front of the window as Miranda, who had been managing the organization's more established efforts to develop guidelines for measuring and reporting natural capital, switched on her standard-issue Dell computer, prompting a neatly organized desktop to blink onto the screen.

Through numerous interactions supplemented with semistructured interviews during my year in Geneva, I got to know Miranda as resolutely objective, with a proud and unwavering faith in the ability of technoscientific management programs to address various social and environmental problems. She sees natural capital—things like forest covering and fish stocks—as fairly straightforward to measure and value. Bioeconomists, she told me in one interview in the autumn of 2015, have given us reliable-enough estimates of the regeneration rates of things like salmon and pine trees, while ecologists, climate scientists, and data analysts have provided reliable estimates of the carbon sequestration rates of oceans and rain forests. Her unwavering belief in the ability of markets to incentivize companies and other actors to develop profitable and sufficient solutions to crises like water shortages and sea-level rise exemplified the prototypical "green capitalist," a person who believes it is possible "save our collective, planetary selves without having to eschew the cherished free market system."[1] Because she so thoroughly embodies the ideals of green capitalism and because she was so forthcoming in our conversations about sustainability, Miranda features prominently throughout this book. We got along quite well, and I enjoyed being around her. Relatedly, I never questioned her commitment to making the world a better place, and she seemed deeply and genuinely passionate about her work. But I also believe Miranda's approach to sustainability, which is typical of my informants, is deeply flawed. As we know from Tania Murray Li's work on development projects in Indonesia, even a sincere "will to improve" does little, on its own, to prevent profoundly unjust outcomes.[2]

Miranda lifted her watch up to her face and announced that it was time to start the meeting, bringing an abrupt end to our chitchat. She had prepared a short presentation for those of us working on the social capital project about the principles of natural capital valuation and the ways in which our efforts might be more closely aligned. After an overview of some of the methods used in natural capital valuation, including their strengths and weaknesses and advice on when to use which evaluative tools, she told us about the progress she and her colleagues have made over the years and how they had become "thought leaders" in the field of natural capital measurement and valuation, an indispensable resource for corporations, banks, and international organizations. But she ended her presentation on a bit of a skeptical note: she was worried that attempts to "align" natural capital valuation with ongoing attempts to develop methodologies for measuring and valuing social capital might undermine decades of effort to legitimize the former, which at the time was just starting to be embraced by industry and policy makers.

In the months leading up to this meeting, I had been shadowing Susanna, one of Miranda's colleagues who was managing a project to develop new social capital accounting tools for multinational corporations. In response to Miranda's skepticism, Susanna spoke up, noting not only the rapid progress being made in the field of social capital measurement and valuation but also, just as important, the growing public interest in these types of metrics. This prompted Miranda to launch into a critique of social capital's methodological limitations that was so fluid that it seemed rehearsed. How, she demanded, could we ever hope to compare the biological and geochemical processes that constitute the "stocks and flows" of natural capital with the cultural and emotional processes that constitute the "stocks and flows" of social capital? The measurement and valuation of natural capital is based on a modern, objective, technoscientific view of the world, whereas social capital relies on subjective assertions and abstract theories from the humanities and noneconomic (or "soft") social sciences. The former appeals to reason, logic, observation, and rationality, while the latter appeals to emotion and imagination and culture and politics. She concluded her critique with a simple question that sheds light on one of the critical presuppositions at the heart of neoliberal sustainability and the theoretical concern at the heart of this book: "How can you expect to value something if you don't even know how to measure it?"

Ultimately, this organization's efforts to design a general protocol for measuring a company's impacts and dependencies on social capital failed due in large part to the slippery definition of "social capital" and all the different things it would need to include in the context of corporate sustainability. Most attempts to measure things like social and environmental impacts fail, which makes sense given their reliance on establishing benchmarks, on the one hand, and their commitment to constantly improving the definitions of and methods for measuring KPIs, on the other hand, rendering earlier benchmarks obsolete. Nevertheless, as this chapter shows, even failed attempts to standardize and quantify the different dimensions of sustainability reinforce the idea that sustainability is something that can and needs to be measured in the first place. I argue that my informants' preoccupation with metrics—even when their attempts at quantification fail—shifts concerns about social and environmental impacts into a regime of neoliberal government, allowing corporations and corporate-adjacent organizations like the banks that invest in them and the NGOs that partner with them to reframe sustainability as a primarily economic problem that can only be solved by subjecting it to the dynamics of the market.

Capitalism for Good

The impetus behind the social capital project was the idea that if natural and financial capital were being measured and reported in corporate sustainability reports, social capital should be measured and reported, too. This represented a rather explicit embrace of the triple-bottom-line approach to sustainability, the idea that sustainability is the consideration of all three of these dimensions. It also explicitly embraced a metaphor of capital, reimagining the social dimension of sustainability as something that could be managed in a way that yielded a return on investment. According to Susanna, sustainability without the social dimension was not sustainable at all; it was "merely viable," a reference she made to a more detailed version of the Venn diagram of sustainability that was popular at the time, which labeled the areas where only two of the three circles overlap as viable (economic and environment), bearable (environment and social), and equitable (social and economic).[3]

Given the importance of "aligning" the measurement and valuation of social capital and natural capital, it is necessary to understand how natural capital emerged as such an important force in global sustainable development debates. Here, the political ecologist Sian Sullivan's work is indispensable. In her critique of the book *Natural Capital: Valuing the Planet*, Sullivan observes that the "measurement of what exists is seen as key to rational and efficient management, whilst counting, calculating and pricing things are seen as purely technical practices that are beyond ideology," noting how this contradicts work among critical scholars who have shown how metrics do not merely describe the world but often contribute to its formation and governance.[4] Natural capital, according to Sullivan, "fabricates" nature as an objective, technical "matter of fact," promising to save nature "through its enrolment and technical rendering in natural capital accounts" while at the same time "offering routes whereby market growth can be sustained and amplified, in part through the better valuing of 'natural capital' that such accounting practices promise to perform."[5] Following work by Andrea Mennicken and Peter Miller, she theorizes ongoing attempts to quantitatively and financially account for nature and society as "a *territorializing* activity, through which calculative, market and privatising regimes of governance extend into new areas of social and ecological life."[6] Reframing the natural environment as natural capital submits nature to the logic of capital.

In the attempt to align methods for measuring and evaluating social capital with methods for measuring and evaluating natural capital, the social capital project contributed to the reproduction of "economic and accounting practices" that "contribute the building blocks for an ideological construction of the world that serves particular interests and frames out others."[7] Perhaps unsurprisingly, the interests that this ideological construction serves are the interests of capital, and often explicitly. Several informants insisted that capitalism may not be perfect, but it is the best system "we" have ever had for lifting people out of poverty and improving people's lives, repeating a line of thinking often advanced by technocapitalists like Bill Gates and often wielded against people who advocate degrowth and other anticapitalist alternatives. In that same vein, two of the most influential theories of corporate sustainability— creating shared value and stakeholder theory—were both developed with the explicit intention of saving capitalism from its opponents. Writing at the beginning of neoliberalism's ascent in the early 1980s, R. Edward Freeman prefaced his classic account of stakeholder theory with the observation that "managers in today's corporations are under fire," and one of his book's concluding questions was whether a "revision of managerial capitalism" might one day allow managers to think about their duty to stakeholders rather than just stockholders. Nearly thirty years later, in a world still reeling from the 2008 financial crisis, Freeman prefaced an updated version of his book by claiming that, "more than ever, we need a story about 'responsible capitalism'" and that stakeholder theory was "a good place to start."[8] Around the same time, in 2011, Michael Porter and Mark Kramer popularized the notion of "creating shared value" as a way of reinventing capitalism, which they saw as "an unparalleled vehicle for meeting human needs, improving efficiency, creating jobs, and building wealth" that was currently "under siege." A commitment to creating shared value would yield an "evolved" and "more sophisticated form of capitalism."[9]

Measuring the social and environmental impacts of capitalist development is a key part of efforts to give capitalism a more human or caring face. Through an analysis of the tools and techniques that "value entrepreneurs" develop to account for "social value" across different contexts, the sociologist Emily Barman has argued that scholars should pay attention to the relational and contextual aspects of efforts to measure things like social capital rather than approaching measurement devices as if they necessarily reflect a particular ethical or economic value.[10] Here, she pushes back against the "reflection assumption" implicit in the theoretical agendas of both marketization scholars, who see measurements of social value as reflective of and motivated by the hegemonic logic of financial markets, and moral markets scholars, who argue that people try to engage with markets in ways that address their own ethical concerns. As Viviana Zelizer showed in her classic study of the changing social value of children, it is difficult to identify a clear line between the cultural and economic factors that determine social value, even in a world where market logics are increasingly pervasive, because of the way these dynamics intersect with each other and evolve across time and space.[11] Barman's contention is that understanding the way different actors define social value is not sufficient for anticipating the kind of devices they will come up with to measure it. People who balk at the idea of putting a price on something like health or educational outcomes have no problem embracing the market as a way of achieving their goals, while people who push corporations to be more compassionate might reject monetized indicators of their social performance.

Different people working in different contexts come up with different ways of measuring social impacts that do not fit neatly with what one might expect—a Swiss private banker who thinks it is wrong to monetize corporate social responsibility or a worker at a left-wing NGO who thinks the best way to promote social change is to put a price on it. Few, if any, of the people I have interviewed and observed since starting this research in 2015 have agreed on the precise elements of social or environmental responsibility, and many of them were happy to admit that their personal views about what matters when thinking about sustainability might diverge from what other people think is important. That raises a different set of questions that the rest of this chapter addresses: What are the consequences of debates about which dimensions of sustainability should be measured and how we should measure them? Does it matter what kinds of measurement devices these different groups of sustainability professionals develop in the different ethical and institutional contexts in which they work? As I argue in this chapter, these debates leave something important in their wake, namely, the idea that sustainability is something that not only *can* be measured but *should* be measured, which leads to the emergence of accounting infrastructures that afford a particular mode of neoliberal sustainability governance. This leads to a broader point about an ideological embrace of "the market" as the only way to achieve sustainability and to a commitment among sustainability professionals to providing the kind of quantitative data they believe will enable the market to generate sustainable outcomes, rather than engaging more directly in generating those outcomes themselves. The diversity of the measurement devices that sustainability professionals develop as a way of measuring things like social capital or social impact obscures the way these never-ending disputes about metrics transform sustainability into a debate about how and what to measure, precluding more fundamental discussions about the kinds of ideological structures that all these measurements end up reinforcing.

"You Can't Measure Everything"

Companies have a lot of leeway in determining what kinds of data they publish when it comes to sustainability reporting, and one of the motivations of my informants who work to promote more rigorous social and environmental accounting standards is to make these accounts look like financial accounting, where measurement and reporting rules are much stricter and much more standardized. Scrolling through the seemingly infinite number of potential indicators included on the website of the Global Reporting Initiative (GRI) one day in 2016, I asked Chantal, a corporate sustainability manager at a multinational industrial agricultural company, how she chooses what to measure and report. It was the third time I had interviewed her about her job, the first two times over the phone and this time in person while she was in Geneva for a small conference on global agriculture and sustainability, where we were sitting in the foyer of the World Trade Organization during a break between sessions, surrounded by the multilingual chitchat of sustainability professionals who were busily networking over coffee and pastries. I had taken out my laptop and pulled up some documents outlining various GRI standards, a set of reporting and disclosure guidelines on "material topics" for companies and other organizations. In my own attempts to navigate the GRI standards, I found the options available to companies a bit bewildering, and I hoped Chantal could offer a concise way to make sense of them all. Instead, she laughed and said that it was indeed overwhelming, and she described the huge expenditures of time and money that companies are increasingly pressured to invest in these kinds of initiatives.[12] Some of the indicators are very relevant to agro-industrial companies like hers (e.g., GRI 204: Procurement Practices or GRI 417: Marketing and Labeling), while some of them are clearly less relevant (e.g., GRI 418: Customer Privacy). Most of them, however, are in what Chantal called a "gray area," by which she meant that it is possible to make a case for including them but also relatively easy to ignore them.

Chantal described two main considerations when choosing whether to measure and report particular indicators: first, she and her team tend to collect data about indicators that are easiest and cheapest to measure; second, they disclose what has the least (negative) impact on their company's reputation, which can impact its share price. It is a delicate balancing act. To avoid charges of greenwashing, they should disclose their performance in areas where they "could stand to improve" but never in areas where improvement is impossible. Industrial agriculture, for example, uses substantial quantities of water; in drought-prone areas of the world, this often exacerbates water shortages and increases pressure on local communities. It is best, then, to not disclose GRI 303-2 ("water sources significantly affected by withdrawal of water") but to disclose instead GRI 303-3 ("water recycled and reused"), which points to a challenging area but in a way that paints it in a relatively rosy light. These kinds of choices are necessary, she tells me, because "you can't measure *everything.*"

Chantal's comment highlights the challenge of coming to terms with the nearly infinite dimensions of sustainability, of choosing from among long lists of possible indicators and potential components to paint a more "complete" picture of a company's or a product's sustainability performance, but also highlights the power that companies have in determining what "counts" as sustainable through their determination of what gets measured and reported. Out of the three dimensions of sustainability, my informants usually claimed that the social aspect is the trickiest to measure. It can be disaggregated into numerous subdimensions—gender, education, health care, labor rights, and so on—that are themselves able to be disaggregated into even more sub-subdimensions: wage disparities and gender-based discrimination, funding for childhood education and continuous training for workers, and so on. These subdimensions do not have clear boundaries. Gender-based violence on tea farms, for example, is as much an issue of gender as it is of labor rights; child labor is as much an issue of labor as it is of education, since many of the children who are forced to work at different nodes of global supply chains must often miss school to do so. Even if you could account for these different aspects of a company's social impacts, all that information would overwhelm even the most committed analysts, and it could even undermine the goal of tracking a single company's improvements over time or comparing the social impacts of different companies, which are implicated in different social issues on the basis of the sector they are in or the places in which they operate.

Gendered Accounts

Amanda is a sustainability analyst at a multinational energy company that, during my fieldwork in Geneva, was engaged in an aggressive PR campaign, trying to promote itself as a "responsible" energy company. Energy companies, especially those involved in conventional energy generation through the burning of fossil fuels like coal and natural gas, often use the language of responsibility instead of sustainability, wary of the ease with which critics might accuse them of greenwashing if they claimed to be sustainable. In doing so, they tend to emphasize their social impacts rather than their environmental impacts, like providing stable employment to skilled workers or investing in infrastructure like roads and hospitals. During an interview with Amanda in 2016, she told me that a key part of her company's sustainability strategy was gender equality. When I asked what exactly that involved, she told me somewhat elusively that the company was "investing" in the professional development of the its female managers and executives, including a new mentorship program aimed at the retention of women employees and developing more progressive maternity leave policies that go "above and beyond" what is required by most of the national regulations that they are subject to. In practice, this involved little more than tracking the number of female managers and executives. I asked whether she considered herself as part of that sustainability strategy, either benefiting from it as a woman with a successful career in the company or contributing to the formulation of the strategy as a sustainability expert:[13]

AMANDA: Well, I don't think it really works like that, exactly. What matters is that these kinds of things are things that we can measure and keep track of. We know how many women work for us, how much we spend on retention and training programs; we know how much it costs to hire and train someone to replace a new mother. It's easy. That's data we already have. It's data that we'd have anyway. And it's easy, then, to say, "Oh, last year we hired this many women, and this year we hired this many. This many quit. This many stayed." Et cetera. That kind of comparability over time is super important, obviously, and it helps set us see how we're doing compared to other companies.

MATTHEW: Okay, but if it's data you already have and programs you're already doing, what makes it sustainable? When I think of an energy company's sustainability policy, I think of windmills and solar panels. Is that too simplistic?

AMANDA: Well, obviously sustainability means a lot of things. For us— look, we work a lot in coal, a lot in natural gas. That's never going to be as "sustainable" [air quotes] as windmills and solar panels, no matter what you do. No one is ever going to see us that way. So we have to do what we can. We have to set realistic goals that have social impacts, which is obviously just as important for sustainability as environmental impacts.

For Amanda, the idea that sustainability can be broken down into its component parts (people, planet, and profit; or social, environmental, and economic) is taken as axiomatic, indexed by her use of the word "obviously" several times when talking about her company's sustainability strategy. This was no doubt as much a result of her professional experience in corporate sustainability as her postgraduate training in sustainable development, which tends to start by introducing students to the triple-bottom-line model of sustainability. In those settings, the triple-bottom-line model is presented as critical in and of itself vis-à-vis notions of sustainability that focus too "simplistically" on environmental problems alone or approaches to management that focus too myopically on a single, financial bottom line. Poor performance in the domain of environmental sustainability can be offset by excellent performance in the domain of social responsibility, reinforcing the "weak sustainability" approach that not only characterizes most corporate sustainability initiatives but is a condition of possibility for the comparability and substitutability of social, environmental, and economic impacts that such initiatives instantiate.

I also talked about the relationship between gender diversity, sustainability, and financial performance with Maarten, who oversees the responsible investing operations of a large international asset manager. I first contacted Maarten when I was living in Geneva because his LinkedIn profile said he was working there, but he responded that he had recently moved to his bank's New York City office and that we should meet in person when I returned to New Haven. When I got back to the US in the fall of 2016, however, it ended up being quite difficult to schedule a time to meet, and he asked if it would be all right to have an interview over the phone instead. When we finally settled on a time, I asked him to tell me if a responsible investment is worth more financially than an irresponsible investment, a question that was admittedly meant to be a bit provocative, since it highlights the indeterminacy of words like "responsible" and "irresponsible." He replied that responsible investments are "obviously" more valuable than irresponsible investments, so I asked him how, exactly, his company measures and values responsibility. He rattled off a list of well-known principles and guidelines before sheepishly confiding that, actually, there is really no way to value "this kind of stuff." Walmart, he argued, outperforms many of its competitors financially, but he asked rhetorically whether that has anything to do with its well-developed (and, in business school classrooms and popular strategy books, widely lauded) climate-change policy and, if so, how much of its financial success is attributable to its climate policy. Wouldn't Walmart perform well even if it had no explicit climate-change policy? He turned to another example of something that "obviously" affects financial performance but is difficult to measure: "You have some academic research that can show, for a cross-section of companies, that more [gender] diverse boards make better decisions. But for the specific, individual company, how much of a premium do you put on that? It's not like the standard toolkit of finance. It's sales. It triangulates directly in the bottom line."

Amanda and Maarten both think that gender is an important, valuable element of corporate sustainability. They both believe that a gender-diverse workforce is "material" in the sense that it improves a company's financial performance, and both seem to think that it is good from a social perspective to have more women managers and board members. They also both seem to think that gender diversity among a company's management staff is relatively easy to measure, which is why they offered it to me as an example of a dimension of sustainability that can be measured. But they also seemed motivated by very different things, even though they both worked in the private sector. Amanda never directly linked her company's position on gender equality to its financial performance, even if the indirect links were clear: if a company has a demonstrably progressive gender policy—evidenced by generous maternity leave and a large number of women managers—it will be able to attract the best female talent, who will see that they can balance having children with having a career and will also believe that there are opportunities for upward mobility. Maarten, on the other hand, was very interested in the direct economic benefits of social and environmental responsibility, whether it is a company's climate policy or the gender diversity of its leadership team. Whereas Amanda seemed content with her company's gender policy generating these indirect economic benefits, Maarten wanted evidence that there was a direct economic impact, and not just at an industry level.

If tasked with developing devices to measure the social impact of, say, a board diversity policy, Maarten and Amanda would probably come up with different solutions. Amanda's indicators might emphasize the loyalty that such a policy cultivated among women or minority employees, while Maarten's might be more focused on the financial benefits of such a policy, reframing its social impact in explicitly monetary terms. But even if they were to come up with different ways of measuring and evaluating gender diversity, they would both be contributing to a conceptualization of gender diversity within corporations as something whose social value can ultimately be accounted for in a way that lets these kinds of comparisons happen and be used to make claims about the cause-and-effect relationship between more gender diversity and more profits.

Capital-S Social

In a sense, Miranda was right: the difficulty with measuring social capital is that it seems impossible to define "the social" in a way that decomposes into meaningfully measurable components. A few months after our meeting, where Miranda had expressed her skepticism about social capital, the social capital team had a daylong brainstorming session. We talked about different approaches to social capital, what we liked about them, and what we did not like. I brought the "academic" perspective, which I think the team liked because it lent a bit of scholarly legitimacy to their otherwise floundering efforts. I had been doing research on definitions of "social capital," and I gave a "high-level introduction" to a tradition in sociology that extended from Bourdieu's well-known theory of cultural capital through more recent work spanning economics, sociology, political science, and psychology.[14] This overview included a description of three different forms of social capital famously outlined by the sociologist James Coleman: obligations and expectations, informational channels, and social norms and sanctions for violating these norms.[15]

We took each of these forms of social capital in turn. Susanna asked us to think about what obligations and expectations there were in the context of sustainable development. We talked about how, as relatively privileged Western consumers, we are obligated to purchase things like sustainably produced products and energy-efficient cars and appliances. To the extent that it is feasible, we should take the train when we travel. We should ask the people who manage our retirement accounts if it is possible to invest in a responsibly managed fund. Stephen, a colleague who worked part-time with the social capital team, summed it up nicely: we have an obligation to "vote with our wallet." Nellie, who had been in the meeting a few months earlier with Miranda, Susanna, and me, wondered whether it was just consumers who were obligated to be sustainable. Weren't companies obligated to be sustainable, too? Stephen was quick with a rebuttal. Companies have an obligation to their investors—a fiduciary duty to maximize shareholder value—as well as an obligation to comply with the law. Our role in all this was to make sure that there was a clear business case for sustainability, to prove to companies that the best and easiest way to meet their obligations to investors was to be as sustainable as possible.

Susanna cut in, building on Stephen's point to emphasize the importance of the work we were doing on the social capital project. Having consistent and reliable indicators of the company's impacts on society would make it easier to make this business case. We would be able to show objectively that companies that performed better socially also tended to perform better financially, especially in the long term. Nellie, however, did not seem content leaving these things up to chance. What about companies that performed better financially despite—or even because of—poor social indicators? She raised the issue of "sin stocks," a term used to refer to companies that trade in things like weapons, alcohol, gambling, and pornography, which tend to perform well on the stock market due to high margins and consistent consumer demand, especially during recessions, when other companies perform poorly. Stephen responded with the example of Diageo, the beer and spirits conglomerate that owns popular brands like Guinness, Smirnoff, Tanqueray, Crown Royal, and Baileys, which for the past several years had been a beacon of corporate sustainability, signified by its inclusion in the Dow Jones Sustainability World Index and the FTSE4Good Index. Stephen's point was that alcohol companies can be sustainable, too, especially when they recognize that being sustainable can help them be more profitable, as Diageo clearly had. By the end of the conversation about obligations and expectations, it was clear that companies had an obligation to make money, sustainability professionals had an obligation to demonstrate and facilitate the business case for sustainability, and consumers had an obligation to drive the business case by shopping responsibly. This was "the market" working like it was supposed to.

We moved on to a discussion of information channels, the second of Coleman's forms of social capital. "Information," argues Coleman, "is important in providing a basis for action. But acquisition of information is costly. At a minimum, it requires attention, which is always in scarce supply. One means by which information can be acquired is by use of social relations that are maintained for other purposes."[16] As I read this definition aloud from the notes on my computer, Susanna nodded along vigorously, as this was where she saw her role most clearly elaborated. Stephen and Nellie agreed. The role of organizations like theirs—and the goal of the social capital project we were working on—was to make it so the information (the data) that companies provide about their social impacts could provide a basis for action on sustainability. The cost of acquiring this information, according to the team, was only indirectly financial: the issue was not that companies could not afford to collect and analyze this information (indeed, most of my informants were happy to admit that sustainability is typically a small, even marginal, part of corporate budgets); rather, the challenge was that companies did not know how to measure and report this information in a meaningful way, and they ended up wasting a lot of time and money producing inconsistent data about poorly defined indicators. By developing a single standard for defining, measuring, and reporting social capital, companies would finally be able to produce information about their social impacts that could be used as a foundation for data-driven sustainability strategies. A shared protocol would facilitate information sharing not just about social impacts per se but about measuring and managing social impacts. Stephen liked the way this conversation was going, concluding that the real value of our work would be to show that there was a business case for social responsibility across different sectors, which we would only be able to do once those different sectors had a common way of measuring and reporting their social impacts.

We finally turned to a discussion of norms and sanctions. Nellie pointed out that she did not really understand the difference between expectations and norms: Weren't our expectations of a company or a consumer determined by our understanding of what is normal? I struggled to answer her question, but I said that, in my reading of Coleman's typology, the focus on norms highlighted the way norms can inhibit other, abnormal actions. "Norms that make it possible to walk alone at night," Coleman observes, "also constrain the activities of criminals (and in some cases of noncriminals as well)."[17] Susanna was interested in the role that our work might play in the establishment of new norms, specifically around the normalization of standardized measurement and reporting. She saw a direct parallel with Coleman's example of the norms that make it possible to walk alone at night and the norms that might make it possible for conscious consumers to shop with confidence. Stephen agreed, claiming that if this kind of reporting became a norm, companies that refused to disclose their social impacts might be sanctioned, not by some regulatory authority but by the market itself, since they would potentially fail to attract investors who also face increasing pressure to be more sustainable. Excited by the prospect of creating something that would have such a big impact on the way companies operated, Stephen concluded that our work that day was not merely a technical exercise; we were contributing to a new way of thinking about the "capital-S Social," bringing it more in line with Miranda's approach to thinking about nature itself as a measurable form of capital.

Objectifying the Social

The accounting theorist Michael Power has developed a model for thinking about how something like "social capital" emerges as an object that can be accounted for. His model consists of four phases: object formation, object elaboration, activity orchestration, and practice stabilization via the accretion of a transorganizational sociotechnical infrastructure. The example that Power uses to develop his model is the impact case studies (ICSs) that are conducted as part of the British government's Research Excellence Framework (REF). The REF assigns a score to British universities that is meant to demonstrate the impact of their research and is an important indicator in determining not only how much public funding the different universities receive but also how successful the careers of its individual researchers will be. A government report published in 2006 established the need for universities to measure their impacts (object formation), followed by debates about what scientific impact actually meant, expanding the report's definition from a narrow concern with economic benefits to a broader concern with social, economic, and cultural benefits outside the academy (object elaboration). During this process, the focus on impact as something that should be measurable and verifiable remained strong, and over the next few years, the ICS started to institutionalize, forcing researchers (and the growing class of academic administrators) to reconceptualize impact as something with particular traces (such as invited lectures at a government agency or a newspaper article about some bit of research), which they collect and narrate in an increasingly standardized way (activity orchestration). As universities all start to report impact in the same way, new infrastructures emerge to make the measurement and reporting of this data easier and more centralized, while also locking these methods in place (practice stabilization through infrastructure). On the basis of this model and on the experiences of a pseudonymized British university in dealing with the REF, Power suggests that the "specific form and content of new accounting statements is likely to be more fragile than the infrastructures to which they give rise," that the "importance of accounting to processes of subjectivization" ("the production of subjects who orient themselves towards an object and make it material") "increases with the accretion of infrastructure," and that the accretion of these accounting infrastructures "creates routines which shorten organizational time horizons."[18]

Power's model and subsequent propositions resonate with my observations of the social capital project and other discussions about defining and measuring so-called noneconomic indicators, especially the parts regarding the accretion of accounting infrastructures. It is difficult to identify the moment when social impact or social capital emerged as an accounting object in the context of corporate sustainability, but it is surely around the same time as the triple-bottom-line model of sustainability started to gain traction in the corporate world. One bottom line— the financial bottom line—was a well-established accounting object at that point, but the social and environmental bottom lines had to be recognized and negotiated. For environmental impacts, there were some obvious things to measure, such as wastewater, energy use, pollution, and so on, and many of the debates in natural capital or environmental impact accounting have focused less on what to measure than how to measure it. Negotiations around what counted as social capital were often more contradictory and confusing. Few people seemed to agree what kind of indicators might convincingly demonstrate a company's impacts and dependencies on social capital. As Miranda had already observed, social capital was a step behind natural capital: she conceded that much of the data included in natural capital indicators—fish stocks, pollution emissions, and so on—were exceedingly difficult to measure, but at least, in the narrative projected by Miranda, we knew what we were looking for with natural capital. That technical, quantitative, scientific approach was quite similar to the way financial capital was understood; there was no need for subjective interpretation. Social capital, on the other hand, faced not only the challenge of measurement but also the challenge of definition, of knowing what to try to measure in the first place. What counts as social capital is a matter of opinion, and opinions have no place in these kinds of decisions.

Ultimately, it was impossible to resolve this tension, and the social capital project was abandoned in favor of the more familiar notion of human capital, which would allow companies to focus more narrowly on indicators like employment statistics, funding for worker training, workplace disputes and resolution mechanisms, rates of union membership, and so on. However, despite the object of social capital failing to materialize as a concrete policy object, the debates about how to define and measure it reinforced the idea that the relationship between corporations and the societies in which they operate needed to be understood as something measurable and verifiable, hence the relatively comfortable embrace of a different set of human capital indicators that were easier to measure and whose metrics were more familiar. Discussions about the weaknesses of the proposed framework to measure and report social capital focused on the difficulty of defining and quantifying its different components, the solution to which was either to define them in a way that was easier to measure or to simply choose other indicators that were easier to measure or already had established measurement methods. In the end, this organization opted for the second option.

In talking about the "accretion" of accounting infrastructures, one gets the sense that this process happens slowly and a bit unintentionally, a by-product of negotiations about what an accounting object is and how it should be accounted for, leaving these durable infrastructures in their wake. But in working with Susanna and her colleagues, the establishment of these infrastructures emerged as a rather explicit goal. From the outset, they were endeavoring to create a direct channel of reliable and consistent sustainability data originating in companies and ending up in the hands of consumers, regulators, and investors—in a word, the market. The fragility of metrological regimes belies the durability of the accounting infrastructures on which those regimes depend and the intentionality with which sustainability professionals construct those infrastructures.

Value Propositions

Koen is the regional director of a boutique consulting firm that analyzes corporate sustainability reports, news stories, social media posts, government documents, and other sources of information to generate ESG analyses that many of the world's largest financial firms are willing to pay rather substantial fees to access. When we first met at a conference in Geneva, I noticed on his name tag that he was based in Belgium, where my in-laws live and where I visited fairly regularly for holidays. He told me to connect with him on LinkedIn and to send him a message next time I was in Belgium. A few weeks later, I was spending a long weekend visiting my husband, who was working in Brussels at the time, and Koen invited me for lunch in a lakeside Italian restaurant in a swanky suburb just outside the city. One of the challenges of business anthropology is that informants are often not only fluent in the same sorts of analytical vocabularies as the ethnographer but also constantly on the lookout for lines of questioning that have potentially ulterior motives that might lead them to divulge some insider knowledge. There were more than a few times during our long lunch when Koen's eyes glinted and he had to suppress a smile, well aware of the kinds of topics I was trying to "trick" him into broaching. I think he thought I was trying to get him to admit that sustainability was all greenwashing, to get a good quote for my dissertation to show that he and his colleagues were all in on a joke that the rest of us outside the industry had not quite grasped. But after a round of Belgian beers and multiple assurances that our conversation would be anonymized, Koen finally began to open up. He knew that I was not after his company's trade secrets, and he knew that I was not after a job, like a lot of young people ostensibly interested in his views on sustainable development apparently were. "Let me be frank," he said with a chuckle. "Is a lot of this stuff bullshit? Yes, definitely." He paused for a moment to contemplate his next sentence. "But what we're doing, the data we provide, really makes companies more sustainable." He attributed this to two forces: first, managers can make better decisions when they have objective and reliable data about their companies' sustainability; second, investors are able to make better decisions about their investments when they have that same data about companies, which pushes companies to be even more sustainable, generate more data, and so on.

The kind of data that Koen was talking about came from disparate sources and in diverse formats. His firm collects newspaper stories about corporate scandals from major international newspapers like the *Washington Post*, *Le Monde*, and the *Financial Times* but also, he told me, from smaller regional and local newspapers, where an observant analyst might discover reporting about an event that eventually becomes a global scandal. Social media has become more important for Koen and his colleagues' work. If they notice something before it goes viral, they might be able to "get ahead of it." They combine this kind of analysis with more conventional forms of financial analysis, reading the sustainability reports and financial statements of major companies, following legal proceedings and regulatory disclosures, and maintaining a watchful eye over several databases. "We spend a lot of time on Bloomberg terminals," he said, but because Bloomberg's sustainability coverage at the time was, in Koen's words, "thin," they also had to look elsewhere for sustainability ratings. Different rating agencies often provide wildly different estimates of the same company's sustainability performance, which means that Koen and his colleagues have to spend time understanding the different methodologies used to construct those ratings, using their own judgment to determine which methods are the most rigorous. Even if they think a particular rating is too simplistic or has ignored an important variable, sometimes it remains influential in investor decisions, so it must be accounted for in Koen's advisory work.

Sometimes, Koen told me, the market responds to ratings and rankings that he personally thinks are quite superficial, especially lists like *Corporate Knights'* annual ranking of the world's one hundred most sustainable companies. And even though most of the world's biggest companies were quickly signing onto the Global Reporting Initiative, their sustainability reports varied substantially in quality, with some doing "the bare minimum" while others seemed to try to inundate readers with irrelevant or difficult-to-decipher information.

Koen's company was doing well, attracting a steady stream of new clients and retaining old ones. I was curious, however, if he felt like there was a risk that investors would eventually move all of this research in-house. He thought it was unlikely, given the high costs of collecting the kind of information that his company analyzed. The amount of money clients had to spend on subscriptions and consulting fees was substantial but also substantially less than what they would have to pay to hire a team to do that work themselves. On top of that, they would still have to pay subscription fees to other service providers, and they would still have to hire "independent" consultants and analysts to come in and legitimize their sustainability decisions. Koen said that his company's biggest "value proposition" was its ability to turn all of this data into something that makes sense to investors, offering a way for investors to think about the sustainability performance of a company alongside its financial performance (which, as investors, they already know how to do).

Koen was approaching sustainability from a different angle than Susanna and her colleagues working on the social capital project, and yet both reinforced the idea that data about sustainability should be measurable and verifiable, and both contributed to the accretion of the same kinds of infrastructures that allow data about a company's sustainability performance to be compared with data about its financial performance. From both perspectives, the issue was the messiness of the data about sustainability and the difficulty this posed when trying to integrate sustainability concerns into strategic decision-making processes. Their approach to the problem may have been similar, but their approaches to the solution really were different: whereas Koen and his colleagues sought to provide the service of analyzing sustainability data and corralling it into a financially legible set of indicators, Susanna and her colleagues were focusing on data sources, trying to figure out a way for companies to report their social impacts in a way that would obviate the need for people like Koen to charge high fees for cleaning and analyzing that data in the first place.

Data for the Market

Despite these different approaches and despite the debate about whether social capital measurement could be aligned with natural capital measurement, everyone seemed to be working with the same goal in mind. They wanted to ensure that data about sustainability—whether those data are reported by companies, derived by a consulting firm, or measured by natural scientists—made sense from the perspective of the market. Neoclassical economists imagine the market as uniquely able to take in data about social and environmental factors and make sure that the impacts of financial decisions are efficiently and optimally distributed. In my own postgraduate training in environmental economics, a field that focuses on topics like the economic value of clean air and the financial incentives for conserving things like old-growth forests or specific endangered species, many of our homework assignments or "problem sets" dealt with figuring out the point at which a supply curve and a demand curve or a cost curve and benefit curve intersect. The idea was that if you could do this relatively simple calculus, then you just needed sufficient and accurate data to determine, empirically, how the market values things as different as clean air and panda bears. Much of the innovation in the field of environmental economics seems to happen around the production and analysis of new data sets. Preferences and values are "revealed" through this kind of analysis, with the market facilitating those revelations: whether, when given the choice, consumers prefer oat milk over soy milk, how much they are willing to pay to have their preferences, and what kind of variables influence those preferences. This preoccupation with measuring consumer preferences erases many of the differences between the things people consume in their daily lives, suggesting that the choices they make about things as different as food, education, and medical care are equivalent in a meaningful way.[19]

The amount of data about sustainability is overwhelming, a result of the complexity of global supply chains and the opacity of the financial industry, exacerbated by the difficulty of defining what sustainability is in the first place. It is in response to this that the motivation of quantification among sustainability professionals shifts from economization ("aimed at producing calculating selves who think and act in terms of efficiency, utility calculations, the maximisation of returns") to marketization (aimed at "reconstitut[ing] subjectivity in terms of choice, competition and competitiveness").[20] Put differently, sustainability professionals are not gathering all this data to inform their own calculated, efficient decisions but to allow the market to make those decisions for them by revealing the most efficient paths. Here, it is the market itself that emerges as the infrastructure of sustainability, there to take all this data about sustainability and channel it, like capital itself, toward the most efficient and optimal ends. Anyone working in sustainability will concede that markets are imperfect; the solution, however, is not to abolish markets but to do whatever possible to enable them to be more perfect, to provide them with the data they need to make better decisions and generate more sustainable outcomes.

What is the role of a sustainability professional in a world where the market is endowed these kinds of capabilities, in a world where the idea that you cannot manage something until you can measure it has morphed into the idea that once you have measured and disclosed your social and environmental impacts, the market will manage it for you? This, after all, is precisely what my informants believed, especially to the extent that they conflated efficiency—which they saw the market as uniquely capable of achieving—with sustainability. As we will see particularly clearly in chapter 4, the market becomes an actor in its own right, offering incentives and making decisions on its own terms, even as this helps actors like corporations and investors obscure their own power and influence. The task of sustainability professionals comes to revolve around giving the market what it needs to make these decisions and incentivize sustainable actions. Put differently, in a world of neoliberal sustainability where the market is responsible for generating positive social and environmental impacts through incentivizing socially and environmentally responsible behavior and directing investments to socially and environmentally sustainable operations, the role of sustainability professionals is simply to make sure the market has the information it needs to do all these things.

Conclusion

Discussions about how to measure and evaluate social impacts are ongoing in corporate sustainability and sustainable finance circles, often facilitated by nongovernmental organizations like the World Economic Forum, the World Business Council for Sustainable Development, the Global Reporting Initiative, and the Sustainability Accounting Standards Board. Each of these organizations takes a different approach to measuring social capital, and the methods they come up with are all different. The World Economic Forum's 2019 Global Competitiveness Index (GCI), for example, used the Legatum Institute's Prosperity Index to assess countries' "social cohesion and engagement, community and family networks, and political participation and institutional trust" on a scale from 1 to 100, one of twenty-six indicators that makes up the first of the GCI's twelve pillars. The imputation method used for deriving this social capital score is a linear regression equation using easy-to-quantify data like mean years of schooling and GDP alongside harder-to-quantify indicators like incidence of corruption, yielding values like 49.88 for Serbia and 57.78 for Barbados.[21] Others, like the 2013 "agenda for [social capital] measurement" of the Organization for Economic Cooperation and Development (OECD), focus more on developing guidelines for how governments, companies, and community organizations can better select which existing indicators are most relevant in their specific contexts, insisting that collecting data about social capital "needs to go beyond the measurement of 'social capital' generally, as the different concepts sometimes covered by the term social capital (personal relationships, social network support, civic engagement, and trust and cooperative norms) are conceptually distinct and are relevant to different research questions."[22]

The OECD report concludes with a familiar refrain: "there is still a pressing need to develop better and more harmonised measures of personal relationships, social network support, civic engagement, and trust and cooperative norms."[23] This sentiment of having much more work to do is ubiquitous. Implicit in Chantal's claim that "you can't measure everything" was a belief that we should still measure what we can while trying to figure out ways to measure what we cannot. Through these endless discussions about what and how to measure something like social capital or social impact as part of an integrated sustainability strategy, where companies, regulators, and NGOs come together at workshops, webinars, and stakeholder feedback sessions to quibble about indicator definitions and materiality assessments, the idea that sustainability is something that has to be measured in the first place gets reinforced as an implicit but fundamental assumption about what sustainability is. Even if these initiatives fail to produce the kinds of concrete definitions and quantified indicators that they set out to create, the infrastructures of measurement and reporting that define and facilitate neoliberal sustainability get reinforced. Quantifying things like companies' impacts and dependencies on natural and social capital is an attempt, in the words of one former financial services CEO, to "measure the unmeasurable, and then to compare the incomparable," with the ancillary goals of "appealing to the financial markets' penchant for hard data" and demonstrating the business case for sustainability.[24] The prioritization of efforts to define and measure social impact is inseparable from the prioritization of "the market" and powerful market actors like banks and corporations.

3

Certifying Sustainability

You can't bullshit me with a lot of statistics.
—James Purdy, "Daddy Wolf"

Shelf Life

Most mornings, my husband has a cup of Lipton Yellow Label tea with his breakfast. A small green frog, the symbol of the Rainforest Alliance, is prominently displayed on the box, signifying that the tea inside has been certified as complying with the Rainforest Alliance sustainable agriculture standard. Inside, the individually wrapped tea bags make more specific claims about Lipton's sustainability efforts. One wrapper claims that Unilever, the company that owns Lipton, uses "96% renewable energy in [its] plantations in Kericho." Another wrapper describes the contents of the sachet as "sustainable tea leaves grown in sunshine goodness," while yet another claims that "[Unilever] planted 1.3 million trees in Kenya in the last two decades."[1]

As nice as these impacts might sound, they have very little to do with the technical requirements of the Rainforest Alliance's certification scheme. The farm requirements, for instance, cover things like farm management (topics here include administration, gender equality and grievance mechanisms, and so on), farming practices (including planting and rotation schedules, pest and agrochemicals management, and so on), and environmental aspects (including energy efficiency and emissions reduction, river and forest protection, biodiversity protection, and so on). The standard stipulates how farmers define improvement indicators, how often they must measure those indicators, where the data from those measurements have to be uploaded, and how often they have to submit to external auditing of both their records and their farm management and improvement plans. Farms need to be geotagged, with things like crop areas and water bodies specified using GPS (global positioning system) data. The standards are exceedingly detailed, stipulating, for instance, that illiterate farmers are allowed to provide information about their age, gender, and wages orally instead of written.[2] In recent years, there has been a growing emphasis on the production and dissemination of quantitative indicators within these standards, driven by a narrative of transparency and traceability that equates sustainability with the proliferation of accessible data *about* sustainability.

Complying with these kinds of standards is labor intensive, and it can be very expensive, especially for small-scale producers whose margins are already low. They must invest in new accounting systems and production infrastructures that keep certified and noncertified tea separate, both physically and in their records. This requires further investments in hiring and training workers who are able to navigate these requirements. On top of all this, they have to pay for independent auditors to come and certify both their records and their practices. From the perspective of farmers and farmworkers, there is little evidence that the benefits of standardization outweigh these substantial costs. Although standards like those produced by the Rainforest Alliance are typically referred to as "voluntary," farmers who refuse to adopt a particular standard risk being excluded from global commodity markets. This was the case in Kenya, where, in 2007, Unilever's decision to source its popular Lipton tea exclusively from Rainforest Alliance–certified farms sent shockwaves through tea industry, which is one of the country's main sources of income and employment.[3] According to a report by the International Trade Center, in the eight-year period between 2008 and 2016, the area of Rainforest Alliance–certified tea farms grew by a mind-boggling 3,200 percent, from 14,000 hectares to nearly 470,000 hectares globally, including more than 85 percent of Kenya's tea farms.[4] At an expo for the coffee, tea, and cacao (CoTeCa) industry in Hamburg in 2018, I met a representative from the Kenya Tea Development Authority, a powerful cooperative organization that represents Kenya's hundreds of thousands of smallholder tea farmers, who produce most of the country's tea. When I asked her why so many farmers had chosen to adopt the Rainforest Alliance certification, by far the country's most popular standard, she told me that farmers had not really had a choice. Unilever is the biggest buyer of black tea in the world, much of it sourced from

Kenya, so if it refused to buy Kenyan tea, who would? It did not help when other major buyers like Tata Global Beverages and Finlays quickly followed Unilever's lead in committing to sourcing exclusively from certified sustainable producers.[5]

As such, these kinds of standards have become powerful tools of governance in global supply chains, empowering corporations at the expense of marginalized and dispersed producers, who often have little recourse.[6] While the social, environmental, and economic benefits of these standards are tenuous from the perspective of farmers, critical work on global value chains has shown how the rapid growth of sustainability standards tends to empower multinational corporations, especially "lead firms" that are able to influence standards development processes.[7] As I would learn later on in my fieldwork, the only reason the Rainforest Alliance began certifying tea was because Unilever encouraged it to. Sustainability certifications play an important role in determining which products are considered sustainable. In a world of sustainability standards, few consumers understand what distinguishes one certification scheme from another. Standards development organizations compete to attract companies to adopt their specific standard. As one informant told me, it is a question of taking up as much "shelf space" as possible, which is why these organizations typically have active marketing departments that work with brands and supermarket chains to promote their standard as the most sustainable, while also working closely with companies to ensure that the standard is not too stringent or too costly.

In this chapter, I take a biographical approach to sustainability certifications, following them through the moments of consultation, revision, and publication that make up their social lives. How is it that certifications can promise to generate positive social and environmental impacts for dispersed farmers across the Global South while also serving to increase the power and profits of multinational corporations whose investors are based predominantly in the Global North? As I argue in this chapter, the increasingly data-driven approach adopted by leading standards developers reinforces the power dynamics of neoliberal sustainability by relying on "the market" to deliver sustainable outcomes, enhancing the power of lead firms and other powerful market actors. Specific moments in the social life of a certification scheme make this possible, namely, a formalized stakeholder consultation process that transforms small farmers into beneficiaries and that stands in contrast to the less formal ways companies and other powerful actors are able to convey their own interests.

Biographies of Certification

Objects like engagement rings and handmade rocking chairs mean different things to different people, moving in and out of different spheres of exchange or regimes of value over the course of their lifetimes. For one person, an engagement ring is a priceless gift that signifies a commitment of lifelong love between the giver and the receiver, while for a child who inherits the ring (or even more for a person who finds the ring years later in a pawn shop or at a secondhand jewelry shop), its value might be much closer to the sum of the market price of the diamonds and gold that constitute it. This observation—that objects move in and out of different regimes of value—has motivated much of the anthropological literature on value and its relationship to values, prompting a strong empirical focus on what Arjun Appadurai has called "the social life of things."[8] One method for understanding the social life of things is to take a biographical approach. According to Igor Kopytoff, "In doing the biography of a thing, one would ask questions similar to those one asks about people: What, sociologically, are the biographical possibilities inherent in its 'status' and in the period and culture, and how are these possibilities realized? Where does the thing come from and who made it? What has been its career so far, and what do people consider to be an ideal career for such things?"[9] These questions are similar to the kinds of questions we regularly ask about sustainability certifications, especially those regarding the legitimacy of standards and labels, the inclusivity of standards development and revision processes, and methods for assessing the efficacy of different certification schemes.

Kopytoff refined his biographical approach by drawing on his own work among the Suku of Zaire, tracing the biography of a typical hut from its erection on the occasion of a marriage and its subsequent transformation over the years into a guesthouse, a hangout for teenagers, a kitchen, and finally a chicken coop or goat shed, with these distinct uses corresponding to the hut's degrading physical state over its approximately ten-year life span. Putting a guest in a hut that should be used as a kitchen, Kopytoff notes, would signify what the host thinks about the visitor's status. Within a given culture, there are certain "biographical expectations" of things, and there are responses when those expectations are not met. In a different context, he observes that most people might negatively react to a Renoir painting ending up in an incinerator or a museum basement, arguing that "the cultural responses to such biographical details reveal a tangled mass of aesthetic, historical, and even political judgements, and of convictions and values that shape our attitudes to objects labeled 'art.'"[10]

The same might be said of the convictions and values that shape our attitudes to things we think of as "sustainable," like a box of Lipton tea with a little green sustainability label in the corner whose affirmative wrappers make us feel good about our consumption choices. There is a large body of work in anthropology and geography inspired by the kind of biographical approach Kopytoff advances, following things (especially agricultural products) like green beans and matsutake mushrooms to better understand their social lives. Different spheres of value are governed by different moral codes, and understanding how things move between different spheres of value reveals important insights about power and its assertion, particularly in supply chains, where commodities take on different meanings as they move along the chain.[11] As Kopytoff notes, "Biographies of things can make salient what might otherwise remain obscure," recalling Henry Sussman's description of the "task of the critic" as rendering explicit what might otherwise remain unsaid.[12] Thinking about the biography of certification schemes themselves, as opposed to the commodities like tea and coffee whose supply chains these standards help govern, attunes us to the moments and methods in a standard's life span when corporate actors in particular exercise and reinforce their power over others. In doing so, we gain insight into a key aspect of these biographies, namely, how things (like a sustainability standard) move between different regimes or spheres of value, how the tensions between these spheres are resolved or managed, and how these processes mediate the relationship between the "cultural biography" of a particular certification scheme (or some other technology of governance) and its broader "social history."[13] Taking a biographical approach to certification schemes helps us understand the way standards come to benefit lead firms and other powerful corporations in global supply chains by identifying the moments when these actors are able to influence the design, implementation, and enforcement of market-oriented certification schemes, thereby further entrenching the structures and infrastructures of neoliberal sustainability.

Sustainability standards are constantly moving between different spheres of value, which offers actors like multinational corporations the opportunity not only to assert their power but also to hide it. Sometimes, standards are seen as tools to increase profits, while at other times, they are seen as schemes to generate positive social and environmental impacts. They can occupy different spheres simultaneously. For consumers, certification schemes represent an opportunity to buy more responsibly produced tea, while for tea brands, these same certifications represent an opportunity to attract a market segment that spends more on products and mitigate against charges of unsustainability by being associated with an established sustainability initiative. Even from the same perspective, they can occupy multiple spheres. The managers of a multinational tea brand may well expect their commitment to a particular certification scheme to have a positive financial impact, but they undoubtedly also hope that their participation will yield positive social and environmental impacts. Sometimes, standards are seen as technical and objective, while sometimes they are seen as ethical and subjective and deeply personal. At some moments in their lifetimes, standards are merely technical documents whose production and revision are governed by a strict set of rules, often by yet another standard.[14] In these moments, the development of a standard is narrated as something rational and coherent, a formal process in which different stakeholders express their interests and concerns, with an established system for analyzing those concerns and translating them into a standard that is acceptable to the different actors. The goal of standards developers is not to respond to the interests of individual farmers or individual corporate sustainability managers but to collect enough data to generalize these interests through structured stakeholder engagement and feedback sessions, yielding an ideal typical stakeholder whose interests are represented in the standard's final version.

Consequently, standards developers can distance themselves from negative outcomes that happen as a result of the standard's adoption. Several people I interviewed at different standards development organizations, for example, thought it was unfair that a farmer who planted household crops too close to a river might be decertified if they were caught during an audit, but they tended to adopt a rules-are-rules approach. They speculated that this would get even worse with the growing automation of on-farm monitoring and auditing, which, in the not-so-distant future would leave even less room for exceptions and human error. Standards development and the resulting certification schemes in this value sphere are not about individual farmers but about a technical understanding of production systems and even entire landscapes.[15]

In other moments, however, sustainability is intensely affective and personal, firmly rooted in local contexts and individual lives. During a research trip to London that I took in 2019, a tea buyer I interviewed about her company's sustainability strategy suggested that I should visit a photography exhibition at the Mall Galleries near Buckingham Palace, which had been sponsored by Twinings to showcase the impacts of its "Sourced with Care" campaign. I went a few hours later after a different informant suddenly canceled our planned interview. Just to the right of the gallery's reception desk, I descended four or five steps into a small exhibition space, where I read an overview of the company's campaign and its vision "for healthier, happier, empowered and sustainable communities in [its] supply chain." There was a wooden bench with a basket of free Twinings tea samples, each individually wrapped in colorful, glossy paper. Hanging on the wall, unframed, were large photographic portraits of tea pluckers from Kenya, China, and India. Under each picture was a cardboard plaque with a brief description of the portrait's subjects and their work, as well as a story about how the Twinings "Sourced with Care" campaign had improved their lives. The caption under a photograph of a Kenyan woman with a huge grin and a wicker basket strapped to her back, for example, claimed that "through the Sourced with Care programme, in partnership with producers, not-for-profit organisations, international NGOs, industry bodies and others, Twinings have positively impacted 352,159 people in communities from which they source." Under another photo, this one of an Indian woman with an umbrella balanced on her headwrap, the caption read, "Lalita lives in Assam, India, she works as a tea plucker. Many of the families living on tea gardens lack access to basic services, such as clean water and adequate sanitation facilities. Twinings works with producers and not-for-profit organisations to construct toilets for families on the tea gardens, so people like Lalita can have the privacy they rightfully deserve." Elsewhere in the exhibit, captions below the photographs described programs sponsored by Twinings and its partners that taught women proper hygiene and helped establish schools for local children and training programs for the families of tea pluckers. It only took about fifteen minutes to look closely at every picture and read the captions and other material that Twinings had provided. As I left the gallery, I pocketed a handful of tea bags to take back to my hotel room.

Sustainability standards move between these different spheres—not just the social, environmental, and economic spheres discussed throughout the book or the spheres of the singular and the common that interested Kopytoff but also, as we have just seen, between what we might call the technical sphere and the social sphere, or the objective sphere and the subjective sphere. Like the Twinings exhibit, feel-good stories about the impacts of a sustainability campaign on individual farmers make for good marketing material, but the technical, data-driven approach overrides those stories. (Recall the informant who, in the introduction, dismissed the "Sourced with Care" campaign as relying on "anecdotes" rather than data.) An increasingly automated system for monitoring, auditing, and certifying farms might see some farmers decertified for minor, even arbitrary infractions—certainly not the kind of story a tea company would feature in its corporate sustainability literature—but the ability of this system to contribute to the realization of the sociotechnical imaginary of data-driven impacts that is so fundamental to neoliberal sustainability becomes much more important than these kinds of one-off impacts, which have to be reframed as "case studies" in a broader sociotechnical system of objectively measuring and managing impacts.

The promise of sustainability—typified by impassioned narratives about the positive impacts of certification—is couched in stories of people whose lives are improved, species that are saved from extinction, and so on. This stands in stark contrast to the kind of language used to describe the process of designing and revising standards, which is all about establishing KPIs and measurement baselines, soliciting and analyzing feedback from diverse stakeholders in an objective and apolitical way, and harnessing new digital technologies that can ensure transparency and traceability in global supply chains. The biographical details of individual farmers become data points in an ever-expanding data set, with the collection of data an even more important goal than making sure those data show improvements.

Corporate Governance

As it turns out, the only reason the Rainforest Alliance started to include tea in its certification scheme was at the tea giant Unilever's behest. According to a former Rainforest Alliance employee, at the time Unilever decided to pursue sustainability certification, the company was trying to enhance its corporate brand recognition (as opposed to just focusing on the recognition of the brands it owns, like Hellman's mayonnaise and Lipton tea), and it wanted sustainability to be a key part of its new public face. In line with that goal, it had invited representatives from several sustainability organizations to meet and discuss their various approaches to sustainability. Unilever expressed an ambitious plan of buying and selling sustainable tea, and it was interested in working with the Rainforest Alliance. At the time, however, the Rainforest Alliance's standard did not cover tea, so the Unilever representative suggested that it expand the scope of its certification program and "partner" with Unilever to promote sustainability in the global tea industry. Since then, hundreds of thousands of hectares of tea farms have been Rainforest Alliance certified, with around 90 percent of Kenyan tea currently certified according to the organization's standards.

Standards are typically revised every few years an in attempt to stay on top of pertinent social and environmental issues but also to integrate the latest science and technologies into the certification process. The revision of standards is also standardized, governed in part by a group called the ISEAL Alliance, which is a sort of a standardizer's standardizer that pushes for greater transparency in the revision process and publishes rules for stakeholder engagement, with the goal of ensuring that some stakeholders (like Unilever) do not have more influence than other stakeholders (like small farmers). There are successive rounds of public and private consultations and comments, and several drafts of a revised standard will circulate among different actors before the final version is approved. On the surface, it all seems relatively straightforward. An organization like Fairtrade International or Rainforest Alliance publishes several successive versions of a proposed standard online for anyone to comment on, whether critically or in support, before eventually approving and publishing the final version, including guidelines for compliance and certification. Almost immediately, the process starts again, with these organizations soliciting feedback from various stakeholders on the strengths and weaknesses of the updated standard, which will be used to structure future revisions.

This seems like a fair, transparent process, but I quickly learned that the rules are different for different actors. During a short visit to the headquarters of one sustainability standards organization, several people told me that I needed to meet with their colleague Daniel, since he was in charge of marketing the certification scheme to brands and supermarkets, with a specific focus on products like tea and tisanes, chocolate, and coffee. The office had a system of rotating desks, meaning that you carried your laptop home every afternoon and brought it back each morning, sitting at whichever desk was free in the open office plan, sometimes referred to as "hot desking." It took a while to find where Daniel was sitting, but with the help of someone I had interviewed earlier that day, we located his desk. She introduced me—"This is Matthew. He's visiting from Copenhagen Business School and wants to talk to you about tea"—and left us to chat.

While it was true that I wanted to talk to Daniel about certified tea, I had an ulterior motive, as well: Unilever was proving to be a tough nut to crack, and with the exception of a few interviews with procurement managers, sustainability analysts, and marketing interns scattered around the company's vast global network of offices, I had not been able to secure an invitation to do the kind of participant observation that most ethnographers consider their methodological bread and butter. I did not expect to get this kind of access, but I was hoping to at least secure an invitation to one of the company's two headquarters in Rotterdam and London. Daniel, as it turned out, was in close contact with Unilever, Tata Global Beverages, and other major tea companies, as well as supermarkets like Sainsbury's, Tesco, Albert Heijn, and Carrefour. We talked for a few minutes about the challenge of marketing what he described as a rigorous sustainability standard when supermarkets like Sainsbury's were developing their own, competing labeling schemes. Whereas the standards that his organization develops are based on principles of transparency and broad stakeholder engagement, he accused companies like Sainsbury's of developing their own standards to get around these requirements. Conscious consumers, however, have a hard time telling these labels apart, and on a supermarket shelf, one label seems as good as any other.

I was planning another trip to London to conduct interviews with people involved in sustainable tea procurement, and I promised I would try to chase down a Sainsbury's representative when I was there. I then mentioned that I had been having a difficult time getting in touch with anyone from Unilever who might be in a position to help me negotiate access to one of its offices for a few days. Daniel was not surprised, and he pessimistically suspected that I would never find anyone to agree to host me for more than a brief interview and, if I was lucky, a tour of the office. He offered to put me in touch with his main contact at Unilever, but when he shared the details, I realized that I had already talked to this person a few months earlier. I mentioned to Daniel that I had spoken to his contact on the phone a few times but that our conversations had never been very generative and that this particular informant seemed hesitant to stray too far from Unilever's corporate line, even when pushed to reflect in more abstract terms about sustainability challenges in the tea industry that I suspected he would have been quite familiar with as a sourcing manager for the world's biggest tea buyer. Daniel chuckled and agreed but said that when the man needed something, he could be more charismatic. This was especially true around the time standards were being revised, when it was not unusual, according to Daniel, to receive brief, informal emails from representatives of organizations like food companies and supermarkets asking to meet over lunch or a coffee to discuss the newest proposed version.

Differential Access

This kind of direct, behind-the-scenes influence over the standards development process is something not every stakeholder enjoys. A few days earlier, I had seen a group of people I later learned were cocoa farmers from Côte d'Ivoire sitting in front of a screen and a projector in a corner of the building's cafeteria, where one of the organization's employees was giving a presentation on their revised standard. The farmers had been flown in to participate in the standard revision process as part of commitment to stakeholder engagement. The idea was that these farmers could comment on the draft standard in person, with the ensuing discussion forming a basis for the next round of revisions. It was a very formal and structured process, each step standardized and regulated. When I asked an informant about it in an interview later that afternoon, she said that stakeholder engagement was a normal part of the revision process, and it gave farmers an opportunity to learn about any major changes to the standard so they would have time to prepare for them before being required to implement them. In contrast to the picture of stakeholder engagement as a process of give-and-take between standards developers and standards users, this informant's brief description of the process made it seem like stakeholder engagement was merely an opportunity to inform farmers of decisions that had been made on their behalf.

Farmers' experiences sharing their concerns about a revised certification scheme are clearly very different from the way companies like Unilever express their opinions to standards developers. This makes sense given the political economy of certification schemes, which compete with each other to attract subscribers, customers, and funding, reducing the price premiums that producers themselves are able to demand for certified products.[16] Within this political economy, multinational corporations, known in the global value chain literature as "lead firms," act as gatekeepers because they are able to dictate which sustainability standard producers have to adopt through their influence in global commodities markets, as Unilever did with Rainforest Alliance certification in the Kenyan tea industry.[17] In the context of this gatekeeper power, standards development organizations tend to self-regulate, in the sense that they design certification schemes that are attractive from the perspective of these lead firms: schemes that allow companies like Unilever to credibly claim that their products are sustainable without increasing costs and even allowing them to charge a sustainability premium. The costs of certification shift from multinational corporations to dispersed producers, leaving it to farmers and estate managers to bear the costs of both complying with a standard and having their compliance audited by an approved auditor. Thus, in practice, the one thing producers really want—higher prices for their certified products—is often the one thing popular standards do not explicitly stipulate.

As Daniel's description of Unilever and other companies' backdoor access suggests, however, standards developers do not have to *guess* what companies want; companies tell them fairly directly. In any case, the organizational structure of standards development organizations makes it unlikely that the interests of multinational corporations would be ignored. The Rainforest Alliance's board of directors, for instance, is rather elite, mostly consisting of wealthy philanthropists and executives or former executives of banks, real estate investment funds, tech companies, corporate law firms, and consultancies. Several board members work or have worked for the same companies whose supply chains the Rainforest Alliance's standards ostensibly govern, such as Tata Consumer Products and Kraft Foods. Boards like this are ultimately responsible for approving the final version of a revised standard, including any last-minute changes they might deem necessary.

If there is anywhere that small producers themselves enjoy this kind of preferential access, it is with sellers who buy directly from farmers and farm cooperatives. A few days after I talked to Daniel, I visited a shop that specializes in direct-trade and single-origin tea, coffee, and chocolate. The shop was founded by a mother and son who were both interested in sustainable agriculture, the latter of whom had pursued a degree in sustainable development and had eventually persuaded his father to leave his corporate job and join them in running the small business. I had emailed the son, Jamie, when I was planning my research trip to ask if he was available for an interview, and he told me to drop by whenever they were open, since he was usually there and would be happy to talk about their philosophy.

When I walked into the shop, a man who I later learned was Jamie's father was sitting with a group of three men who I later learned were cocoa farmers from Latin America. They were passing a cacao pod between them, before one of the farmers cracked it open and handed out the cocoa beans that, when fresh, are coated in a delicious sticky white goo (the mucilaginous pulp that many plants produce to protect and nourish their seeds), which tastes a bit like Jolly Ranchers. At the counter, I introduced myself to the person I correctly guessed was Jamie, with whom I had corresponded a few weeks earlier. He told me that he was free to talk about their approach to sustainability, but he apologized in advance that we would probably be interrupted several times, as he would have to get up and help any customers who came in while his father was busy with the farmers. The farmers, he said, were visiting not just as suppliers but as friends. The family makes several trips a year to visit the different farms where they source their products, and in the process, they had become quite close. I was reminded of an interview I conducted with the owners of a family-run boutique chocolatier in Belgium several years earlier, who had grown so close with some of their suppliers that they often travel to celebrate holidays together. In these long-term, direct-trade relationships, this sort of familial relationship seems common, complicating the predominant market relationship that tends to structure the governance of global supply chains.

I told Jamie a bit about the project I was working on and explained that I was interested in understanding the role that sustainability standards like Rainforest Alliance and Fairtrade play in the global tea industry, especially in Kenya, where my colleagues were doing more situated fieldwork. He chuckled and said that he might not be much help, since, with the exception of a few organic coffees and chocolates, few of the company's products were actually certified. "All of them could be, of course," he added, claiming that everything it sold exceeded the requirements of standards developed by organizations like the Rainforest Alliance and Fairtrade International. A few days earlier, the proprietor of another local tea shop made a similar claim, telling me that while few of her teas were certified, they were all "unofficially" organic and fair trade. The aforementioned Belgian chocolatier did not parse her words: she and her husband follow much-stricter rules than industrial chocolate producers that can afford auditors to go out and certify that their chocolate complies with what she described as "bullshit" standards. So while her company may not be able to label most of its chocolate as certified sustainable, she assured me that I would be hard-pressed to find more sustainable chocolate anywhere. For the boutique shop owners I met over the years, it was obvious that this kind of personalized approach to cultivating strong relationships with producers was better than relying on impersonal mainstream sustainability standards that multinational corporations are eager to use in their marketing strategies.

When I asked Jamie to explain what he meant, he said that the only way to procure the kind of products he was committed to selling in his shop was to pay farmers a premium price, which lets them develop farming practices that ensure the delivery of consistently high-quality products but also save enough money to buffer themselves against a bad season or other unpredictable conditions. According to Jamie, when farmers receive a fair price for their products, it is "natural" for them to invest in social and environmental sustainability, and they do not feel pressured to underpay workers or use dangerous pesticides. Regardless of the commodity, he told me, sourcing the best-quality products relies on building relationships with smallholder farmers and farmer cooperatives. Building these relationships meant that it was impossible to think of trade in purely economic terms. Jamie claimed to know the names and birthdays of several of his suppliers' children, many of whom he had met on repeated trips to production sites.

Jamie grew up in an upper-middle-class European family whose patriarch, a grandfather who lived on a large piece of land in the countryside, had instilled a love of nature that evolved into a passion for sustainability. From there, he had pursued university degrees in sustainability science and sustainable development, cultivating an understanding of sustainability that was in many ways technocratic and market oriented. This background is similar to that of many of the sustainability professionals working in places like Geneva and New York and London, who also tend to come from privileged backgrounds and tend to have studied sustainability from the perspective of economics or the natural sciences. Indeed, Jamie's theory of sustainability was exceedingly market based, in the sense that he believed that paying a higher price for higher-quality products is what allowed farmers to be more sustainable. What differentiated Jamie's way of thinking about the social aspects of sustainability was that, for him, these aspects were intimate and familiar. Unlike the sustainability professionals we met in chapter 2, whose main task seemed to be defining and measuring indicators of social impacts, leaving those impacts to be managed by the dynamics of the market, it was difficult for Jamie to describe his relationship with producers as anything other than friendly and even familial. I had the feeling that if Jamie were ever given the chance to undercut or take advantage of his suppliers—some of whom were sitting across the room laughing with his father like old friends—he would have a hard time doing it. This would be a difficult model to reproduce on a global scale, and it would probably make things like tea and chocolate a treat for the wealthy rather than something normal people can afford. However, the lesson from Jamie's relationship with the producers who sell to his shop is how these relationships are improved by refusing to see each other as atomistic, disconnected actors in a constellation of relations that the market manages. It is an idealistic and perhaps even slightly naïve way to think about what a sustainable supply chain could look like, but it also serves as a potent reminder of what most supply chains patently are not. In any case, there are worse things than a bit of idealism.

Expert Stakeholders and Legitimate Standards

Recent scholarship on multistakeholder initiatives (MSIs) has shown that multinational corporations tend to play an outsize role in the kinds of social and environmental sustainability standards these initiatives attempt to develop. A recent review of the multidisciplinary literature on MSIs shows how power asymmetries between the different stakeholders that constitute an MSI lead to the privileging of corporate interests, particularly when it comes to the politics of standards development, which tend to play out "backstage."[18] Although the legitimacy of these standards depends on the perception that diverse stakeholders were involved in their development, in reality, as we saw earlier, corporations enjoy privileged access through both backdoor access to standards development and enhanced proximity both geographically (with corporate offices in the same cities or countries as the headquarters of major standards developers) and culturally (with NGOs boards made up of corporate elites).

Although companies have more direct access to standards development organizations than farmers do, which ends up privileging the interests of these companies in the resultant standards, it would be a mistake to assume that most companies pay too much attention to the process of standards development. An employee of a major tea trader I interviewed in the Netherlands in early 2020, for example, was not aware that the forthcoming version of the Rainforest Alliance standard, which governs the production of much of the tea that his company trades, was going to have more intense disclosure requirements for both producers and buyers. Rather than corporations actively managing the standards development process, and because they enjoy the kind of privileged access that allows them to express their concerns directly to standards development organizations in a way that the more marginalized beneficiaries of sustainability initiatives rarely are able, they are often a kind of imagined interlocutor among standards developers. Standards developers make assumptions about what companies will find acceptable, what they might disagree with but still comply with, and what might be so strict that it drives them to a competing standard. This means that even if a large company could swoop in and essentially veto parts of a standard with which it refuses to comply, it rarely actually has to do that.

In Washington, DC, I interviewed Nathalie, who works for a standards development organization that develops technical and environmental standards for a range of organizations. At the time, she was working on a new standard to facilitate the recycling of plastic waste, and she seemed to have a clear sense of what companies might find acceptable with regard to the stringency of a proposed standard: "If you create a standard that companies like Microsoft like, then that means it might not be rigorous enough environmentally. But if you create something that, you know, all the NGOs or the Greenpeaces of the world like, then companies are going to say, 'We can't meet those requirements,' kind of thing. So, you have to figure out that place in the middle where it's, you know, accurate, rigorous, transparent enough, but also, you know, manageable, doable." Other informants made similar observations. During a trip to London, I met with two members of the social impact team for a well-known sustainability standard. During our interview, one suggested that sometimes she wishes she could have more of an impact but that ultimately it was more important that the standard had broad uptake by companies. It was better, according to this informant, to have a smaller impact on a large scale than a larger impact on a small scale.[19]

Standards developers have a clear sense of what companies will accept in a standard and what will cause them to adopt a competing (and probably less stringent) standard, and they operate accordingly. Many of them admit that farmers simply want more money for their certified products, but if that would drive companies away from a certification scheme, it would not really help the farmers at all. An organization like the Rainforest Alliance, despite its mission to help producers and protect the environment from exploitative farming practices, ultimately depends on the willingness of major corporations like Unilever to adopt its standards over other standards like Fairtrade International, which means that standards developers always feel and respond to corporate pressure, even when the corporations are not applying pressure directly. Stipulations that corporations would oppose, such as high premiums paid directly to farmers, never even make it into draft standards because standards developers know from the outset that it will be fatal not just to the standard but potentially to the organization that owns it.

The implicit threat of these influential corporations refusing to participate in a *voluntary* certification scheme is one reason that standards development processes and other MSIs end up being structured in a way that privileges companies over other actors. Within these processes, companies are able to represent themselves, while the interests of producers and other marginalized groups are mediated by "experts." When I asked Nathalie how she "find[s] that balance" between being rigorous, on the one hand, and doable, on the other, she responded,

> I think it's all about having the right stakeholders in the room and getting that kind of broad representation. . . . For this plastics work, we probably need to have oil companies represented. We need to have manufacturers. We have recyclers, and we have waste pickers. We need to have consumers. So, I think most people would trust us to pick, you know, to make sure that we have the right representation on a group like that. . . . But you do have to do your homework, especially if you're going to go into a new area like plastics. We need to make sure that we understand the value chain of plastics to make sure that we're not skipping over stakeholder groups and, you know, just talking to a lot of people.

Increasingly aware of the way the "stakeholder" discourse maintains existing power relations, I decided to push Nathalie a bit about who counts as an expert stakeholder in these kinds of conversations.[20] At the time, I was living in Copenhagen, where immigrants and homeless people could often be found sorting through waste in public trash bins looking for recyclable plastics, with each bottle earning them between one and three Danish crowns (between about fifteen and forty-five US cents). Surely people who spend much of their time collecting and sorting recyclable plastics should be considered experts when it comes to recycling plastics.

For Nathalie, an expert was "somebody with a good reputation, [who has spent time] on the particular issue and who is broadly trusted, because, you know, if your standard isn't going to be trusted, then no one's going to buy into it." I returned to her claim that "recyclers and waste pickers" were invited to the stakeholder consultation process, and I asked if this included homeless people who might be considered experts in this area, noting that they were a big stakeholder group that might really be impacted by a standard that affected plastics recycling.[21] I asked if these kinds of stakeholders had been consulted during the development of the new plastic standard, to which Nathalie responded, "We have. We've consulted at least with, um, people or organizations that work with the waste pickers. So, there's a lot of organizations that kind of help organize waste pickers in, say, India. So, we've certainly spoken with those people, and then as we get into more of the identifying pilot-project phase, we'll probably talk more directly with them." During this process of developing a standard for plastics recycling, the interests and experiences of people like waste pickers are mediated through more formal organizations, and Nathalie sees the waste pickers themselves as relevant stakeholders mainly when the standard is being piloted. Like the farmers who can only influence the standards development process through the formal channels of scheduled public consultations and public comment periods—that is, during very specific and clearly defined moments in the standard's biography—these highly mediated interactions serve to create spaces of negotiation that appear broadly representative but are in fact tightly circumscribed by more powerful interests. This is particularly insidious in cases where expertise is wielded on behalf of marginalized groups—that is, when the experts in question take responsibility for the well-being of others—since it makes it harder to criticize their conclusions and the resultant policies or standards.[22]

As Elizabeth Fortin observes, "Despite such standards representing just one version of the world among many, their status as 'standards' represents the achievement of 'legitimacy' or 'symbolic capital'—a form of power—for those who . . . have managed to secure particular forms of knowledge embedded within them. . . . Questions as to how this is achieved, whether through contestation or composition, are crucial for understanding such standards processes."[23] MSIs tend to reflect the interests of the most powerful stakeholders, and appealing to the "legitimacy" of these initiatives and the standards they generate is an important strategy for depoliticizing these inherently political processes.[24] What emerges is a standards development process that requires input from diverse stakeholders in order to be seen as legitimate but also requires the interests and experiences of the least powerful of those stakeholders to be filtered through structured consultations and mediated by formal organizations.[25] The power to determine what counts as a rigorous sustainability standard is inseparable from the power to define and determine what counts as a socially and environmentally sustainable product.

The Promise of Certification

The logic of certification is fairly straightforward. An informant who works for a well-known sustainability standard explained it to me as we walked from her office in Washington, DC, to a nearby café for lunch one afternoon in the spring of 2019. I had scheduled a series of interviews during a weeklong visit to the city with people working at different standards development organizations (SDOs) in the city. (Rainforest Alliance, Fairtrade International, and Fair Trade America all have offices in the US capital.) I knew this particular informant from earlier research, so as we walked, I was able to open up a bit more than I was normally able to in the mostly semistructured, one-off interviews I typically conducted as part of the tea project, and I expressed some friendly skepticism about the actual impact of these kinds of sustainability standards. I told her that it seemed like producers shouldered most of the costs of certification—from the expenses involved in actually complying with sustainability standards to the cost of hiring auditors to come and assess their compliance to investing in the necessary infrastructures for keeping track of certified and uncertified products.

She nodded along in agreement, and when I finished, she was happy to admit that there were problems with the standards development and certification process. But for her, the problems I had outlined were not a function of the standards themselves but a problem of uptake and enforcement. She told me that in an ideal world, producers of certified tea would be rewarded by market forces, since they would be able to sell their tea for higher prices. Complying with sustainability standards might require producers to invest a lot of money up front, and auditing might be expensive, but it also gave farmers an "opportunity" to learn better business practices and become more effective, profitable entrepreneurs. Her defense of standards was textbook neoliberalism: markets harnessing consumer demands for sustainable products to reward individual entrepreneurs with more money for their certified products. Relying on the market to distribute the costs and benefits of certification "efficiently" helped ensure that all the different stakeholders were able to use a standard to meet their own, diverse needs. In this worldview, standards have a very specific role to play, which is less about forcing changes from the top down than enabling the market to incentivize those changes from the bottom up.

For that to work, these standards must contribute to ensuring that the market has all the information it needs to incentivize sustainability decisions. This data-driven approach to sustainability standards has become mainstream. In the Rainforest Alliance's efforts to "reimagine certification," for example, the collection and analysis of data emerges as a fundamental dimension of sustainability. In a 2020 interview published on the Rainforest Alliance website, the organization's former chief sustainable supply chain officer, Britta Wyss Bisang, emphasized the central role of data in its "new approach" to sustainability. Digitized data, according to Wyss Bisang, has emerged alongside visual inspections, document checks, and interviews as a "fourth pillar" of auditing. As impactful as certification has been in the past, she claimed that it needed to "evolve further" to become even more impactful: "Certification has to become more data-driven, more improvement-oriented and better tailored to the needs of producers. . . . Based on data-driven insights into what the sustainability needs are, companies need to co-invest in improvements that contribute more to sustainability. . . . Finally, the data generated through this new and evolved certification will hopefully also be useful to generate institutional funding and link certification more strongly with landscape and community-wide programs." This commitment to datafication is reflected in the revised version of the organization's standards, which went into effect in 2020. One of the main "innovations" of the 2020 standard was the notion of "continuous improvement," which requires farmers to set improvement targets in addition to the traditional pass-fail approach to certification. A key feature of this continuous improvement scheme is what the Rainforest Alliance refers to as Smart Meters: "Smart Meters give farmers a way to set goals for their farm based on what's most beneficial and feasible within their specific context. Rather than having predefined targets set by the Rainforest Alliance, farmers themselves will set the targets for these improvements and define the necessary actions needed to achieve them."[26] Farmers will conduct a baseline assessment and define targets for Smart Meters before their first certification or in the first year of certification (depending on the requirement), plan and implement actions to achieve the targets, and monitor results. They will then use the data collected on Smart Meter requirements to reflect on yearly progress and to adapt measures in case little or no progress is shown. This creates a feedback loop that enables farmers to continuously improve their practices. If this all sounds a bit vague, that is because it is. At the time of writing this (summer 2022), there is still a year to go before certificate holders will be required to use the Smart Meter reporting system.

Beneath this unambiguously neoliberal ideology of entrepreneurial self-improvement, farmers are subjected to an increasingly invasive regime of monitoring and surveillance. Another new part of the standard, the Supply Chain Risk Assessment (SCRA) tool, includes an assurance system that requires expansive data collection and analysis:

> As a part of the assurance system, data is collected through the SCRA which is embedded in the registration and profile completion process. The SCRA evaluates the potential risks of an organization's operations on individual site level in order to determine the type and frequency of verification required. A company's profile is based on the activities, location and crop information captured through this process in combination with other internal and third-party data (volumes, compliance, social risks, and others) specific for each individual operation. The organization's profile will result in a contextualized checklist of both mandatory and available self-selected requirements.[27]

In this view of what it takes to make supply chains sustainable, farmers become data providers to an organization that insists on a positive relationship between the proliferation of data and the market's propensity to reward farmers for providing that data: "The data collected from Smart Meter indicators enables farmers to better display their efforts and quantify the benefits of more sustainable practices which contributes to better market access and prices for their goods."[28] The precise mechanisms that enable better market access and prices for their products, however, are never explicated. Indeed, when I described the data requirements contained in the new standard to a Dutch tea trader in early 2020, he was flummoxed. Revealing too much information about production and trade would make it impossible for farmers to maintain what little competitive advantage they have left, suggesting that the proliferation of this kind of data might actually disempower producers vis-à-vis other, more powerful actors, further confirming the observation that these kinds of certification schemes enhance the power of lead firms like Unilever to "not only [define] the product and process parameters to be met along the value chain but also [establish] systems to monitor and control compliance."[29] Although the promise of certification emphasizes the potential market-driven benefits to smallholder farmers and other marginalized actors in global supply chains, the reality of certification is that voluntary sustainability standards enhance the power of multinational corporations by prioritizing their financial interests and, in recent iterations of popular standards, putting farmers in a position where they are required to disclose valuable data about things like wages and input costs in order to maintain access to global tea markets.

It is unclear whether these standards even have many real social or environmental benefits. Proponents of voluntary certification schemes claim that complying with sustainability standards helps ensure better-quality products, allows producers to demand higher prices for their goods, promotes autonomy and self-dependence, stimulates improvements in farm management practices, and generates a host of social and environment impacts from worker rights to biodiversity production, which are often addressed explicitly and meticulously in these standards. These purported benefits, however, are tenuous. When I asked another Dutch tea trader if there was any relationship between sustainability certifications and the quality of the tea a farm produced, he responded emphatically, "No." The sustainability manager of a large British tea importer had a hard time telling me what the best sustainability standard was, but she singled out Fairtrade as one of the worst, claiming that it promises farmers a premium for their certified tea but then leaves it in the hands of byzantine committees and approval processes. My informants who worked for standards development organizations often cited a study by researchers at Wageningen University on the benefits of Rainforest Alliance training for Kenyan tea farmers. However, an activist I interviewed who was critical of the Rainforest Alliance and other market-driven certification schemes questioned these results, claiming that Unilever and the Rainforest Alliance facilitated the researchers' access to farmers and that the farmers would therefore be hesitant to critique the training programs in interviews and survey responses. Even the evidence for certification's financial benefits—higher wages and higher commodity prices—is unconvincing.[30]

Nevertheless, standards organizations are committed to regimenting this kind of data-driven approach to sustainability, and this is reflected in their operations. When I asked Joshua, who works in the US office of a multinational standards development organization, what a typical workday was like, he said that it consisted mostly of meetings and emails and reading over reports from auditors and farmers. Much more exciting, he told me, was when he was able to take field trips to see the effects of his organization's work firsthand. In addition to meeting farmers and talking about how certification had helped them, these field trips offered a valuable opportunity to train farmers to collect and upload data about their operations. Making sure they were providing the right kinds of data was so important, he told me, that the organization was planning to launch a training program that all certified producers would attend as part of the certification process. Joshua's trips and these imminent training programs had a disciplinary effect, turning farmers into providers of data that would be legible to the market. The fragility of these emergent metrological regimes requires this kind of training and engagement, clearing the path for raw data to be transformed into quantitative indicators for tracking and auditing sustainability performance, and the kind of disciplinary work that Joshua and his colleagues promote is a key part of this.

The Machine in the Garden and the Drone above the Farm

Over lunch one Friday in the office cafeteria, I introduced myself to Emily, Michael, and Bruno, three employees of a standards development organization where I spent a week conducting participant observation and ethnographic interviews in the spring of 2020.[31] I told them about my research on the role that sustainability standards play in the governance of the Kenyan tea supply chain and asked them about their work. Michael chuckled, telling me that he was "just an accountant" and that most of his days were spent processing reimbursement claims from colleagues who had recently traveled abroad for work. He then quickly excused himself and went back to his desk, wishing me good luck with my research. Bruno and I turned to Emily as she told me that she was a data analyst, using GIS (geographic information system) technology to map the adoption and impact of her organization's sustainability standards, and that she spent most of her time working on new ways to promote traceability in global agro-commodity supply chains. Bruno interrupted her by leaning over and squeezing her shoulder. "Emily's our drone and satellite girl." She rolled her eyes as he continued, "So you better not make her mad, or she'll send one to your house!" Emily laughed, jokingly threatening Bruno, "You better watch out! I know where you live."

We spent the next ten or fifteen minutes talking about the kinds of data Emily analyzes and why. GIS tools allow her to correlate spatial data derived through GPS coordinates and satellite imaging with social, environmental, and economic data collected through audits, surveys, disclosure requirements, academic research, and other methods of data collection. She raised concerns about transparency and traceability that are familiar to anyone involved in the development and management of global supply chains, arguing that these qualities were necessary to facilitate sustainability in the global agro-food industry and that new technologies like the drones and satellites that Bruno had joked about moments earlier, when deployed in tandem with blockchains and artificial intelligence, were the best way to promote them. She gave a number of examples of issues she thought these kinds of technologies could help solve, from the pervasiveness of child labor on Ivorian cacao farms to the rapid encroachment of soy plantations into the Amazon rain forest to the "illicit" collection of firewood from the Mau Forest Complex to power tea-processing factories in Kenya. Collecting and regularly updating the GPS coordinates of certified farms, for example, would allow certifiers and other interested stakeholders to monitor these farms remotely through satellite imaging and drone surveillance.

Later in our conversation, Emily casually mentioned that the organization had been exploring the possibility of genetic tracing for cocoa, listing it as one of many examples of how they were working with academic researchers. I stopped her and asked if she could elaborate on genetic testing, since it was the first time I had heard it mentioned in the context of sustainability standards. She admitted that she did not know much about it but claimed that, according to her understanding, genetic tests would let them better ensure that cocoa farms were not using child labor to harvest and process cocoa. I was perplexed. She insisted again that she was not "exactly sure how it works," as she had only heard it mentioned in a workshop she had attended, but she speculated that analysts might be able to detect genetic material from people working on the farms, which would allow them to determine whether the registered workers had picked the chocolate or whether someone else had, potentially a child.

As it turns out, Emily's guess about how this kind of traceability might work was incorrect, and genetic testing of cocoa has nothing to do with the residual genetic material of workers. Rather, the identification of chloroplast markers in cocoa samples is "a reliable and cost-effective approach to identify the farm haplotype composition of the sample," which could in theory allow chocolate to be traceable back to specific farms.[32] Even though I might have made the same guess as Emily if someone had asked me how genetic traceability might help ensure that cocoa was not harvested by child slaves, it is nevertheless worth thinking a bit about what this kind of mistake signifies. Admittedly, Emily and I were having a casual conversation about some of the solutions she and her colleagues were exploring to make supply chains more sustainable. None of us sitting around the table were experts in genetic tracing, and I had put her on the spot, perhaps inadvertently pressuring her to give me an answer. If we had discussed it further, we probably would have concluded that the privacy implications of this kind of technology were unacceptable. Even if it were possible to extract and analyze traces of human DNA from processed cocoa beans or even chocolate, it would require a vast data set of genetic material from farmers and other workers in the cocoa supply chain, many of whom are seasonal and informal. That means that any worker who comes into contact with any of the inputs that eventually end up in a lab-tested bit of cocoa would have to submit a sample of hair or saliva to a third party that manages that database and shares it with other relevant stakeholders, like auditors and certification bodies, that can cross-check any DNA found in the cocoa with the DNA database of all the workers in a certified supply chain. The conditions of possibility of this kind of traceability system are frankly horrifying, something that Emily herself would almost certainly have agreed with. However, the fact that this was even offered as a possibility hints at how sustainability professionals' embrace of data-driven solutions threatens to erase or at least minimize a broader concern for the social implications of these potential technological fixes.

At a different standards organization, Lucas, who had recently led the development of a new sustainable cocoa standard, also described drones as way to promote economic efficiency. In-person audits of farms and factories, which is what certification has traditionally relied on, are not only a huge expense for the farmers who must pay for private auditing services but also rife with opportunities for mistakes or even outright corruption. Audits that are scheduled in advance give producers plenty of time to hide prohibited practices. Like Emily, Lucas offered child labor in the cocoa supply chain as an example, claiming that "the day after you have been auditing, the children can be in the field again." As a solution to this, he suggested a technologically advanced system, where drones and satellites supplement in-person audits to facilitate more continuous monitoring and reporting. He likened his proposed system to the way banks detect for credit card fraud through the constant monitoring of clients' transactions.

In in a different context, these kinds of technological imaginaries would seem dystopian, like something out of a bad sci-fi novel. But for informants like Emily and Lucas, the proliferation of invasive data collection, storage, and evaluation infrastructures seems like an obvious, unquestioned aspiration, overriding any potential social harm. Speculations about the adoption of these technologies becomes naturalized, their political implications rarely, if ever, critically examined except to the extent that organizations' data-management plans comply with standards like the European Union's General Data Protection Regulation (GDPR) or other data rules. At the same time, these kinds of technologies are seen as the key to solving the multidimensional problem of unsustainability across scales, from climate change to local development challenges, linking a present populated with suffering subjects to a future wherein those subjects, both human and more-than-human, can thrive. Understanding the role that these sociotechnical imaginaries play in the dialectical relationship between an unsustainable present and a sustainable future is crucial.

In *The Machine in the Garden*, Leo Marx famously identified a defining tension between what he called the "pastoral ideal" and industry-driven progressivism in nineteenth-century American literature. Within this pastoral ideal, the sights and sounds of rural life—the toll of church bells and the whoosh of scythes—fit rather seamlessly into the settler-colonial mind-set of the American landscape as a bountiful estate whose riches could be exploited through hard work. The violent intrusion of "the machine" in this landscape—typified by a scene in Nathaniel Hawthorne's "Sleepy Hollow" in which a screaming train interrupts the narrator's peaceful stroll through the otherwise bucolic countryside—has remained an important trope ever since. For Marx, the pastoral and the progressive are dialectically related, yielding a politics that we recognize today as what James Scott has referred to as "high modernism" or what John Bellamy Foster, Brett Clark, and Richard York have referred to as "ecological modernism," both of which rely on technoeconomic fixes that tend to ignore or even entrench the structures that generated the problems they are meant to solve.[33]

In Emily and Lucas's worldview, drones hovering above a tea estate collecting data about who is (not) working in the field and gene sequencers used to test imported cocoa are more than just minor "technical adjustments" that reinforce the status quo.[34] They are critically important tools for resolving the tension between an ideal of happy, healthy farmers plucking tea on verdant farms and the neoliberal impetus to let the market govern—and harmonize—the increasingly fraught relationship between society, the environment, and the economy. Rather than the technical impinging the pastoral, in this imaginary of technologically mediated, data-driven sustainability, technology is necessary to save the pastoral, even if the pastoral in this particular instance is the rolling green hills of an industrial tea plantation.

This turns Marx's dialectic on its head: for writers like Hawthorne, Emerson, and Melville (Marx's interlocutors), industrialization's ethical and ecological encroachments on the pastoral ideal were nascent and even largely hypothetical; for my interlocutors, however, those encroachments are already firmly established, and they form the grounds on which their interventions are based. Among sustainability professionals, it is well-known and widely accepted that a relatively small number of companies are responsible for the vast majority of historical greenhouse gas emissions that have led to irreversible climate change and even that overconsumption in the West, especially among the wealthy, drives deforestation, biodiversity loss, modern slavery, and a host of other socioecological issues.[35] Technologies of transparency and traceability promise to restore the balance, generating data that lets the market hold everyone accountable, punishing bad actors and rewarding the good ones. Like attempts to solve the problems of capitalism with a better version of capitalism, my informants embrace this new, technologically advanced industrialization—sometimes referred to as "Industry 4.0"—as the solution to the problems created by earlier forms of industrialization.[36]

One of the consequences of this imaginary is that technologies of data collection, storage, and analysis come to be uncritically embraced as key elements of global sustainability, even when these technologies involve invasive monitoring and surveillance regimes. This is why the definition of sustainability matters: if the dominant way of thinking about sustainability is through quantitative measurements of social and environmental impacts, then there must also be a technopolitical infrastructure in place to measure and evaluate those impacts. In this world of data, imagining and enacting alternative visions of sustainability become even more difficult.

Conclusion

Toward the end of 2019, rumors started to swirl that Unilever was looking for investors to buy its tea business, which included well-known brands like Lipton, PG Tips, Tazo, and Pukka. In a statement to Reuters at the time, a Unilever spokeswoman insisted, "contrary to reports, we are not exploring the sale of our tea business."[37] This was probably a bit of a fib, since by the end of 2021, Unilever had in fact sold its tea business, ekaterra, to the private equity firm CVC Capital Partners.[38] The *Financial Times* suggested that the Unilever tea deal was a "test of private equity's conscience."[39] Before CVC emerged as the buyer, two other large private equity (PE) firms pulled out of negotiations, citing labor issues on Unilever's East African tea plantations as a specific reason. The PE firm Advent International excluded the Kenyan plantations from its relatively low final offer, while the Carlyle Group pulled out completely. Reporting in *Nation.Africa* did not pull any punches: the deal with CVC allowed Unilever's CEO to avoid "a potentially embarrassing 'failed transaction' after two of the final three bidders chickened out amid claims of poor work conditions in Unilever's tea plantations in Kenya," so "when suitors expressed interest in Unilever's tea business, it was a perfect opportunity for its management to . . . both shake off the bad reputation from human rights concerns and save the company the agony of dwindling earnings from the beverage amid evolving consumer tastes."[40] As recently as early 2022, I struggled to find any coverage linking the problems on these plantations to the Rainforest Alliance standard, even though Unilever—and its tea business in particular—is one of the NGO's crowning achievements.

Despite Unilever achieving its goal of sourcing tea exclusively from sustainable certified farms and despite being ostensibly one of the best sustainability performers in the industry, the company's Kenyan tea farms were ultimately so rife with labor issues—from gender-based discrimination to the lingering specter of postelection violence in 2007 that affected many of Unilever's workers in Kericho County—that even private equity firms were hesitant to be responsible for them. Some observers might interpret this as an obvious failure of voluntary certification schemes, given that Unilever's Kenyan plantations are Rainforest Alliance certified. Alternatively, it could be the case that these standards are working exactly like my informants claim: by requiring data-driven transparency and traceability, the market—personified by its most powerful actors, private equity firms—was able to essentially punish Unilever for the labor violations that supposedly occurred on Kenyan tea plantations under its watch. Better-managed plantations might have attracted a higher price, but in either case, the market needed reliable social indicators to determine ekaterra's value. As someone involved in the negotiations to sell ekaterra told the *Financial Times*, "The whole ESG [environmental, social and governance] lens across these sorts of investments is so much more of a factor than it was before."[41]

But in fact, it was not the Rainforest Alliance's reams of required data that allowed the market to accurately account for (and price) the labor issues in Unilever's tea business. It was reports from organizations like the United Nations and the Netherlands-based SOMO (Stichting Onderzoek Multinationale Ondernemingen, or the Center for Research on Multinational Corporations), the Kenyan Federation of Women Lawyers, and the Kenyan Human Rights Commission. The continued growth of these kinds of market-oriented sustainability standards is relatively clear case of what political ecologists like James Ferguson, Arturo Escobar, and Tania Murray Li have described in various contexts as the persistent expansion and enthusiastic embrace of neoliberal development schemes, even as they fail to achieve their stated goals or to work as they are supposed to.[42] In these cases, a specific vision of expert-derived, market-oriented development solutions becomes further entrenched with each (failed) attempt to enact that vision. When it comes to actually achieving the kinds of development goals that farmers themselves want—namely, higher prices for their products—actors that push back against the downward pressure of market forces have tended to be the most successful. While the Rainforest Alliance responded to farmers' demands for higher prices by adding a convoluted "sustainability differential" to the most recent version of its standard, which one informant critical of the Rainforest Alliance dismissed as an "accounting trick," in 2021 the Kenya Tea Development Agency simply mandated a minimum auction price, which stands to increase farmers' income by around 25 percent.[43]

Standards development organizations play an important role in determining which specific "vision of sustainability" becomes dominant in the "contested multiplicity of 'sustainabilities'" that characterizes global value chains.[44] But that influence is often behind the scenes, and standards tend to end up reflecting the interests of companies even without their overtly explicit input. Even if these schemes fail to deliver what they promise, as many of them do, businesses and their investors "charge ahead" with plans that reinforce the idea that the solutions to socio-ecological crises are both convenient and profitable. "Corporations," according to Heidi Bachram, "ever conscious of cost and image, seek quick-fix solutions that do not require radical changes to fundamental business practice," all while "the majority of these projects are being imposed upon the South."[45]

Multistakeholder initiatives do little to mitigate that imposition. Their highly mediated engagement of marginalized stakeholders like smallholder farmers vis-à-vis the relatively direct engagement of tea brands and other major corporations reinforces the power imbalance between companies and producers by obscuring those relations behind a veneer of inclusivity. But there is something even more insidious at play, and something even more fundamental at stake, in the way these standards operate: they contribute to the accretion of sustainability's definition as something that can only be understood through quantitative metrics and indicators, as something that is objective and neutral rather than subjective, ethical, and political. Debates about the kinds of data that farmers will be required to provide to comply with future standards or what kinds of technologies might be developed to collect and analyze that data or who counts as an expert when it comes to determining what data to collect and what to do with them once they are collected might seem mundane. These debates leave little room for other, more critical approaches to sustainability to germinate and flourish, such as the idea that farmers should simply be paid a fair price for their products. This leads to what the political scientist Eve Fouilleux and the sociologist Allison Loconto have called a "competition regime of governance," which "has had the effect of limiting the political debates to predominantly trade and market-compatible options."[46]

Within this competition regime of governance, thinking even metaphorically about the biography of sustainability standards helps us think about how—by prioritizing the technical over the social—a preference for analyzable, quantitative data erases those aspects of sustainability that do not fit neatly in a spreadsheet. The legitimacy of these standards depends on the inclusion of multiple stakeholders. As we saw earlier, however, different stakeholders have different access to the standards development process, with the most influential stakeholders tending to benefit the most from the implementation of whatever standard they helped develop. Imagining sustainability as something that can only be understood through indicators that have to be constantly measured, analyzed, and disclosed circumscribes debates about what sustainability can and should be. It facilitates a narrative of impacts as market driven, in which the role of sustainability standards shifts from intervening directly in production processes to providing enough data to allow the market to intervene more organically through monetary incentives to both farmers and corporations, which are imagined as having an equally "shared responsibility" for sustainability outcomes, as they are in the current version of the Rainforest Alliance standard, for instance. The continued datafication of sustainability empowers multinational corporations at the expense of smallholder producers and the people who work (often informally) on large plantations, perpetuating a trend that is now well documented in the critical literature on neoliberal sustainability. A biographical approach helps orient us to the moments when these power dynamics get reinforced but also when they might be contested. For instance, the boards of standards development organizations might be reorganized to prioritize the voices of producer organizations. The ISEAL Alliance, which governs standards revision processes, could develop strict and prohibitive sanctions (such as expulsion from the alliance) for organizations that grant backdoor access to corporations, or it could ban private financing for nonprofit standards organizations. Since private standards tend to stop short of requiring direct payments of sustainability premiums to farmers themselves, producer-country governments could require it instead. Regardless of what a sustainable supply chain might look like, the main goal should be to prioritize—rather than merely to include—the voices of marginalized producers, so that they have the power to say what counts as sustainable. In short, the biography of sustainability should be written by those for whom the biography matters most.

4

Moralizing Sustainability

In a human sacrifice to deity there might be at least a mistaken and terrible beauty; in the rites of the moneychangers, where greed, laziness, and envy were assumed to move all men's acts, even the terrible became banal.
—Ursula K. Le Guin, *The Dispossessed*

Richesse Oblige

I was sitting next to Mr. Guo at dinner in the private dining room of a swanky hotel in Beijing. The dinner was hosted by the organizers of a small, invitation-only workshop on impact investing that had been designed to bring together academics and practitioners. There were a dozen other people at the table, including well-known management and finance professors from Europe, the US, and China; a handful of graduate students and junior scholars (like me); and a few impact investors, all of whom were there to learn more about impact investing and, of course, to network. Among the practitioners, Mr. Guo was by far the most successful. After selling a popular internet venture and "making more money than [he] knew what to do with," he had lived a life of luxury, buying expensive cars and houses and taking lavish holidays in places like Bali and the Swiss Alps. A half-empty pack of expensive Hongtashan cigarettes sat on top of two cell phones, a new iPhone and a new Huawei, which were on the floor under his chair. When the waitress came to take our order, Mr. Guo glanced over at the foreign conference organizer, who was still studying the Chinese-language menu with a puzzled look on his face, unsure of what to order or how much. Without hesitating, he turned to the waitress and began rattling off a long list of dishes in Chinese, much more than we would end up eating. He had only skimmed the menu, and the waitress had to interrupt him a few times to say that the restaurant did not have what he had ordered. Otherwise, she dutifully recorded his order on her tablet. A few moments later, she returned with a tray of cold appetizers, prompting Mr. Guo to tell us that he had been a bachelor for most of his life, claiming with a wry grin as he gazed at the young waitress that he had been quite a playboy. As far as performances of wealthy middle-aged internet tycoons go, Mr. Guo's was Oscar-worthy.

In Ellen Hertz's ethnographic research on the Shanghai Stock Exchange, people like Mr. Guo are prominent characters. They are known as *dahu*, or "big players," men (mostly) who are extremely rich and seem to eschew many of the moral obligations that characterize contemporary Chinese social relations. They brag about their extramarital affairs and bring their girlfriends to breakfast rather than hiding them in luxury apartments and buying their silence with expensive gifts. They spend money on themselves but not their friends and colleagues, refusing to cultivate interpersonal relations of reciprocity, or *guanxi*. Like the wolves who populated Wall Street in the 1980s and 1990s (or the "finance bros" who have replaced them today), the prototypical *dahu* is not meant to perfectly represent every Chinese financier but is instead a figure that lets us analyze the financier's role in Chinese society. In that vein, as Hertz observes, "If *dahu* have [a moral] obligation, it is to earn and to spend their money actively and freely, that is, without regard to the dense network of relations which characterizes economic and social exchange in Shanghai generally."[1]

Whereas *dahu* "respect the [Maussian] obligation neither to receive nor to give," Mr. Guo professed a deep commitment to promoting different kinds of social enterprises in China and abroad.[2] At one point during dinner, he said that he had considered pursuing an academic career, but because he did not think he would be able to produce anything as good as *The Communist Manifesto*, he had abandoned that goal. Then, he had asked himself if he should try to get as rich as Bill Gates. Although he seemed convinced that he could make that much money if he put his mind to it, he dismissed Gates as "boring." He told us that it was easy to get rich but that it was a real challenge to make a positive impact on the world. This was surprising, since lots of people I have interviewed and observed over the past few years have pointed to Bill Gates as precisely the kind of "effective altruist" the world needs. Mr. Guo, however, seemed wholly unconvinced by this Gatesian fantasy of a philanthrocapitalist utopia, even as we became too tipsy from the constant flow of Tsingtao beer to remain focused on its shortcomings.

The next day, only slightly hungover, we all met at the university to discuss the future of impact investing. A few prominent academics offered their analyses of the "impact investing landscape," their talks peppered with references to social theory, academic finance research, and the occasional industry report. As the day wore on, a theme emerged: impact investing has been slow to go mainstream not because it is unprofitable but because, like "sustainability" more generally, "impact" is poorly defined, too ambiguous for investors to get behind. After lunch, Mr. Guo took the stage. Whereas the academics had stood behind the podium and pointed to their PowerPoint presentations or paced back and forth, Mr. Guo easily commanded everyone's attention. His PowerPoint presentation looked like it had been professionally formatted. He regaled us with a sobered-up version of his life story, euphemistically referring to his decision to sell his internet company as "getting some financial freedom," smirking to let everyone know that what he really meant was that he had become exorbitantly wealthy. He joked, again, about his inability to write a book as good as *The Communist Manifesto* and insisted, again, that he could have been as rich as Bill Gates if he wanted but that Bill Gates was boring.

This time, he elaborated: whereas Gates simply throws money at problems hoping that they will be solved, Mr. Guo uses his social and financial acumen to solve problems efficiently, creatively deploying his (and other rich people's) wealth to generate positive impacts. Whereas Gates, in other words, is a philanthropist—even if he embodies the kind of hyperutilitarian, "effective" philanthropist we will hear more from in chapter 6—Mr. Guo imagines himself harnessing the power of the market to generate social and environmental impacts, which he considers more sustainable because it does not depend on the whims of a single rich person. His theory of the causal relationship between impacts and investments turns on an understanding of the market as a self-regulating entity, as something that, given certain inputs, can be expected to yield certain outputs. The market, in other words, emerges in Mr. Guo's worldview as an ethical subject capable of yielding ethical outcomes because of its ability to yield efficient outcomes, but only if it has the right information (and, crucially, the right kind of information) to do so.

Behind him, a photo flashed onto the screen of poor people in China's rural hinterlands. He asked why these communities were being excluded from the immense wealth that was being created in urban financial centers, suggesting not only that it was unethical that they were being "left out and left behind" but that investors like him could use the market to improve their lives and livelihoods. Unlike Hertz's *dahu*, Mr. Guo seemed deeply concerned about "the dense network of relations which characterizes economic and social exchange" in China. By relying on the dynamics of the market to generate impacts, however, Mr. Guo's own ethical subjectivity is mediated by the ethical subjectivity of the market itself. As Giulia Dal Maso has recently argued, understanding the particular subjectivities of different groups of investors is crucial to understanding the variegations of contemporary capitalism, especially in the context of rampant financialization.[3]

The biggest challenge for impact investing, according to Mr. Guo, is that investors and analysts have not developed tools to measure the impact of their investments. This means that it is difficult (if not impossible) to integrate impact as a tangible or "actionable" dimension of the investing process, since it does not "fit" in the financial models that investors use to make investment decisions. Impact, in other words, remains illegible in the hegemonic and hegemonizing gaze of conventional finance. Mr. Guo echoed the preceding speaker's academic argument that "the biggest challenge for the operationalization of impact investing is the measurement and management of impact." This turned out to be one of the workshop's key takeaways. Over the course of three days, nearly every speaker called explicitly for the development of standardized methods to measure and evaluate social and environmental impacts, which they saw as more or less the only thing keeping impact investing from going mainstream.

Understanding the calculative devices that sustainable finance practitioners develop and use to evaluate and valorize the impacts of their investments is key to understanding the plurality of values—including moral values and economic values—that exist at any given moment within financial markets.[4] But it is also important to consider what the compulsion to define, quantify, and measure these impacts tells us about the ethics of sustainable finance in particular and the ethics of finance more generally. In this chapter, I show how sustainable finance practitioners' preoccupation with quantifying and measuring social and environmental impacts both moralizes the process of investing and shifts the moral obligation to be impactful onto the market itself, what Ananya Roy understands as the "ethicalization of market rule" and the subsequent transformation of "the market itself . . . into an ethical subject."[5] If the informants we met in previous chapters seemed myopically concerned with the quantification and measurement of sustainability indicators, the informants we will meet in this chapter, who work in different areas of sustainable finance, will seem positively obsessed. It offers the clearest case of a phenomenon described elsewhere in the book, that is, the embrace of the market as an ethical subject that can generate outcomes that are ethical because it can generate outcomes that are efficient. The market as an ethical subject becomes a constitutive, relational element in sustainability professionals' own ethical subjectivities, not just in sustainable finance but in sustainability more broadly.

The Present, Past, and Future of ESG

Concerns about the reliability of techniques to measure social and environmental impacts pervade the field of sustainable finance, which the industry group Swiss Sustainable Finance (SSF) defines on its website as "any form of financial service integrating environmental, social and governance (ESG) criteria into the business or investment decisions for the lasting benefit of both clients and society at large."[6] What this means is that sustainable finance is essentially standard investment practices with an ESG twist—the inclusion of an ESG rating on a financial report, for instance. Investors tend to think of ESG integration as another form of risk management, expounding a neoclassical argument that the more information investors have about the market and its participants, the more efficient their investment decisions will be. Because of that, sustainable finance qua ESG integration can be difficult to distinguish conceptually from fundamental investing, especially to the extent that investors have always collected firm-specific information as a form of risk management.[7] Nevertheless, ESG analysis is becoming increasingly mainstream as financial institutions come to see their social and environmental impacts as another form of risk that needs to be managed. Major firms like BlackRock and Goldman Sachs have turned their attention to ESG investing over the past few years. Business schools, too, are starting to offer classes in ESG analysis, though these courses are typically considered marginal by the finance departments themselves. At the business school where I taught between 2018 and 2021, for instance, I supervised several master's theses for students in finance programs who struggled to find finance professors willing to supervise their projects, and the university's ESG minor is housed in a department whose main strengths are organizational communications and value chain studies.

It is useful here to consider both the history of ESG and the way ESG advocates narrate and mobilize that history as the basis of their assertions about the future of sustainable finance. A recent article on the "social origins of ESG" traces the history of ESG to socially responsible investing (SRI) initiatives that began as early as the nineteenth century, when faith-based organizations in particular started to impose restrictions on the kinds of enterprises in which their money could be invested. This kind of exclusionary investing gained momentum in the twentieth century in the context of the civil rights movement in the US, the Vietnam War, apartheid South Africa, and environmental concerns, among other things. The article's authors claim that the term "ESG" first appeared in a 2004 report by the United Nations Global Compact (UNGC), which is "a voluntary initiative based on CEO commitments to implement universal sustainability principles and to take steps to support UN goals."[8] The report invited financial analysts "to better incorporate environmental, social and governance (ESG) factors in their research where appropriate and to further develop the necessary investment know-how, models and tools in a creative and thoughtful way." Recognizing that the world has become "increasingly complex and interconnected," the authors of the report bemoaned the failure of the financial industry to "[develop] a common understanding on ways to improve the integration of environmental, social and governance (ESG) aspects in asset management, securities brokerage services and the associated buy-side and sell-side research functions," a failure that was "due partly to the complexity and diversity of the issues involved."[9]

This 2004 UNGC report, along with a 2005 report by the UN Environment Program's influential Finance Initiative (UNEP-FI), form the "backbone" of the UN Principles for Responsible Investment (PRI), a set of six principles launched in 2006 that "were developed by investors, for investors," and "offer a menu of possible actions for incorporating ESG issues into investment practice." Like the Global Compact, "signatories" of the PRI commit to these principles without any oversight or repercussions for failing to adhere to them; and like the four core principles of the Trade for Sustainable Development Forum discussed in the introduction, the Principles for Responsible Investment focus more on integrating and reporting ESG indicators than ensuring that those efforts lead to any actual "sustainable" outcomes. On a section of the PRI's website that is full of so much corporate jargon that it verges on nonsensical, the PRI claims that the widespread adoption of its principles will help "address unsustainable aspects of markets that investors operate in, to achieve the economically efficient, sustainable financial system that responsible investors and beneficiaries need": "We work with our signatories and other stakeholders to challenge barriers to a sustainable financial system and drive meaningful data throughout markets."[10] The PRI thus imagines that it can achieve its aims by pumping the market full of "meaningful data." Scholars and practitioners alike take the rapidly growing number of signatories over the past fifteen years as a proxy or "barometer of the growing awareness of ESG issues among investors and their inclusion in investment decisions."[11] This growing awareness, they argue, translates to a growing demand for ESG data. This, in turn, "has spurred the creation and growth of an entire industry of ESG data vendors in a relatively short period of time," and "those looking to use ESG data for the first time may find it challenging to navigate the wide range of offers available in the ESG data market."[12]

This history grounds claims about the future of ESG investing, especially the challenges its proponents believe it will have to overcome in order to generate positive social and environmental impacts alongside competitive financial returns. Awareness leads to demand, which leads, in turn, to an overwhelming proliferation of data. (Note the similar trajectory of more traditional approaches to SRI, which also started with an awareness of some social ill—from the divinely prohibited to the politically sensitive—and led to a demand for more information and the subsequent launch of several ethical investing consultancies.) Hacking through this jungle of often-contradictory indicators becomes the main goal, and the principal task, of those who are interested in ESG invest-ing. By foregrounding questions about the quality of ESG data, there is less scope to critically examine the assumptions about what the integra-tion of these data in investment processes can actually achieve, and the idea that better data will lead to better social, environmental, and finan-cial performance comes to be taken for granted, much as it was in nearly all of the presentations I observed in Beijing.

"We Rely on Data"

My research project with Norebank, which included around thirty inter-views with members of the sustainability team and several portfolio managers in 2018 and 2019, had a bit of an unusual start. I reached out to a member of the sustainability team via Twitter and explained that I was an anthropologist studying corporate sustainability and sustainable finance and that I would be interested in hearing more about what his employer was doing with regard to sustainability. We set up a meeting for a few weeks later, which I approached as just another interview with sustainability professionals working in different financial institutions. I was surprised when this informant, Johan, started our discussion by asking about anthropological approaches to finance and what kind of project I had envisioned collaborating on. "We're so fucking bad at sus-tainability," he said with a chuckle, clarifying that by "we," he did not mean his bank in particular but the financial industry as a whole. As he described the difficulty of integrating ESG into the investment process, he suggested that a different perspective—an anthropological perspec-tive, apparently—might be exactly what was needed to figure out what was going wrong. I had not expected to start a new side project on ESG integration, but I went along with it. Serendipitous access to these kinds of spaces, after all, is rare.

I explained how more and more anthropologists had turned their ethnographic gaze to corporations and other financial institutions over the past few decades, and I described some of the observations these scholars have made. Johan was particularly interested in the anthropol-ogist Stefan Leins's observations about the precarious role that finan-cial analysts play in the investment process: economic theory says that there is no way to beat the market, but the job of financial analysts is precisely to try to make predictions about an unpredictable market in order to beat that market, putting them in the uncomfortable position of having to constantly justify their own work by narrating the market as a coherent set of relations between different actors.[13] Johan thought this would be a really interesting avenue to explore with the sustainability team during a future meeting that he volunteered to set up for me, where he assured me that I would be able to ask more questions and get a project started. I asked what Norebank had been doing with regard to ESG integration. He responded that ESG was very difficult to measure, which he interpreted as a threat to the legitimacy of the bank's sustainability claims. "You cannot tell the world you're doing this [sustainable investing] if you can't measure it." He asked, "What kind of data is to be trusted?" before telling me, "We can't go out and talk to every company. We rely on data." He moved on to a discussion of "good" versus "bad" data, suggesting that the most challenging part of his team's work was making sure they were able to find "the right data." His preoccupation with accurate, consistent, and reliable data, especially firm-level data, turned out to be the key issue for both the sustainability team and the portfolio managers at Norebank.

A few weeks after my meeting with Johan, I met with Sammy and Tobias, who lead Norebank's ESG analysis team of around a dozen people. They were the faces of the ESG team, and in later interviews with portfolio managers, when I asked about their interactions with the ESG team, they often responded by talking specifically about their interactions with Sammy and Tobias. Their jobs revolve around collecting, "cleaning," analyzing, and communicating ESG data to the bank's portfolio managers, who are often skeptical of the so-called added value of ESG integration. These data come from disparate sources, from sustainability indexes like those provided by Morningstar and the Dow Jones Sustainability Indexes (DJSI), from sustainability analytics companies like Sustainalytics and RobecoSAM, from Bloomberg terminals, and from their own research on specific companies' various social and environmental scandals. The data they collect often tell contradictory stories, and their job is to find out which data and data sets are the most reliable, to tidy them up, and to make them "look like" the kinds of financial indicators that portfolio managers are not only more familiar with but also find much more convincing and trustworthy in the context of their role, which is to do nothing other than increase the financial value of their portfolios.

As I heard from numerous members of the sustainability team and from many of the portfolio managers, "speaking the same language" is crucial, which helps explain why most of the sustainability team has a background in conventional finance. It also explains why the sustainability team feels so compelled to make sure the ESG data they share with portfolio managers is quantitative, which the managers find more trustworthy because they associate numbers with objectivity and rigor and which they perceive as more legitimate in the context of investing. There are vast amounts of data about companies' ESG performance. At least a dozen companies offer subscription services for ESG analytics, and there are always news stories and corporate reports that need to be analyzed in-house. On top of collecting and "cleaning" these data, the ESG team also performs a lot of emotional labor, constantly tempering their own personal commitments to sustainability by insisting (to themselves, I suspect, as much as me) that their approach to ESG was "value driven, not values driven." This phrase popped up several times in interviews with both the ESG team and portfolio managers, who seemed to have to remind themselves that their job is to make sure the market has the data it needs to accurately price social and environmental externalities, which is the right thing to do both ethically and economically.

I met with Sammy and Tobias several times during the course of my research, and they always seemed excited to have someone to talk to about sustainable finance. They appreciated my critical approach, at one point telling me that while they were used to being criticized by portfolio managers who sometimes thought they were trying to do "too much," they had never been criticized for doing "too little," which is apparently how they interpreted my questions. We talked about academic literature in the social studies of finance, and I shared articles, books, and lectures from my course that I thought they might be interesting. At one point, Sammy asked me for advice on doing a PhD, which he was considering because "there's so much we don't know yet about ESG." As if I were not sufficiently convinced that their jobs were difficult, during our first meeting, Tobias pulled up a picture on his iPad and handed it across the table. It was a graph with companies' ESG scores according to MSCI on the y-axis compared to those same companies' ESG scores according to

FTSE on the x-axis. (MSCI and FTSE are both well-known providers of stock-market indexes.) There was a huge disparity between the two indexes' ratings, meaning that many of the companies that MSCI rated as high ESG performers (i.e., relatively sustainable) were low ESG performers according to FTSE, and vice versa. Tobias grinned. "Crazy, huh?"

The reliability and objectivity of ESG data was not the only problem for finance professionals interested in integrating ESG considerations into their investment decisions. A few months later, during a Skype interview with two portfolio managers that Sammy and Tobias set up for me, Jim complained that ESG ratings were like credit ratings to the extent that they only told you how a company had performed in the past and were therefore not very helpful in making "prognoses" about a company's future performance. ESG indicators, he told me, are "lagging" rather than "leading." I asked if he could pinpoint the moment during the investment process when ESG indicators are most important. He responded by saying, "We are sort of aware of all the different aspects of risk in a company [we invest in] from the beginning, and of course I would say that it's something that's important. It's part of our investment decision all the way through, and we are aware of that. We are maybe not aware of it in a systematic way, but we're definitely aware of it." He continued that ESG could "definitely be a reason . . . for not investing in a company": "We might say, 'Well, this is just too big a risk to take, because we feel that at the end of the day, it will be a negative trigger to the share price, and we won't invest in the company." His colleague Roland interjected,

That's the real issue that Jim brings up here, that everything we do is to try to look into the future and forecast what is going to happen with this company. And our traditional background is to do it from a financial point of view, so [we] do prognoses of the revenue and the earnings and so forth and the cash flow and then discount it back to see its value: Is that higher or lower than the current price? That's what we do. So for us to think that the ESG issues are really relevant, then it should be part of this prognosis.

ESG, in Jim and Roland's view, is synonymous with sustainability, and in order for sustainability-as-ESG to be "really relevant"—in order for portfolio managers to be "systematically" aware of sustainability—it has to be legible from the perspective of "traditional" or conventional investors, who personify the perspective of the market. In other words, it is not sufficient for Jim, Roland, and other human investors to be "aware" of a company's social and environmental impacts; the market must be aware of those impacts, too. For these portfolio managers, it was important to start from a conventional investing mind-set, in which the only real ethical obligation is to increase the financial value of their clients' investments. From that perspective, ESG matters only insofar as it helps increase the client's return on investment, which explains why it typically enters the equation to shore up decisions based on more traditional investment models.[14] But even if ESG is mobilized in service of this status quo, it still needs to be legible to the market, part of a "prognosis" that takes place on analytical rather than merely ethical grounds. The translation of social and environmental impacts into quantitative indicators—what Jim is alluding to when he talks about being aware of different aspects of risk in a systematic way—is a precondition of the market's awareness, like the way any particular receptor can only receive signals in particular forms.

The most straightforward way to render sustainability legible from this perspective is to think of it as a form of risk, which makes it relatively easy to incorporate, discursively at least, within the conceptualization of investing as a consideration of risk and return, a basic tenet of contemporary finance. The financial legibility of these otherwise-nonfinancial domains, as Sian Sullivan argues, is a key condition of their leveragability as sources of financial value.[15] Sarah Bracking has shown how risk plays an increasingly important role in what she calls the "climate finance *dispositif*" and what we might think of as a more general sustainable finance *dispositif* or apparatus, a key component of which is the "moral propositions" that underlie sustainable finance practitioners' political-economic claims.[16]

In one of the first interviews I conducted during my research in 2015, the head of sustainability at a Swiss private bank situated his own work trying to integrate sustainability concerns in a longer history of the financial industry's continued evolution. It was only halfway through the twentieth century, he told me, that investors started to systematically consider risk and return, instead of just returns, which changed the way investing was done. Now, sustainable finance was doing something similar, instigating a "new normal" in the investment community. I have heard this claim numerous times since then, the idea that sustainability would become as central to investment decisions as risk and return. And yet, it has never been clear how sustainability is separate from risk; indeed, most investors I have talked to over the past five years have, like Jim and Roland, approached ESG integration as another component of risk management. During an interview with a portfolio manager at Norebank who focuses on large European companies, I told him what the Swiss banker had told me a few years earlier, and he laughed, telling me that I should have asked him, "What's the difference between risk management and ESG?" For this informant, there was no difference. If ESG was in fact a new way of managing investment risks, he asked rhetorically, wouldn't portfolio managers, whose compensation depends on the financial performance of their portfolios, have embraced it wholeheartedly? Rather than thinking of this as confusion on their parts, it is more helpful to understand it as an effect of the commensurative impulse. The goal of the ESG team's work—the reason they were so concerned with "speaking the same language" as the portfolio managers themselves—was because they wanted ESG risks and financial risks to be interchangeable in the models investors use to make decisions.

This resonates with other analyses by anthropologists and geographers of risk in the context of sustainable finance.[17] What this scholarship has quite clearly demonstrated is that sustainable finance practitioners in numerous contexts feel compelled to "translate" both the socioenvironmental contexts and the socioenvironmental impacts (the causes and effects, the conditions and consequences) of their investments into particular forms of risk that are legible within the dominant mode of investment decision-making, whether they are legal risks, climate risks, reputational risks, or so on. The production and dissemination of quantitative, data-driven reports that translate various aspects of economic life into forms of risk that are legible to investors is a key part of this, reports that narrate "acceptable engagements" with nature and society that render these domains legible in particular, "actionable" ways.[18] Indeed, this is the primary task of Norebank's ESG team and, according to many of the people who presented at the Chinese impact investing conference, the biggest challenge for the impact investing community, the biggest impediment, in other words, to their collective, market-generated impact.

Moral Markets and the Ethics of Efficiency

A key driver of my informants' preoccupation with quantification and datafication is the idea that, with the right kinds of data, the market will be able to generate the most efficient outcome not only from an economic perspective but also from a social and environmental perspective. Economic theorists have long conflated mathematical efficiency with social optimality, facilitating the commensuration and comparison of economic and social values. The anthropologist Horatio Ortiz shows how this peculiar notion of efficiency—as the point on a graph where supply meets demand or where (marginal) costs meet (marginal) benefits—easily shifts from an economic value to an ethical value.[19] Building on this idea, David Graeber theorizes "infravalues" and "metavalues." Efficiency, in Graeber's reading, is a "tacit interior value" (infravalue) that is a means to an end rather than an end in and of itself; and yet it can be translated into a metavalue (a criterion by which we can choose one value structure over another) in practice, as "efficiency" has indeed become a "metavalue" in the work of economists, bankers, development agents, "neoliberals," and sustainable finance practitioners. Not only that, but efficiency (as metavalue) plays an important role in determining what other values are worth pursuing (e.g., equality, development, sustainability).[20] The commensuration of socioecological and financial impacts is inseparable from the commensuration of these distinct ethical and economic values.

As Christian Berndt and Manuel Wirth argue in the context of social impact bonds (SIBs), one way to interpret the growing interest in different modes of sustainable finance, especially in a world still dealing with the fallout of the 2008 financial crisis, is to see them as "strategic attempts to re-moralize and humanize markets and capitalism," narratives of which, they claim, create a kind of "discursive veil, hiding from view entanglements with those two institutions that protagonists appear to be so keen to distance themselves from—the financial market and the state."[21] My informants, however, do not seem keen to distance themselves from either the financial market or the state. Especially when it comes to the financial market, they tend to do exactly the opposite: they explicitly and consistently situate themselves in the middle of the market, which, for them, is precisely the conduit through which the ethicality of their investments is generated. They see the market as yielding the most efficient—and thus the most ethical—distributional outcomes, where they are concerned with not only the distribution of capital but also the distribution of social and environmental impacts.

This is a crucial point. It builds on observations in anthropology and related disciplines that markets not only reflect various moral values but are increasingly ethicalized themselves and that one of the main tools that market actors use to do this is the quantification and measurement of factors that, until quite recently, they insisted were nonfinancial, things like social and environmental impacts. Roy makes this point quite clearly in her introduction to a set of essays on neoliberal poverty alleviation programs. A system wherein some actors profit (often immensely) from their ostensible efforts to combat poverty—as in the impact investment imaginary, especially—will strike many observers as obviously problematic. The same might be said of efforts to "do well by doing good" more generally, where investors claim to be able to reap substantial windfalls from investing in socially and environmentally friendly companies. As Roy observes, "The conversion of [social and environmental issues] into spaces for enterprise and profit is both complex and fragile. It requires elaborate practices of calculation and rationalities of risk, as well as nimble forms of expertise. It requires formatting social infrastructures as an infrastructure for global capital. . . . It requires converting the urgent temporalities of need into repetitive contracts of long-term profit. Prone to dissent and disorder, bottom billion capitalism and disaster capitalism are thus always under construction, never guaranteed." The fragility of this conversion, according to Roy, "necessitates the ethicalization of market rule," which refers to "the struggle to retool practices of calculation and rationalities of risk to take account of, and even mitigate, the exploitative character of bottom billion capitalism." The same could be said of any of the other "forms" of capitalism we have encountered so far: caring capitalism, green capitalism, stakeholder capitalism, and so on. Analyzing the rise of microfinance as both a "highly popular poverty intervention" and as "an asset class yielding robust rates of return in financial markets," Roy interprets sustainable finance as a form of global finance's self-disciplining, representing the "ethicalization of finance" and, consequently, the transformation of "the market itself" into "an ethical subject."[22]

Understanding the emergence of the market as an ethical subject is crucial to understanding the ethics of sustainable finance and the quantification and measurement of impacts that defines it. One thing my informants share is a more or less explicit acceptance of the idea that investing is an ethical practice but the insistence that the impact of investing should not rely on an individual's morality, which they dismiss as philanthropy. Whether they work in sustainable finance, corporate sustainability, or sustainable finance, sustainability professionals often invoke some episode from their own life or a personal ethical orientation as a way to explain their interest in sustainability. At the same time, my informants at Norebank were very hesitant to evaluate their employers' sustainability efforts through the lens of their own personal moral convictions, careful to rely on "objective" sustainability indicators that would allow the market to yield sufficient outcomes on their behalf.

This was clear in my conversation with Jim and Roland, two of the portfolio managers at Norebank whom I introduced earlier. During the interview, they struggled to give examples of when ESG indicators had been useful, but they were able to speculate about when ESG integration might help (or might have helped) them decide whether to invest in a company or not or even whether to divest. One example revolved around executive pay, which they saw as a prototypical example of the "G" (governance) in "ESG." It can be difficult in Europe, they told me, to hire executives from the US and the UK, because in the Anglo-Saxon system, executives expect much-higher levels of compensation than many Europeans are willing to tolerate, demanding tens of millions of dollars per year in different forms of remuneration (salary, stock options, etc.), whereas their European counterparts are often happy with a fraction of that. Roland recalled that, when he worked at a different bank, one of the companies it invested in wanted to recruit an executive from the US, but it ended up hiring someone else because the candidate wanted $100 million in "fixed and variable pay." This, he told me, was absurd, eliciting a laugh from Jim, who told me, "We think a little bit differently about pay in our society."

Jim and Roland vacillated between ethical-cultural logics and market logics, demonstrating the fuzzy boundaries of these ostensibly distinct realms. Jim was worried that an executive who made $100 million a year would lose the incentive to work hard and suggested that paying someone that much money would not be in the best interest of shareholders, no matter how talented the executive might be. A moment later, Roland said, "If we look at senior management earning $100 million, it is probably not sustainable for a company rooted in this part of the world to have that kind of inequality." He immediately corrected himself: "But that's a personal view," before reiterating Jim's earlier point about incentive structures, telling me that executives, too, "need something to strive for." If they were thinking about investing in a company that paid its senior management hundreds of millions of dollars a year, they would be forced to ask whether "the incentive program is structured in the right way" in order to prevent well-paid executives from "maximizing in the short term" before they "run away with half of the bank, and then afterwards, we have nothing left." Here, Roland had to reframe his own personal opposition to exorbitant executive pay as something that was simply bad for business.

Another example revolved around a mining company in Latin America, where a leaky dam had polluted hundreds of square miles of land and, in Roland's words, "killed some people." Although they had not invested in the mining company, it was a supplier to some other companies they had invested in, raising thorny ethical questions about the boundaries of responsibility. Nevertheless, Roland felt compelled to conceptualize pollution and homicide in terms of risk, specifically the financial risks that an investor would have to deal with if they decided to invest in that particular mining company or other companies to which it supplied raw materials. He explained,

> You can say this is a financial risk, a foreign company operating mines that have these dams that can leak, and it could create a huge mess. So you can say that's an ESG risk translating into a financial risk, and you will have to take that into account when doing your financial calculation. That's an example of where it becomes a very financial objective, but it is still an assessment of what is risk is behind these dams. That's one risk within a mining company, assessing how these dams are constructed. Is

there a risk that they will leak? And if they leak, what will be the financial implications of this? That is a sort of an environmental risk translating into the financial.

In both cases, Roland and Jim's ambivalence is apparent, an ambivalence that is only resolved through recourse to the market's own ethicality. In the first case, the incentive structure of the labor market yielded, in their "personal opinion," the most ethical outcome precisely because it was the most efficient in economic terms. They imagine the "G" in "ESG" allowing them to account for that and then, crucially, allowing the market to determine the right outcome. In the second case, ESG indicators (here, emphasis was on the "E" and "S") help "translate" the ecocidal tendencies of the modern corporation into a measurable and manageable financial risk. In both cases, my informants were careful not to make ethical judgments about leaky dams and overpaid executives from their personal perspective but to think about these issues in terms of "objective" indicators that the market is able to use to make its own judgments. That is, rather than deciding not to invest in a mining firm because they personally believe that ecocide is wrong or deciding not to invest in a company that pays its CEO $100 million a year because they are ethically opposed to the kind of inequality that such a high salary would reflect (and contribute to), Roland and Jim want the market to yield these outcomes on its own, using the kind of ESG indicators that their colleagues in the sustainable department work so hard to produce and disseminate. For these actors, it is indeed the case that the "intention of doing good is not enough. . . . It is ultimately the market that has to make sure that what is good is also efficient."[23]

Sustainable (Inter)Subjectivities

In the context of sustainable finance, the ethicalization of market rule relies on a few intersecting assumptions: first, the concomitant status of "efficiency" as both an economic and an ethical value, one that subsequently grounds other ethical evaluations; second, the belief that the market, as long as it has complete and accurate data (or what economists like to call perfect or near-perfect information) about social and environmental concerns, will yield efficient—and thereby ethical—outcomes;

third, the tacit conflation of efficiency with sustainability; and fourth, the presumed inevitability of sustainability under the condition of perfectly or near-perfectly informed markets. The market is an ethical subject to the extent that it makes sense of complex information about the social, environmental, and economic dimensions of investment opportunities, and it yields the efficient distribution of capital. In this context, efficiency is ethical, so the market's ability to determine these efficient outcomes imbues it with an ethical subjectivity. The market's ethical subjectivity is an important element of investors' own ethical subjectivities, since engaging with the market as an ethical subject that yields ethical distributional outcomes is important in justifying their own moral commitments to sustainability as a data- and market-driven enterprise, perhaps especially in cases of unsustainability.

It also explains why my informants view attempts to impose "subjective" rules on investments (such as, "Don't invest in oil companies because they are bad") as unethical because they are (economically) inefficient. Failing to frame investment decisions in a way that corresponds to the logic of the market, in other words, renders those decisions unethical because they do not take advantage of the market's ability to identify efficient outcomes, opting instead for outcomes that might be inefficient. By relying on the market to identify the most efficient and thus the most ethical investment opportunities, sustainable finance practitioners mitigate their own ethical responsibility for outcomes that are ultimately less than ideal: it is not their fault a mining corporation destroyed a watershed by dumping toxic chemicals or that a CEO was incentivized to maximize the value of a company in the short term at the expense of its long-term viability, nor is it the market's fault per se; rather, it is a failure of companies to adopt standardized reporting frameworks and to accurately disclose their social and environmental impacts, a failure of data providers to provide complete and consistent data about ESG issues, a collective failure to agree on a sufficiently rigorous and easily measurable definition of "impact," or some other data-centric failure that negatively affects the market's ability to achieve efficiency.

Data, after all, are how "the market" sees, how it doles out moral judgments and governs those who fall under its gaze. This gaze is not panoptic, but there is almost a sense among my informants that a panoptic market would be more sustainable because it would then have access more perfect information. The sociologists Marion Fourcade and Kieran Healy have described contemporary organizations' compulsion to collect vast amounts of data as the "data imperative": organizations collect data because of institutionalized myths about what organizations should look like. "Organizations," they argue, "believe they should be in the data collection business, even when they do not yet know what to do with what they collect," and "it does not matter that the amounts [of data] collected may vastly exceed a firm's imaginative reach or analytic grasp. The assumption is that it will eventually be useful, i.e. valuable."[24] For my informants, however, it is not about what their organization will do with these increasingly vast amounts of data but rather about what the market will do with them. Perhaps the "data imperative," then, is at least partially motivated by the ethical subjectivities of people working within organizations, who see their own ethicality as mediated by what they believe is the exclusive ability of markets to yield efficient, and thus ethical, outcomes. My informants' engagement with the market as an ethical subject depends on their assumption that it will act in a certain way. Indeed, their own ethicality depends on their assumptions about how the market works, its internal logic, how it makes sense of information, and what kinds of decisions it will make based on that information—how, in other words, it behaves. Thus, to the extent that my informants invoke the ethical subjectivity of the market in their own narrative accounts of what is right and wrong in the context of their work—such as allowing the market to determine whether to invest in a dirty mining company or leaving it to the market to make sure that poor children in rural China are not excluded from the rapid economic development of urban areas—the ethics of ESG are inherently intersubjective.

And yet, if intersubjectivity is the "existential foundation for all possible sociality," what does it mean that "the market" constitutes one of my informants' primary intersubjective engagements?[25] Here, the anthropologist Alessandro Duranti's account of intersubjectivity is helpful, specifically his claim that intersubjectivity is a "precondition for interaction," that is, a condition of possibility for, rather than an effect of, communication.[26] Interacting with the market is ultimately what sustainable finance practitioners are trying to do, evidenced by their interest in "translating" social and environmental concerns and "speaking the same language" as those whom they see as more familiar with the market and their commitment to "harnessing the power of markets [to] protect our environment and prevent its rapid destruction," as a recent op-ed in the *Financial Times* described the salvific potential of sustainable finance.[27] To the extent that intersubjectivity is a precondition for interaction, and to the extent that intersubjectivity presupposes multiple subjects, the market as an interactant is also, necessarily, a subject.

For Duranti, intersubjectivity is "participation in a world inhabited by Others . . . even when the Others are not physically co-present." His goal in theorizing intersubjectivity is to "found a truly interdisciplinary study of human sociality," and while intersubjectivity may very well be "foundational to human-specific modes of interaction . . . , the agents or selves in question don't need to be individuals, or even humans."[28] For Kockelman, instead, intersubjectivity is merely a shared awareness of something and a mutual awareness of that shared awareness. This does not require an assumption of mind reading, against which Duranti cautions us, but rather an assumption of semiotic interpretability. What ESG investors are trying to achieve with all their hard work of collecting and analyzing ESG data—a goal shared by all those involved in the development of ESG reporting standards and ESG investing frameworks and so on—is to make sure the market is aware of social and environmental issues by making sure those issues are accounted for and to make sure the market is aware that investors are also aware of these issues, so it will reward them by increasing the financial value of their sustainably managed portfolios.

As ESG investing commands an increasingly prominent role in discussions about sustainable futures, it is important to think about ethical intersubjectivity involving the market as a condition of possibility for ethical interaction beyond the market. This mode of intersubjectivity relies on assumptions about how the market behaves—assumptions that are often wrong or assumptions that in turn rely on other, unrealistic assumptions. In the case of sustainable finance, these assumptions are as numerous as they are untenable: the assumption that a free market yields ethical outcomes, the assumption that a "free" market can exist at all, the assumption that more data will make markets more efficient, and the assumption that sufficient amounts of sufficiently high-quality data will ever be available. Alongside these assumptions about the market's behavior, my informants' ethical subjectivities also rely on assumptions about their colleagues, including assumptions about their colleagues' assumptions. In order for Norebank's sustainability analysts to act in a way they deem ethical, for example, they have to make assumptions about how the market works, and they have to make assumptions about the assumptions of portfolio managers responsible for acting on (or ignoring) their analyses. These assumptions (about assumptions about assumptions . . .) are a complex but ethnographically tractable key to (ethical) intersubjectivity. And throughout all this, it is important to remain critically attuned to the market's remarkable ability to transform from a proxy for human actors to an actor in its own right, as well as to the politics of this shifty transformation. However the market might appear to behave, and however it acts and interacts with others, behind its quasi-algorithmic determination of what is efficient and thus what is ethical, real people are affected by investments in mining companies, social development projects, companies with overpaid CEOs, and all sorts of other ventures. People's livelihoods are destroyed, and their environments are polluted; and in the midst of all this, it is clear that the ethics of sustainability extend far beyond the human, that our fates are intimately and inextricably linked—a forceful reminder of the entanglements of being, knowing, and doing discussed elsewhere in the book.

Contingent Commensurability

Anthropologists like Stacy Leigh Pigg and Fabiana Li have shown that commensuration is not a natural or straightforward process, even if the results of commensuration often get naturalized through subsequent discourses that presume commensuration.[29] Rather, problems and solutions must be carefully framed in specific ways that facilitate commensuration. The negotiations around ESG integration in Norebank reveal the substantial amount of work that goes into this framing. The ESG team is constantly on guard to make sure they are "speaking the same language" as the bank's portfolio managers, spending much of their time cleaning and organizing quantitative data that they think will make sense to their more numbers-minded counterparts. Similarly, portfolio managers like Roland and Jim were quick to correct themselves when they slipped into a register that they considered too subjective or too far removed from the data-driven approach to sustainability that they were trying to embrace. Sustainability professionals put a lot of work into framing the problem of unsustainability as something that can be understood through quantitative indicators. This underlies their framing of sustainability as something that can only be achieved by the market, which makes sense of these indicators to yield the most efficient, and thus the most sustainable, outcomes. The framing of the problem and the solution in this way is necessary for the commensuration of social, environmental, and financial impacts inherent in their approach to sustainability.

The contingency of commensuration recalls the fragility of the conversion of social and environmental issues into profitable investment opportunities, as well as the metrological regimes on which this commensuration depends. If, as Roy claims, the fragility of this conversion necessitates the "ethicalization" of market rule, it is worth thinking about what the contingency of commensuration necessitates, especially given the extent to which different domains must be commensurated in order to make claims about the substitutability of the efficiency, ethicality, and sustainability of ESG integration. It is not just about framing problems and solutions in a way that facilitates commensuration but is also about constructing and maintaining an infrastructure of assessment and communication that allows this approach to sustainability to take hold both inside and outside Norebank's organizational limits.

During my interview with the marketing and communications managers of the bank's ESG team, my informants seemed anxious to assure me that they were able to speak the same language as both the portfolio managers and the bank's clients. Amanda, who had worked for several different pension funds before joining Norebank in 2018, had only decided fairly recently to switch from her role in fund manager selection to ESG. Throughout our interview, she and her colleague Isabella constantly reminded me that they both had backgrounds in other areas of finance and that they both had postgraduate degrees in financial accounting from prestigious universities. This background was crucial to Amanda's ability to distinguish between greenwashing and what she saw as a real, growing commitment to ESG in the financial industry. A decade earlier, she told me,

My sense of ESG and responsible investment wasn't really that positive because I couldn't really see the value added. It was more that it was covering your ass, making sure you didn't have any investments that other pension funds had excluded or that the media would [pounce on]. And also when I spoke to asset managers—I've spoken to hundreds of asset managers—when they presented their ways of integrating ESG or responsible investment, it was all about exclusions or a process separate from what they actually did. So, for me, it was just, "We do this, then we are able to check these boxes," but there wasn't any value added. But then I transferred to another asset manager doing asset manager selection. I was in the pension fund for eight years and then another local asset manager, and then I joined Norebank two and a half years ago, still doing manager selection. And what I really felt the last three, four, five years is that now many of our external asset managers have really begun taking ESG into consideration in a meaningful way. So, I've seen the shift, and I can see in portfolio managers' eyes that they believe in it, and they see how it can contribute to making better investment decisions. So, for me, that's been very positive. In my previous role [at Norebank], I tried to take on so many of the tasks related to ESG and sustainability, and last summer I decided I would pursue it fully, and I was able to get into the ESG team, which I started in November [2018].

For this informant, asset managers were slowly but surely embracing ESG as a value-adding component of investment decision-making. In her new role on Norebank's ESG team, she focused more on communicating with "external stakeholders," especially clients who might be skeptical of the bank's growing public commitment to sustainability, assuring them that it was not coming at the expense of profits. What was interesting about this interview was my informants' emphasis on their own competence while at the same time emphasizing the value of data-driven sustainability. The way that this informant tacks between her own professional experience in asset management, on the one hand, and her perception that ESG had become a value-adding addition to asset management strategies, on the other hand, reflects larger anxieties about the legitimacy of ESG in high finance.

Throughout my project with Norebank, informants regularly invoked a dichotomy of "value" versus "values," claiming that their ambition was to make ESG integration "value driven" rather than "values driven." What they meant was that their ESG strategy was motivated not by personal, subjective ethical evaluations but by the market's objective valuation of their efforts. The solution to the problem of the market being unable to price things like a threatened species or a remote community's intangible cultural heritage is not to make those things "off-limits" but to develop new ways to account for them in a way that yields to easier valuation. In this context, the legitimacy of Norebank's ESG strategy relied on the legibility of ESG indicators from the perspective of "the market" but also the legibility of the ESG team vis-à-vis the bank as an organization, the people who manage the bank's investments, and their institutional clients. Through the ESG team's insistence that they had the same technical training as "actual" investors and their perpetual struggle to make sure they were "speaking the same language" as portfolio managers, their work highlights the fragility of commensuration and the effort it takes to maintain these metrological regimes. Developing rigorous methods of accounting for social and environmental impacts and publishing rigorous data sets on the nonfinancial aspects of a company or an investment fund is meaningless without all the work my informants put into convincing everyone else that these numerical accounts of sustainability are valuable from the perspective of financial markets. This work is diverse, from the mundane labor of collecting and cleaning and analyzing data sets to the more affective labor of having coffee meetings and working lunches with colleagues and clients to convince them that integrating ESG considerations is a profitable way of managing risks to the difficult-to-categorize labor of spending a year working with a social scientist who is trying to understand why your bank is spending so much time and money on sustainability.

Conclusion

The edifice of neoliberal sustainability relies on the legitimacy and the purported value-added of the kinds of indicators that Norebank's ESG team deals with on a daily basis. In general, ESG is becoming more and more prominent—with consulting firms like McKinsey and EY proclaiming that ESG is "here to stay" and "more important than ever."[30] ESG-managed funds have grown exponentially over the past few years, and yet this seems to have had very little impact on social or environmental indicators, as things like inequality, sea-level rise, carbon emissions, and so on all continue to worsen. In light of that, even the *Harvard Business Review* seems to have grown a bit skeptical, publishing articles that question the impact of ESG reporting and advocate (as you might have guessed at this point in the book) for better measurements and more standardized, rigorous ESG reporting.[31]

ESG analysts and investors must navigate difficult terrain between a "value-driven" approach that prioritizes the financial performance of their portfolios and a "values-driven" approach that is motivated by their subjective, ethical opinions about what is right and wrong. Rather than having to choose a side, however, the polyvalent notion of "efficiency" allows them to reframe this "value-driven" approach as the most ethical approach, collapsing the distinction between "value" and "values." To determine what counts as efficient, they turn to the market, which, in their worldview, requires a huge amount of data in order to make sense of the world and channel capital to the most socially, environmentally, and economically efficient investments, deftly navigating between competing and sometimes conflicting demands. A key tenet of modern economics, which undergirds my informants' understanding of what "the market" is and how it works, is that more information makes markets more efficient. The obsession with quantitative, objective ESG data among my informants at Norebank reflects a commensurative impulse at the heart of contemporary sustainability, one that demands a common metric to understand the relationship between social and environmental performance, on the one hand, and financial performance, on the other. By calculating the environmental, social, and governance aspects of an investment, analysts make it easier to determine the value of those aspects in a way that is legible—in the same way that risk is legible—to "the market." What makes ESG integration ethical from the perspective of my informants and in the context of sustainability is that it facilitates this market-driven efficiency.

The market sits at the center of my informants' ethical intersubjectivities. In order to meet their own ethical obligations, they rely on the assumption that only the market can yield the most efficient and thus the most ethical outcomes, and they see their job as making sure the market is able to do that. From this "intersubjective position," other modes of relationality emerge as a threat that must be dismissed as deficient in various ways. For many people and communities, the market-centered intersubjectivity of neoliberal sustainability is not "translatable" to their own lived experiences, despite the best efforts of ESG analysts and other sustainability professionals to render these lifeworlds commensurable.[32] Even among Norebank's portfolio managers, it was hard to maintain the kind of strict separation of values that such an intersubjectivity demands. In an interview I conducted over the phone a few weeks after Christmas, one portfolio manager told me that his sister, whom he described as a left-leaning environmentalist, was critical of his decision to work for a large bank, which she thought contributed to many of the world's problems. Her critique stung, but when he told this story to me, he justified his work by saying that he had to separate the personal from the professional, as if he could comfortably split himself into two separate people. In fact, the ethical intersubjectivity of a banker vis-à-vis the market and the ethical intersubjectivity of a brother vis-à-vis an accusatory sister were very difficult to reconcile, and this informant had to find fault in his sister's approach. She may have been right, he conceded, in noting that he should probably fly less and eat less meat, but she was wrong that his work was bad, because through his work, capital flowed where it was supposed to, and that was a good thing.

5

Sustainable Lives

Save the children.
—Lu Xun, "Diary of a Madman"

The Good Life

A little over an hour into my flight from Brussels to Geneva in September 2015, the plane popped out from under the clouds, and a picturesque landscape unfolded below: rolling green hills, a glistening lake, and snowy Alpine peaks. As we flew lower, little farmhouses and herds of cattle came into view. It was, as anyone who has visited Switzerland will attest, a beautiful place, with its clean air, clear water, and stately, low-rise architecture. Geneva is a site of extreme wealth and luxury. A substantial portion of the world's private wealth is concentrated there, held in banks bearing the names of rich old families like Pictet, Lombard, de Rothschild, Odier, Sarasin, Mirabaud, and so on. Multinational corporations like Nestlé, Richemont, and Japan Tobacco International are headquartered in and around Geneva, often just a few minutes' walk away from exceedingly well-funded international organizations like the World Trade Organization and the United Nations, with their sprawling campuses covering some of the most expensive real estate on the planet. People who live in Geneva are usually well-off (or in their parlance, "comfortable"). In 2018, Switzerland had the second-highest income per capita in the world (around US$85,000), trailing only Luxembourg (around US$115,000). To give a crude comparison, the global average is around US$11,000.

According to my informants, Geneva was a wonderful place to live and work for young professionals, especially those with ambitions of making a difference in the world. Although the salaries for people working in international organizations and NGOs are not as high as jobs in banking and consulting, they are high enough that workers can live very comfortable lives and, maybe even more important, feel as though they are being fairly compensated for their labor. One of the biggest complaints from people working in sustainability in places like London or New York is that their pay is so much lower than that of people working in the private sector or, for those who work in the private sector themselves, that their pay is significantly lower than that of their non-sustainability-focused colleagues, even in the same organization. This is not the case in Geneva, however, and sustainability professionals there rarely seemed to harbor any resentment toward their unsustainable counterparts. During the winter, Geneva was empty on weekends, with everyone from students to senior bankers going to Chamonix and other ski resorts. My informants took frequent holidays to Spain and Italy, which one person described as "cheaper than spending the weekend in Geneva," as well as more tropical destinations like Phuket and the Seychelles. When the weather was nice, we spent weekends hiking or cycling, swimming in the lake, or lounging in nearby parks with snacks and drinks. They admitted that Geneva could be "a bit boring" sometimes, but everyone seemed to agree that it was "a good base."

In the Parc de la Grange one Saturday, at a birthday picnic for one of my informants, someone pointed to a woman pushing a baby in a stroller while a toddler ran circles around her. "I'd hate to have that job," he said. I asked what he was talking about, and he explained that some of Geneva's wealthier families hire nannies from the Philippines, especially if they have worked somewhere like Hong Kong or Singapore where that is a common practice, in which case it is a matter of "bringing their nannies back with them." (According to a bit of local gossip, the "dumb sons" of Geneva's financial elite are often sent to Hong Kong to get work experience in the financial services industry before returning to cushy jobs in the banks and companies that their families control, creating a thin veneer of meritocracy.) I quickly started noticing which types of people were sitting in the windows of Geneva's restaurants and cafés and which types of people were not, which types of people were lounging in the manicured parks or sipping rosé with their feet dangling into the crystal-clear water of Lac Leman after work and which types of people were nannying the children in those parks or collecting dirty wine glasses. As my fieldwork progressed, it also became apparent who was sitting in the offices of multinational companies and international organizations designing sustainability initiatives and how different these people looked from those whose faces end up on the cover of their sustainability reports.

With the city's cultivated natural environment and comfortable, professional lifestyles, Geneva provided a utopian backdrop against which my informants could design and implement their various sustainability initiatives. It was the place they returned to after taking trips abroad to the spaces where the social and environmental impacts of these initiatives were supposed to manifest themselves, underdeveloped dystopias where they believed their expertise and experience could be put to good use helping the less fortunate. It was a place from which they could view the rest of the world with pity, a place where neoliberal sustainability's "stringent intolerance toward anyone still capable of taking pleasure from simply being alive" was most visible.[1] From this vantage point, sustainability morphed into a kind of *mission civilisatrice* 2.0, a contemporary version of the imperialist conviction (among French colonizers in particular) that the domination of overseas territories was justified by the fact that it introduced Western civilization to otherwise-uncivilized societies. In the context of sustainability, my informants were motivated by a desire not to civilize per se but rather to "improve," to provide the tools they believe are needed to live a good life. Tania Li has documented the perverse effects of this "will to improve" in Indonesia, showing how even well-meaning development agents often end up introducing and reinforcing structures of power that formalize elite control over natural resources.[2] Like Li's development agents, my informants' vision of the good life is predicated on a particular political and moral economy, which they come to be deeply invested in exporting to other places. In their classically liberal vision of what constitutes a good life, certain inequalities are required to encourage people to work hard and to cultivate an entrepreneurial spirit, to give people something they can *aspire to*. Their vision of the good life is one of carbon-neutral luxury, where the status quo is maintained with lower social and environmental impacts. Their goal is to replicate the comfort of their own lives in uncomfortable places, a kind of salvific impulse that sees other ways of living and other kinds of aspirations as inherently lacking, driven by an assumption that, if given the choice, everyone would like to live the life of a Geneva-based sustainability professional with a high salary, good work-life balance, and all the comforts such a lifestyle affords.

But reproducing sustainability professionals' vision of the good life also means reproducing the kinds of extractive and exclusionary dynamics that their good lives depend on. In the book *The Need to Help*, the anthropologist Liisa Malkki examines volunteers with the Finnish Red Cross, including both those who go to help during disaster like the Rwandan genocide or the destabilization of Afghanistan and those who stay in Finland, where they knit blankets and collect toys to donate. Humanitarianism, for Malkki's informants, is a way for people to go "[in] to the world 'out there,' elsewhere," something they are often driven to do, at least in part, because of loneliness or boredom back home.[3] This is quite different from my informants, and yet it points to a similar understanding of the world as something to be engaged with on the terms of those who feel the compulsion to help. Helping is generative, not just of the self vis-à-vis the other selves that populate the world but of the world itself.

This chapter examines the emotions that drive much of sustainability professionals' work, focusing especially on the pity they feel for the people they see as impoverished stakeholders in developing countries and situating this pity in the affective geography of Geneva vis-à-vis the rest of the world. For the feminist political ecologist Farhana Sultana, "environmental degradation and resource crises can produce differentiated emotions that influence the very ways that resources are imagined, accessed, used and controlled on a daily basis."[4] Studying the kinds of emotions these issues provoke among sustainability professionals adds a new facet to the emerging literature on emotional political ecologies, which has focused predominantly on the affective and emotional lives of marginalized people living in the Global South.[5] I show how sustainability professionals working in cities like Geneva, New York, and London express and mobilize a sense of pity for the people whom their work ostensibly benefits (or "impacts"), which reinforces their belief that their commitment to spreading their specific vision of the good life is a worthy cause. I describe this vision of "the good life" and how it gets contrasted against the purportedly dystopian existence of the marginalized stakeholders whom my informants imagine populating the Global

South, ruminating on the field trips they often take to get a "firsthand" experience of their impact. I draw on Judith Butler's notion of grievable lives to think about how the lives of these stakeholders gets assigned a certain degree of sustainability, where an important shift occurs from thinking about sustainability in terms of impacts to thinking about sustainability as the ability to be sustained, turning on even more fundamental modes of commensuration, comparison, and causation.

Through this shift, sustainability professionals come to be the arbiters of what counts as sustainable not only in the sense discussed in the first few chapters of the book but also in the sense of what can and should be maintained, protected, and supported. My informants' efforts to help end up being motivated to a large extent by a desire to create the conditions of possibility for their beneficiaries to achieve the good life, even as these conditions necessarily preclude the possibility of pursuing alternative ways of living well. Sustainability initiatives reproduce and reinforce neoliberal subjectivities and governmentalities, and this chapter reflects on the affective and emotional aspects of these processes in order to shed light on the salvific violence of sustainability that manifests itself in my informants' compulsion to go and help change the world.[6] Taking the speculative nature of sustainability seriously, I also use this chapter to reflect on two short stories, "The Ones Who Walk Away from Omelas" by Ursula K. Le Guin and "The Ones Who Stay and Fight" by N. K. Jemisin. These stories help us imagine what the world might look like when the commensurative impulse is thwarted and when comparison on unjust grounds is resisted.

Living Sustainably

Miranda had strong opinions about what it meant to live a sustainable lifestyle. During one of our conversations in Geneva, we were talking about how difficult it was to define sustainability and how many contradictory ways it can be interpreted, to say nothing of the many ways it can be applied. She admitted that some organizations take advantage of the flexibility of sustainability to greenwash their operations, but the benefits of flexibility, for Miranda, outweighed the costs of rigidity. This was a pretty typical conversation, but what seemed to bother Miranda the most was the idea that living sustainably often seems to imply that people have to make big changes that will negatively impact the way they live:

> I understand sustainable development not to mean "no development." I think we should all be developing super well. We should all be living in the luxury that [the wealthy enjoy], but with a much lower impact. We just need to find a way that everyone can live really well, but within the limits of the planet. That doesn't mean stopping people living well. If you have a choice between two products, you should be able to get the one that you like most but is also the one that is most sustainable. And that should be our target. . . . I don't think it means living a worse life, and I think a lot of people think that because it means making trade-offs [that it means] I'm not going to be as comfortable in my life because I want it to be more sustainable. No. For me, it's very clear. Sustainable development [means] we're all living as well as we can but with a lower impact. It's like Tesla or other options. I mean, we're seeing it every day, these innovations, which are super cool. If you have a Tesla, you've reduced your impact so much, but you're living the life! It's a great product! And I think that's what we should be striving for.

Miranda's ideal, sustainable world is one of luxury, where everyone can drive a fancy car and live in a big house but where these high-consumption lifestyles do not negatively impact other people or the natural environment. It is a vision of sustainability that is contingent on her immediate surroundings—the wealth and security of Switzerland, its pleasant climate, its "neutral" geopolitics, and so on. Externalities are internalized through the entrepreneurial spirit of individuals and the cultural force of markets. Sustainability generates positive social and environmental impacts profitably—"doing well by doing good." In this vision of sustainability, everyone can live more luxuriously in a richer, less polluted, and more socially stable world.

It is worth thinking about the kind of world—and the kind of socio-ecological relationships that define that world—that Miranda believes "we should be striving for" and to interrogate whom exactly her utterance of "we" is referencing. There is broad consensus across numerous academic fields that the world's "planetary boundaries" are being rapidly and perhaps irreparably exceeded, even as critical interventions within this consensus push us to better understand how the responsibility for this situation is unevenly distributed across time, space, and communities. As degrowth theorists have argued, the perpetual pursuit of increased wealth, which is inextricable from the intersecting socio-ecological crises that my informants are trying to address, undermines everyone's ability to pursue the good life, no matter how a good life is defined.[7] And yet, in Miranda's ideal world, not only should everyone have the opportunity to become wealthy (indexed by their big houses with garages full of Teslas), but becoming wealthy should not have much of a negative impact on society or the environment. What degrowth scholars interpret as a delusion, economists take as a fundamental assumption, which sustainability professionals translate into market-driven sustainability initiatives that reflect that assumption.

The "we" in Miranda's future-oriented imaginary of what a sustainable world looks like refers precisely to the kind of people who surround her in Geneva, the kind of people who tut-tut when they see someone driving a big pickup truck (or more likely in Geneva, roll their eyes at a gas-guzzling Lamborghini), whose ambition is to be able to drive a Tesla back and forth between their Internet-of-Things-equipped smart houses in the suburbs of Geneva and their chic, contemporary office spaces downtown, even as they jet-set between international sustainability conferences and family holidays abroad. What Miranda's "we" does is establish the comparative grounds on which she and other sustainability professionals evaluate the sustainability of other people's lifestyles relative to their own. Deviations from the kind of lifestyle embodied by Miranda's imaginary "we" are easily, if not implicitly, evaluated as unsustainable, or at the very least less sustainable than the Tesla-riddled ideal to which she is so committed. The point is not merely that Miranda sees her own lifestyle choices as indicators of sustainability (driving a sleek electric car, eating "mostly vegetarian," buying carbon offsets when she travels internationally for work or vacation, installing solar panels on the roof of her summer house, and so on) or even that she generalizes this as an archetype of sustainable living. The important thing is that Miranda and her colleagues at sustainability organizations, by virtue of designing and helping implement well-funded and influential sustainability programs, have the power to regiment other people's lifestyles in accordance with their own, specific vision of what counts as sustainable and what constitutes a sustainable life. This power is manifest in their ability to craft sustainability projects that draw on their own dreams and desires as inspiration for the goals that others should be pursuing, goals that become baked into the projects they design. In a sense, this mirrors the power of bankers and corporate sustainability managers, who determine what sorts of economic lives are possible by determining what kinds of investment and consumption patterns become valorized. By being in a position to define the terms in which the sustainability of other people's lifestyles is measured and evaluated, sustainability professionals are able not only to formalize a gradient of sustainability that places their own lifestyles "above" other people's lifestyles but also to align and affix that gradient to other gradients comparing things like ethical values, economic values, and so on.

More to the point, by equating "having a Tesla" with "living the life" in a conversation about what it means to live sustainably, Miranda tacitly equates not having a Tesla (or not owning similar markers of a modern, comfortable, sustainable lifestyle) with not living well and not living sustainably. At a different point in our conversation, when we were discussing the large carbon footprint of sustainability professionals who are constantly flying to conferences, she compared her own lifestyle to that of someone who has less impact:

> Even as a person who fundamentally, genuinely believes that we need to respect the earth so much more than we do, that it's our source of life and everything, I go flying and give presentations, and if you think about it, then [I'm having a negative impact due to my carbon emissions]. You have a decision to make as an individual: either you're going to say, "I'm going to reduce my individual impact. I'm going to live in a tiny apartment and never eat food that's been packaged, etcetera, etcetera, etcetera, and I will have zero impact on anyone else, but I know that personally my impact is zero or very low." Or you decide to say, "Well, actually, I know about this stuff, I have stuff that can be shared, and I can influence others, but in order to influence others, I have to just suck it up and say I have to travel to these places in order to get the message out."

Other informants dismissed people like those who "live in a tiny apartment and never eat food that's been packaged" as "granola munchers," "flaming lentil eaters," and "hippies." These are obviously quite different from the people my informants are trying to help through their sustainability efforts, but it suggests that they believe that people who are not pursuing a life of corporate or corporate-adjacent success—with all the middle-class trappings such a life entails—are not living as well as they could be. In this worldview, the poor and working class become exemplars of unsustainability, similar to what Nicole Seymour describes in *Bad Environmentalism* as an increasingly hegemonic vision of liberal sustainability that vilifies working-class "rednecks" because they tend to drive less fuel-efficient vehicles than their bourgeois urban counterparts do. In a sustainable development context, the villains become smallholder farmers who violate sustainability standards by growing household crops too close to rivers or Indigenous communities that practice swidden (sometimes called "slash and burn") agriculture or poor people who cut down trees for fuel to heat their homes and cook their food or foragers who cross the boundaries of conservation zones created (and often violently enforced) by colonial and neocolonial ecologists.[8]

We see the effects of this attitude in sustainable development conferences, sustainability reports, standards guidelines, and other documents where different solutions are proposed. At the Trade for Sustainable Development (T4SD) Forum I attended in Geneva in October 2015, many of the topics discussed both in the official sessions and more casually during lunch and coffee breaks focused on how to make marginalized supply chain actors, especially smallholder farmers in the Global South, operate more sustainably. But it was never clear what they were doing that was so unsustainable in the first place. The few times I asked, the answers centered on vague appeals to participation and inclusion. When I asked what they were meant to be participating in, informants offered ambiguous descriptions of market-based sustainability initiatives like voluntary standards and industry support for farmer cooperatives. One concrete way they could participate, according to my informants, is by making sure they were reporting accurate and consistent data about their operations, from things like labor and wages to fertilizer use and crop yield, lending evidence to critical perspectives on development that expose its radical commitment to the reproduction of neoliberal logics and subjectivities, often at the expense of local and situated knowledges.

This gets enforced with revised sustainability standards that require farmers to participate in the creation of ever-expanding data sets or risk being excluded from the marginally better market conditions for certified producers. It creates a curious correspondence between marginalized producers, on the one hand, and powerful financial institutions, on the other, since the data-driven market-oriented strategy of enhancing smallholder sustainability is the same approach taken to enhancing the sustainability of banks and corporations.

Field Trips

Sustainability professionals often take trips abroad as part of their work, especially those working in sustainable development but increasingly those working in corporate sustainability and sustainable finance, as well. They visit sites of production in the Global South, places like tea estates in Kenya and India, coffee plantations in Peru and Vietnam, and textile factories in Bangladesh and Turkey. These field trips gave my informants an opportunity to experience how other people live, providing an important alternative to their own lifestyles and reinforcing the belief that their particular vision of the good life—decarbonized luxury—and their particular definitions of what counts as living sustainably are correct.

When I interviewed Timothy, who works on the marketing team of a well-known sustainability organization in Washington, DC, he told me how one of the most rewarding parts of his work was the field trips he was able to take to producer countries, where he could see "firsthand" how the standards he helped develop and market were improving the lives of smallholder farmers. I had Googled him a few days before our meeting, and I came across one of his social media profiles, where I saw that he had recently been in Latin America visiting several agricultural production sites. I asked him about this during our interview, and he told me that he had visited the plantations with retailers:

> TIMOTHY: So we were going with a retail group along with a couple of our staff members really just to learn about the impacts that [our standard] has on the ground. And a lot of times you can see it. I mean, you say it to people or you read articles or case studies

about it, but actually seeing it firsthand, . . . that was really our main objective.

MATTHEW: To show retailers?

TIMOTHY: It was both. I mean, it was working with the retailers—that way they have an understanding of the differences of certification—and then also just for our own edification, because I had never been to a Colombian plantation.

MATTHEW: And this was bananas?

TIMOTHY: Yeah.

MATTHEW: So that was the first time you visited a production site?

TIMOTHY: Yep. Yep. For me, I mean, I've been on personal trips where I've been to coffee farms but not for [work]. They weren't [certified]. Well, actually it was. So it was [certified by a competing standards organization], ironically enough.

Timothy was not the only person I interviewed in DC who had been on a field trip in the few months preceding our meetings. More than half of the dozen or so informants based there had recently visited production sites, which was also the case for their colleagues and counterparts working in offices in London, Amsterdam, Hamburg, Brussels, New York, and other big cities in Europe and North America. Field trips to these sites usually have explicitly strategy-related goals. In Timothy's case, it was to show retailers how their participation in a particular certification scheme benefited local communities.

The ethical and emotional "edification" of sustainability professionals through fieldtrips does more than obscure unequal power relations between sustainability professionals and producers. It also presumes that a brief glimpse into the working lives of tea pluckers and cacao farmers, from a quite elevated perspective (as a management trainee, as a tourist, as an auditor, etc.), sufficiently grounds the work of supply chain management and standards development and marketing in "the real world." It presumes that stepping a toe into the periphery, in other words, justifies its management from the center through a gleaned expertise of the managers. It prefigures the relationship between sustainability professionals and the ostensible beneficiaries of their projects by mobilizing the plight of those beneficiaries to reinforce the moral imperative of sustainability professionals' work. The function of these distant stakeholders, in other words, is not to actively contribute to the development of sustainability solutions but rather to passively benefit from them. Javier Lezaun and Fabian Muniesa deliver a scathing indictment of this kind of training, describing business environments such as the ones in which both tea brands and sustainability organizations operate as "theatres" where suffering stakeholders become fetishized playthings for managers to practice their leadership and decision-making skills.[9] And while there is lots to criticize about the way European and American managers engage with and represent marginalized "stakeholders" in the Global South, these trips abroad are also a key part of the "production and reproduction of hegemonic global processes."[10] Much like the study-abroad experiences of MBA students, which Andrew Orta describes as contributing to the production of "business subjects with capacities to unlock the value chain and so manage the margins of commensurability," my informants' field trips to sites of sustainable production helped align their sometimes-competing ambitions of making money, improving the lives and livelihoods of producers, and protecting the local ecologies where they live and work, by rendering those ambitions commensurable.[11]

For my informants, there is a "there" that has problems and a "here" from which the solutions to those problems should emanate.[12] One informant, upon returning from a work trip as a sustainable development consultant to several countries in Southeast Asia, published a long Facebook post describing how she had been inspired by the people she met and their "spirit," how she had seen how much work there is to do, and how her travels had reminded her of how lucky she is to have been born in a rich country to upper-middle-class parents where she was able to get a high-quality education, and so on. Another, who worked for a fund that provided microloans to women artisans in rural Ghana, told me that when he had gone on a trip to Accra—everyone at his company was required to "experience it" at least once—he had been able to see "firsthand" how "awful" life was for "normal Ghanaians" and, crucially, how much the situation there had improved as a result of his company's microfinance-driven sustainable development program. After these trips, sustainability professionals return to their offices in European and American cities convinced that they are better equipped with new knowledge about impacts and, consequently, a clearer sense of what needs to be fixed, how to fix it, and an ethical justification for developing and implementing solutions that will help construct the conditions of possibility for those distant stakeholders to live good, sustainable lives. An edification, indeed.

The Organization of Pity and the Violence of Helping

As Sultana makes clear, political ecologies are shot through with emotion at least as much as they are shot through with power, and the two may very well be inseparable. (Whose emotions count? Whose emotions can be expressed, and whose emotions must be stifled?) During my fieldwork, I became more and more interested in the pity that my informants felt for the supposed beneficiaries of their programs, an emotion that they rarely enunciated but that was evident enough in the way they talked about and recalled their interactions with various stakeholders, who in nearly every account seemed to live resolutely pitiful lifestyles, lacking access to things like safe water, reliable electricity, clean air, dignified jobs, and good educations. The way sustainability professionals' pity for distant stakeholders imbues those stakeholders with the quality of pitifulness is reminiscent of Sara Ahmed's discussion of the way the hatred that white nationalists feel toward Black people imbues those Black bodies with the quality of hatefulness. In *The Cultural Politics of Emotion*, Ahmed theorizes the way emotions move between bodies and how this "affective economy" shapes the bodies it involves. "Emotions are relational: they involve (re)actions or relations of 'towardness' or 'awayness' in relation to such objects." In her illuminating examination of hatred, Ahmed argues that, in order "for the destructive relation to the object to be maintained the object itself must be conserved in some form. So hate transforms this or that other into an object whose expulsion or incorporation is needed, an expulsion or incorporation that requires the conservation of the object itself in order to be sustained. . . . Hence in hating another, this subject is also loving itself; hate structures the emotional life of narcissism as a fantastic investment in the continuation of the image of the self in the faces that together make up the 'we.'"[13] In order for a person to express hatred for something or someone else, they have to be invested, at least to some small degree, in the conservation—the sustainability—of the object of their hatred. The pity that motivates sustainability professionals to go and help producers and workers in developing countries, to be concerned about the anonymous and largely derealized stakeholders who are invoked in the innumerable pages of corporate sustainability reports that they publish, does something similar. In other words, it is precisely a concern for those piteous stakeholders that necessitates both their eradication (by rendering them "sustainable") and their conservation (by maintaining the "stakeholder" as an abstract object in need of their expert assistance). A sense of pity for this imaginary other reinforces the convictions among sustainability professionals that their own lives and lifestyles are archetypically good, that their vision of sustainability is indeed what "we" should be striving for, and that everyone else's lives and lifestyles should be (re)made in their own image.

As it turns out, trying to save something often entails some degree of violence, and the "will to improve" that motivates sustainability professionals to go and save the world is no exception. The cultural theorist Hugo Reinert describes several interventions that took place over the past few decades at the northern tip of Norway to grow the Fennoscandian population of lesser white-fronted geese (*Anser erythropus*), also known simply as lessers. As of 2010, there were only about a dozen breeding pairs, which mate in Finnmark in the summers before migrating to southern Europe for the winter. In the 1970s, the ornithologist Lambart von Essen placed lesser eggs in the nests of a different species of goose, the barnacle goose (*Branta leucopsis*), hoping that it would teach its adopted lesser babies to follow a different migratory path, a path that did not end in the unsustainably managed landscapes of southern Europe but would rather keep the geese in the more tightly regulated landscapes of northern and western Europe. Although the plan worked fairly well, scientists started to realize after twenty years or so that some of the geese were interbreeding. Not only that, but they also realized that some of the lesser eggs originally placed in the barnacle goose nests were genetically suspect, themselves the result of earlier interbreeding while in captivity. The scientists who discovered these problems in the 1990s instituted a moratorium on new releases in 1999. In the 2010s, scientists started a new program, this time focusing on the genetic purity of the lessers they released. One of these new birds, however, named A16, fell in love with a "wild" lesser, one that could have been resident from von

Essen's experiment forty years earlier. Both A16 and her wild lesser lover were "dispatched" (culled, slaughtered) to protect the genetic integrity of the fragile population of Fennoscandian lessers. Reinert theorizes this as an act of salvific violence, "the kind of destructive violence that operates in (and through) the effort to save."[14]

The anthropologist Paolo Bocci observes a similar trend on the Galapagos Islands, where the slaughter of goats was motivated by a desire to save the islands' iconic species, the Galapagos tortoise (*Chelonoidis nigra*). In the name of conservation, hunters shot goats from helicopters, reminiscent of the way settlers in the US nearly extinguished the wild bison population in the name of transcontinental commerce, or what they must have thought of as progress.[15] Practices of care are often fraught, "accompanied . . . by practices of violence and containment," and Bocci highlights the profound irony of the phrase "taking care": one can take care of (i.e., care for) a sick child or an impoverished friend, but one can also take care of (i.e., fix, solve, or eradicate) a problem.[16] These distinct meanings of care seem to converge quite often when it comes to questions of sustainability. More to the point, these kinds of examples help demonstrate the power that a person can have over others on the basis of a desire to help and a belief that their way of helping is the best way to solve a problem. They reveal the dynamics more clearly than I can through my ethnographic interviews with sustainability professionals, because my informants are obviously not proposing that we should actually eradicate people who do not fit their image of a good life. The point is that my informants occupy a position that makes their emotions—whether it is pity or disdain for a person who lives a different lifestyle than they do or a sense of gratitude for their own happy lives—more important in determining the outcomes of a sustainability program than the emotions of the people who ostensibly benefit from these programs.

Sustainable Lives as Lives Worth Sustaining

Contemporary sustainability exhibits a tacit (but nonetheless fundamental) commitment to a particular vision of what constitutes a sustainable lifestyle and the subsequent prioritization of certain lifestyles over others. Given the close relationship between sustainability professionals' ideas about the good life and the programs they design and implement with the goal of cultivating sustainable lifestyles, it does not require much of a conceptual leap to move from thinking about sustainability in terms of social, environmental, and economic impacts to thinking about sustainability in terms of whether a particular lifestyle will (or should) be sustained, that is, whether it should continue existing. From there, the slippage between thinking about lifestyles in terms of their relative sustainability and thinking about lives in terms of their relative sustainability is inevitable. That may seem hyperbolic, but I would argue that the evaluation of different lifestyles and livelihoods in terms of their relative sustainability veers much closer to eugenics, ecofascism, "all lives matter," and related discourses about which kinds of lives are "worth" keeping around than we might be comfortable admitting, with unsustainable lifestyles and livelihoods approached as something that needs to be eradicated. (This is especially evident in the rise of "long-termist" thinking, a trend backed by tech billionaires like Elon Musk that I explore in more detail in chapter 6.) Through the programs that sustainability professionals design and implement, they control the distribution of huge amounts of money to and within marginalized socioecologies. That means that the access to finance on which millions and potentially billions of people depend depends in part on whether sustainability professionals think the lifestyles that those people are living are sustainable. What I want to critically examine in this section is the way these perceptions of the relative sustainability of different *lifestyles* prefigure perceptions of the relative sustainability of different *lives*.

One way to understand how the relative sustainability of certain lives is negotiated and enforced is through the politics of grievability. In *Precarious Life*, Judith Butler highlights the different ways that US conservatives like Rudy Giuliani reserve the word "slaughter" to describe what happened to US citizens on September 11, 2001, but they do not use that same language to describe what the US did (and continues to do) to people in the Iraq and Afghanistan ostensibly in response to 9/11 or what Israel was (and is) doing to Palestinians. More recently, popular commentators have observed that Western governments are quick to label Muslim criminals as terrorists but are hesitant to apply that label to homegrown white nationalists. What this amounts to, according to Butler, is the fact that "some lives are grievable, and others are not; the differential allocation of grievability that decides what kind of subject is and must be grieved, and which kind of subject must not, operates to produce and maintain certain exclusionary conceptions of who is normatively human: what counts as a livable life and a grievable death?"[17] Those who are determined to be ungrievable remain faceless, like the two hundred thousand Iraqi children killed during the Gulf War. Butler asks why, in US newspapers, there are obituaries for dead US soldiers but not the innocent children those soldiers murdered. "If there were to be an obituary," Butler argues, "there would have had to have been a life, a life worth noting, a life worth valuing and preserving, a life that qualifies for recognition."[18] Denying people this grievability, without which "there is something living that is other than a life," renders them less-than-human, objects to be destroyed, populations to be extinguished.[19] The discourse of sustainable lifestyles and sustainable livelihoods does something eerily similar, not only justifying but celebrating the eradication of particular ways of living, those that sustainability professionals and other Western elites do not deem to be sustainable.[20]

In this context, a politics of sustainability is subtended by a politics of grievability, manifesting itself among my informants as an inability to see ways of living that are not on a trajectory toward being more sustainable from the perspective of posh European and North American financial centers as anything other than inherently unsustainable and thus not worth sustaining. Sustainability professionals not only wield the power to define the parameters of what constitutes a sustainable life/style but also have the power (through their access to and control over various forms of wealth) either to force those deviant lifestyles to fit the mold of sustainability that they have constructed or to exclude and erase them from the sustainability discourse completely.

Sustainability, too, relies on declarations of what kinds of lives count and, crucially, what kinds do not, declarations of what kinds of lives we should strive for and whatever the alternative is. Just like modernist development strategies are often premised on the claim that "traditional" ways of doing and knowing are both technically and morally wrong, based on the discursive production of "ignorant" and "backward" subjects qua beneficiaries, the sustainability industry necessarily constructs its targets as ungrievable, as the opposite of whatever we have collectively decided constitutes "a good life," as unsustainable in the sense that they are neither able to be made sustainable nor worthy of being sustained.

To return to Butler's terminology, the sustainability industry systematically derealizes the lives of those whom it deems unsustainable. Derealization occurs in two ways, through what Butler calls a "discourse of dehumanization" and, at the limit of this discourse, the act of erasure or omission. The first is to render abstract (i.e., less real) the lives of the billions of stakeholders who are being impacted by various socioecological crises precipitated over the past five hundred or so years by Western imperialism and industrialization. One way this is achieved is through the process of what Tania Li has referred to as "rendering technical," a "set of practices concerned with representing 'the domain to be governed as an intelligible field with specifiable limits and particular characteristics, . . . defining boundaries, rendering that within them visible, assembling information about that which is included and devising techniques to mobilize the forces and entities thus revealed.'"[21] In sustainability, this manifests itself as the atomization of the stakeholder in terms of its component parts: caloric intake (per capita food consumption), education (per capita spending on education), per capita energy consumption, per capita income, distance traveled between the home and a source of clean water, and so on. Sustainability professionals then set out to collect as much data about these different components as possible, which forms the foundation of their "evidence-based" and "data-driven" impact strategies.

Having thoroughly abstracted the stakeholder through this process of rendering technical, those who remain unintelligible in the terms staked out by the sustainability industry get erased from the narrative altogether. If they cannot improve in the right way, attributing the right causality to the programs designed and promoted by people like my informants, then they are omitted from these programs and erased from the discourse of progress that surrounds them. Smallholders cannot remain subsistence farmers but must become market-oriented entrepreneurs and small business owners; peasants must become workers. An informant I met at the Business and Human Rights Forum offered a good example of this outlook. We were sitting in a UN meeting room called the "Human Rights and Alliance of Civilizations Room" under a dazzling ceiling of colorful stalactites designed by the Spanish artist

Miquel Barceló. We talked a bit about how anthropologists had recently started thinking about questions of corporate sustainability and sustainable finance, which proved fruitful as she told me about a class she had taken as an undergraduate student in anthropology, connecting this with work she had conducted in her current job as the head of corporate social responsibility for a large oil and gas company. She described a survey that her team had carried out among villagers on "an island in Southeast Asia" who rely on fishing for both income and subsistence. A proposed offshore drilling site threatened to impact local fisheries and would have diminished villagers' access to coastal waters. I naïvely asked if the results of the survey had pushed the company to change its plans, but she said in response to these impacts, the company had developed a training program to help (soon to be former) fishermen pursue careers in the oil and gas industry and to teach them about the company's new-found property rights.[22] For sustainability professionals, stakeholders must embody the "green spirit of capitalism," a commitment to becoming the kind of neoliberal subject that sustainability demands, or they risk being excluded from sustainability programs developed by companies, banks, and NGOs alike.[23] In this case, it is less about the grievability of individual lives and more about the grievability of lifestyles and livelihoods that threaten to undermine the goals of neoliberal sustainability. Where is the grief for the eroded relations of care and reciprocity that must capitulate to new neoliberal subjectivities? Where is the grief for the cultural heritage that disappears as traditional fishermen are turned into oil-rig workers or swidden agriculturalists are turned into financial dependents of multinational mining corporations?[24]

The Ones Who Go and Help

How can we make sense of the relationship between the places where sustainability professionals identify problems and come up with solutions, on the one hand, and the places they are trying to help, on the other; between spaces populated by healthy, happy people and spaces populated—at least in my informants' worldview—by sad, suffering subjects? In other words, how do we make sense of what sustainability professionals are doing when they leave the cities like Geneva and Amsterdam where they work and live to go make an impact on the societies and environments of distant, marginalized communities, when they travel abroad to export their vision of the good life?

In my own attempts to think through these questions, Ursula K. Le Guin's story "The Ones Who Walk Away from Omelas" has been a good place to start because it offers a critical interpretation of what "the good life" can involve. In Omelas, we are told, everyone is happy. There is no poverty or hunger, no hatred or injustice. There are wise scholars and elegant music and noble architecture. On the day the story opens, Omelasians are preparing for the Festival of Summer, a joyous affair. But we quickly learn that the happiness of Omelas comes at a high price, specifically the torture of an innocent child, locked away in a cold, dark basement: "They all know it is there, all the people of Omelas. Some of them have come to see it, others are content merely to know it is there. They all know that it has to be there. Some of them understand why, and some do not, but they all understand that their happiness, the beauty of their city, the tenderness of their friendships, the health of their children, the wisdom of their scholars, the skill of their makers, even the abundance of their harvest and the kindly weathers of their skies, depend wholly on this child's abominable misery."[25] When young Omelasians visit the child's prison, they might be angry or sad, but they eventually, collectively, agree that the happiness of all is worth more than the misery of one. Over time, they revise their moral frameworks, starting to think of the torture of the child as a worthy trade-off. Some people are not able to handle it, however, or they do not accept it, and they leave Omelas, although Le Guin never tells us where they go.

Le Guin's story about a society's refusal to deny its own emotional and material comforts in order to assuage someone else's suffering has been interpreted as a critique of capitalism, and it seems especially relevant in the context of what the anthropologist Anna Tsing has called "supply chain capitalism," establishing a rather straightforward correspondence between complacent Omelasians who tolerate the child's torture and Western consumers who buy cheap imported food, clothes, and other products, even as the evidence that fast fashion and factory farming marginalizes already marginalized workers in the hidden abodes of global supply chains.[26] This reading is particularly resonant in Geneva, where three major historical sources of the city's wealth highlight the way prosperity for some often entails the hardship of another: John Calvin's approval of usury, which helped establish the Genevoise financial industry (the influx of foreign capital to hire Swiss mercenaries, which ended up in the hands of these Reformed investors, helped, too); as a home base for private bankers who enriched themselves with Nazi gold during World War II; and most recently as a global hub for tax-evading dictators, oligarchs, and other billionaire plunderers.[27]

But "The Ones Who Walk Away from Omelas" can also be read as a more focused critique of commensuration and of the logic of equivalence that it affords, a critique of constructing and accepting as valid the evaluation of a city's happiness in terms of a child's suffering. In asking whether the happiness of a city's inhabitants is "worth" the torture of an innocent child, Le Guin renders explicit the kind of logic that remains merely implicit in the sustainability discourse, especially in discussions about "offsetting" negative social and environmental impacts, or more generally about internalizing externalities, but also more insidiously in discussions about what "counts" as a sustainable lifestyle. Recalling Espeland and Stevens's definition of "commensuration" as "the comparison of different entities according to a common metric," the social structure of Omelas forces us to think about the common metric according to which one group's contentment can be compared with one person's suffering.[28] Even if that metric is unclear, the fact that most of the citizens of Omelas can accept and justify the torture of child in exchange for some greater good means that they are able to evaluate their own (collective) happiness in terms of a child's perpetual suffering, which indicates that there is indeed some common, if implicit, metric that facilitates comparison between the two. By rendering this commensuration explicit and by exposing the importance of that commensuration in the maintenance of the status quo, Le Guin highlights similar dynamics in our own society, especially the extent to which many Western consumers seem to have accepted that commensuration. It becomes harder to accept the convenience of shopping at inexpensive stores like H&M or Zara, for instance, when forced to recognize that the convenience of fast fashion comes at a high cost for workers in places like Bangladesh, where the collapse of the Rana Plaza garment factory in 2013 killed more than one thousand people, and even when forced to recognize one's own complicity in implicitly accepting that those two things are commensurable. Le Guin's story reminds us that our actions and decisions embed us in a web of relations that impacts and depends on others, particularly in an age of global supply chain capitalism. More important, the story calls into question the grounds of comparison by making it explicit; it is no longer a question of consuming better but one about critically examining and dismantling the foundations on which our justification of and participation in consumer society rests.

In Omelas, people can either remain in their happy city, with the knowledge that their happiness relies on a child's suffering, or walk away, a refusal to be complicit that costs them their guarantee of comfort and security. Some degree of suffering, for Le Guin, seems to be the non-negotiable price of utopia, and people can either accept that and stay or reject it and leave. But are these the only two options? Responding to Le Guin, N. K. Jemisin's story "The Ones Who Stay and Fight" has a different lesson.[29] In a similarly utopian city of Um-Helat, Jemisin's narrator, peering into the city from some other world, also begins with a description of a festival day. It is a colorful scene, full of smiles and laughter, the pungent smell of tamarind and lime juice wafting through the air. But the reader quickly starts to feel a bit uncomfortable. As we learn about Um-Helat's lack of racism, sexism, xenophobia, and other unsavory social dynamics, it all starts to feel too perfect, too happy, as if something important is missing. Right before the scene starts to feel too unbelievable, Jemisin addresses this gnawing skepticism. She introduces a mysterious figure in a dark damask uniform and silver skull piercings, a "social worker" who, moments earlier in the story, had been moving through the crowd. In the background, we start to see evidence of former cities, ruins like crumbling bridges and inoperable trucks with rusted missiles strapped to the back. The social workers' job is to keep Um-Helat from becoming the "worse place that it had been."[30]

The United States and Omelas exist in Jemisin's story, too, places in other universes where various forms of discrimination and oppression persist. Um-Helat is technologically advanced, equipped with radio-like devices that allow Um-Helatians to peek into those other worlds. As shocked as they are by what they see, the "poison," Jemisin tells us, inevitably spreads. Social workers are responsible for making sure this poison does not spread too far, for containing the contagion. They do this with a sharp silver pike, inserted with one quick jab into a contaminated person's spine (so death is painless) and heart (so death is quick).

The point is not to make the person suffer; in fact, it is the avoidance of suffering that motivates the social workers to do their work. For the social workers, "contamination" refers precisely to the toxic belief that there are other people who deserve to suffer, for anything but especially for selfish reasons.

After culling one contaminated citizen, the social workers find his young daughter sobbing on the ground beside him. Instead of asking why her father was killed, she threatens the social workers, promising that she will kill them the same way they killed her father, screaming, "How dare you!" as they look down at her:

> The social workers exchange looks of concern. . . . [They] know, there-fore, that for incomprehensible reasons, this girl's father has shared the poison knowledge of our world with her. An uncontaminated citizen of Um-Helat would have asked "Why?" after the initial shock and horror, because they would expect a reason. There would be a reason. But this girl has already decided that the social workers are less important than her father, and therefore the reason doesn't matter. She believes that the entire city is less important than one man's selfishness. Poor child. She is nearly septic with the taint of our world.[31]

Rather than killing the child, however, the social workers extend a hand. She will have to unlearn the ideology that her father had exposed her to, a lifetime of conscious effort. The contamination can be contained, the poison can be sucked out, even if it takes a lot of work. The social workers bury the man in a beautiful garden, just like they would bury any other Um-Helatian, to reject the notion that his life (and death) were worth more or less than someone else's. Every life in Um-Helat is grievable.

What strikes me as so radical about Um-Helat is its forceful, and in this case quite violent, repudiation of the grounds of comparison on which the importance of the little girl's father can be evaluated in terms of other people's importance, on which the happiness of one can be evaluated in terms of another's suffering. To be sure, comparison still exists, since the only way to conceptualize diversity is to maintain some mode of comparison between different categories, and Jemisin is clear that in Um-Helat, people are perfectly aware of their differences (kinky-haired, light-skinned, etc.). What is missing, however, is the ground on which these categories can be ranked in terms of their relative worth, importance, and so on. In other words, while there is a way to compare different skin colors, hair texture, and so on, Um-Helatians prevent the formalization of those gradients, precluding the correlation between those modes of diversity and other orders of worth. In Um-Helat, the "relations between relations" that link comparison to causality have been carefully and strategically snipped.[32] Disrupting these causal pathways is hard, messy work. It means identifying them and knowing about them without letting them connect. In Jemisin's world, it means comparing people in terms of something like skin tone, while recognizing the threat of allowing that comparison to turn into a ranking, of being causally linked to some other ranking of a person's worth. Perhaps most important, it reveals these causal and comparative grounds as something that we can both construct and deconstruct depending on the social and environmental goals we want to achieve.

Sustainability professionals are different from the people in both Le Guin's and Jemisin's stories. They do not walk away, because they see walking away as too simple, and they dismiss those who try to extract themselves from consumer society as hippies who have little noticeable impact. Nor do they stay and fight, which would require them to critically reflect on the capitalist system in which they are embedded and develop strategies not to tweak it but to act on those reflections and work to dismantle it. Instead, they go and help. Motivated by a sense of pity for distant stakeholders and a belief that their own lifestyles and livelihoods are worth replicating, they mobilize a will to improve the lives of others through programs designed to give them the same opportunities to become members of the middle class. In doing so, they reinforce a way of thinking about trade-offs and the relative value of certain lifestyles vis-à-vis others that leaves little room for seeing other ways of living—other ways of being, knowing, and doing—as sustainable.

Conclusion

At the 2015 Business and Human Rights Forum hosted at the United Nations in Geneva, several of the panels addressed the effects of different development projects on different stakeholders. Noticeably absent from these panels, however, were the stakeholders being discussed, and the conversations were led instead by representatives from companies like H&M, government agencies like the US Labor Department, and NGOs like the Ethical Tea Partnership. An exception was Aye Khaing Win, whose family had been forcibly relocated by the development of the Thilawa Special Economic Zone in Myanmar. In stilted English, he delivered prepared remarks on "multistakeholder advocacy groups" and "training for alternative livelihoods" and complained about "the lack of meaningful consultation and transparency" in the relocation process. His presentation, as I have argued elsewhere, "translated his experience of forced resettlement into both a language (English) and a vernacular (sustainable development jargon) that was comfortable for the corporate and political professionals attending the conference, establish[ing] him as the ideal type of stakeholder that these kinds of initiatives seek to engage with."[33]

That is precisely what was going on in the scenes and scenarios described earlier. Miranda's claims about living in a big, sustainably energized house and driving an expensive, sustainably energized Tesla are as much about what makes a life sustainable as what makes a life unsustainable. But if these are the markers of a sustainable life, what does that say about peasants living at the margins of the global economy or of workers at the center of that economy who are nonetheless marginalized? Their lives might be grievable, but their lifestyles are not. They are unsustainable because they are not the kinds of lives that sustainability professionals deem worthy of sustaining, and thus those lives are often unsustained because those same sustainability professionals have the power to determine who has access to life-sustaining resources. If Dianne Rocheleau and Robin Roth are right in asserting that political ecologies can be understood as networks "shot through with power," then it is in the context of sustainability professionals' role in determining what kinds of lives count as sustainable and the wide-ranging consequences of those evaluations that corporate sustainability is most apparently a question perfectly suited for political ecological analysis.[34]

Sustainability professionals have a relatively clear vision of what constitutes a good life and, just as important, what does not. This vision is based on their own lives, not necessarily how they live per se but how they aspire to live—in comfortable luxury with a negligible impact on society and the environment, indexed by things like sophisticated homes and advanced electric vehicles, as well as professional careers that fit these professional aspirations. For sustainability professionals, this is the archetype of a sustainable lifestyle, and it becomes the benchmark against which they evaluate the sustainability of other lifestyles, establishing a gradient of sustainability in which the lifestyles of sustainability professionals are considered more sustainable than the lifestyles of others. This vision informs the projects that sustainability professionals design and implement with the goal of creating the conditions of possibility for others to live good, sustainable lives. They feel pity for those whom they are trying to help, describing their lives as sad or depressing and mobilizing relatively vast amounts of time and money to find a remedy. They take field trips to visit producers in the Global South, returning to their offices in Europe and the US more convinced than ever that their solutions are desperately needed. They feel disdain toward those who imagine impact in a different way or insist on a different approach to sustainability, a good example of which is the outrage among the professional class toward recent campaigns that involve protesters vandalizing the frames of European art. Moreover, they feel proud of the lives they have crafted for themselves, reproducing their own ambitions and desires in the solutions they promote to various sustainability challenges.

This compulsion to go and help can be understood as a kind of salvific violence, exemplified by the phrase "to take care" of something or someone. In the context of sustainability, many of the solutions aimed at facilitating sustainable lifestyles are violent because they rely on the erasure, the derealization, of the lives that do not conform to (or cannot be made to conform to) sustainability professionals' liberal vision of the good life and their neoliberal vision of a sustainable lifestyle. These lives are found to be unsustainable, not only in the sense that they are not having the right kinds of impacts or being impacted in the right way but also in the sense that they are neither able to be sustained nor worth sustaining. For decades, political ecologists have been interested in the way development depends to a large extent on the establishment and enforcement of a distinction between modern and traditional lifestyles, with development agents insisting that they are the arbiters of what counts as modern and traditional, as developed and underdeveloped.[35] Sustainability does something similar, establishing a rigid distinction between sustainable and unsustainable lifestyles and livelihoods that sustainability professionals themselves are in a unique position to arbitrate.

The point of this chapter has been to highlight the role of emotions in these emergent political ecologies, focusing on sustainability professionals' emotions—their sense of pity but also their hope for a better future—and the role these emotions play in the distribution of various resources, especially financial resources connected to sustainable development funding. Chapter 6 moves on to thinking about the way sustainability imagines the future, how this imaginary actively precludes other possible futures, and how the preclusion of those futures might be resisted in the weird temporalities of the Anthropocene.

6

Sustainable Futures

Although the future is not open, it offers openings.
—Fernando Coronil, "The Future in Question"

Lock-In Effects

Worldbuilding is not confined to the realm of fantasy authors like Jemisin and Le Guin. Every time an insurance CEO gets onstage and tells an audience of policy makers and management consultants that sustainable development is a trillion-dollar investment opportunity, every time a group of researchers decides that a the biggest obstacle to global sustainability is poorly defined ESG indicators, and every time a meeting of corporate and political elites yields a set of goals that prioritizes a way of thinking about development that is rooted in quantitative metrics and public-private partnerships, they are performing a particular vision of sustainability that structures the world we will inhabit in the future. More mundane performances matter, too. Whenever a shopper in the grocery store pays a few cents more for Rainforest Alliance–certified tea, whenever a pension fund pushes its asset manager to adopt a more responsible investment strategy, or whenever an air traveler spends a few extra dollars to offset their flight's carbon emissions, the vision of sustainability as something that can emerge within existing structures of production, consumption, and profit gets reinforced and reproduced. In response to this increasingly stable vision of the future, political and financial resources flow toward particular kinds of sustainability solutions, solutions that are market driven and rely on the anticipation of new technologies for mitigating the various risks associated with climate change and other socioecological crises.

A desirable future is also a matter of perspective. The same can be said for acceptable, tolerable, or even survivable futures. Two or three degrees of global warming might be manageable for small, wealthy communities in places like Scandinavia, but those same changes will be devastating for many tropical and coastal communities, especially those without the access to capital required to finance massive adaptive infrastructure projects. As scholars and activists like Farhana Sultana, Ruth Nyambura, and Vanessa Nakate forcefully remind us, in many places, climate change is *already* catastrophic.[1] In thinking about how to save the world, sustainability professionals make assumptions about what the world will need to look like in order to improve the lives of others and what kind of evidence they will need to determine whether an improvement has occurred, whether a positive impact has been generated or a negative impact avoided. Sustainability is fundamentally oriented toward the future.

This chapter examines the kind of future envisioned within the parameters of neoliberal sustainability, drawing on my informants' understanding of what this future should look like and what it will take to achieve it. I follow their obsession with metrics and markets to its disconcerting conclusion, highlighting the emergent but nevertheless increasingly influential philosophy of longtermism, which, despite its radical message, is rooted in the same kind of economic principles that inform neoliberal sustainability and many contemporary approaches to sustainable development, even if it is not a philosophy that my informants explicitly espouse or probably even align themselves with. I then turn to the alternative futures of queer and Indigenous science fiction, cleaving apart the dissonant temporalities of corporate sustainability and sustainable finance as an entry point into other political imaginaries, as well as unsettling what counts as evidence in debates about sustainability. The goal of this chapter is to highlight these alternatives, to show that the fanciful vision of the future as a place where business as usual has miraculously stopped having its usual effects is not the only possibility. As Andrew Mathews and Jessica Barnes have observed, the future "is not one but many, and those who create futures typically seek to narrow down what the future can be to a relatively limited subset of possible registers."[2] Contemporary methods for predicting environmental futures, they argue, have emerged alongside modernist efforts to distinguish between the scientific and the political, the objective and the subjective, the natural and the cultural. The point here is that the construction of quantitative indicators is not merely a technology of governance in the presence but one that locks in a particular mode of governance in the future.

Kid-Friendly Capitalism

Ray Anderson is a prominent character in the story that sustainability professionals tell about the positive impacts of corporate sustainability. A 2007 profile in *New York Times* described his efforts to transform the industrial carpet company he founded into a "restorative enterprise" that "takes nothing out of the earth that cannot be recycled or quickly regenerated" and "does no harm to the biosphere," suggesting that Anderson was "perhaps the leading corporate evangelist for sustainability."[3] In business schools around the world, from Connecticut (where I observed sustainability classes) to Copenhagen (where I taught them), Anderson's company, Interface, Inc., is often presented as a clear example of the business case for sustainability. Georgia Tech's Scheller College of Business even has a Ray C. Anderson Center for Sustainable Business.

I encountered Anderson's story several times during my fieldwork—during presentations at corporate sustainability and sustainable finance conferences in Geneva, during a class on corporate social responsibility that I audited when I was finishing my PhD, during a conversation with an ESG analyst in the cafeteria of Norebank when I visited its headquarters for a cluster of interviews, and, most recently, during a webinar on the growing demand for critical minerals. The story typically goes something like this: Anderson founded a company that manufactures industrial carpet for offices, schools, and so on. These kinds of places have heavy foot traffic. Carpets wear down quickly and need to be replaced often. But Anderson realized that only a small path gets worn out, which meant that the rest of the carpet in a particular space was still in good condition when the carpet was eventually replaced. His innovation was to produce carpet tiles that could be replaced on an as-needed basis. This not only reduced his company's environmental footprint but also increased its profits.[4] According to the *New York Times* profile, sales went up nearly 50 percent, while landfill contributions were reduced by 80 percent, water use was reduced by a third, and fossil fuel use was almost halved. In each instance, the takeaway was the same: Anderson had definitively shown that sustainability could be profitable, that businesses can, in fact, do well by doing good.

Anderson's profile in the *New York Times* attributed his passion for sustainability to an "*a-ha*! moment!" that is typical of these kinds of biographies.[5] In the mid-1990s, he started to read about environmental issues, which made him realize that his company was contributing to environmental degradation. He also realized that only the private sector was big enough and powerful enough to solve the problem. In a TED talk delivered in 2009, Anderson did not mince his words: CEOs who ignore sustainability might one day be arrested for their actions because "theft is a crime, and theft of our children's future would someday be a crime."[6] Businesses and business leaders need to step up to solve the problem, not for some distant, faceless stakeholder but for their own kids and grandkids, and not as an act of charity but because it makes good business sense.

The kind of future that Anderson and other elites working in sustainability tend to imagine is one in which businesses play a leading role in the realization of a socially and environmentally sustainable society. Like Anderson, many of my informants took the Brundtland Report's famous definition of sustainable development—development that meets the needs of the current generation without preventing future generations from meeting their own needs—to heart, and they regularly invoked their children and grandchildren, as well as their own childhoods, when talking about their interest in sustainability. When I interviewed Chet, the head of sustainability at a pan-African bank whom we met in the chapter 1, about his motivations for pursuing a career in sustainability, he told me about holidays he had taken to different tropical destinations with his parents as a child. He remains an avid outdoorsman, taking regular trips to go hiking or skiing at different vacation spots around the world. He enjoys spending time outdoors with his family, and one of the "main drivers" in his professional life is "helping protect the planet" so his children will be able to make similar memories and enjoy similar holidays with their kids one day.

Advertisements for private banking evoke similarly idyllic futures. One of the first things I noticed upon arriving in the Geneva airport in 2015 was a Barclays ad that depicted a retired couple sitting on plush lounge chairs, their backs to the viewer. The wife gazes happily at her husband, while he sits with his hands behind his head staring out over their infinity pool, which extends past the edge of the photo, at a calm ocean far below. I imagined that they were sitting on the terrace of their Mediterranean villa. "Ever wondered what [return on investment] actually feels like?" the advertisement seductively asks. Another wealth-management ad features a different retired couple, sitting in their lush backyard on comfortable chairs, surrounded by laughing grandchildren. In yet another, a father and son sand the bottom of an upturned boat in a cavernous garage. "Make sure your wealth is working for you," implores the Barclays ad. "Always looking ahead to deliver sustainable performance," promises an Edmond de Rothschild poster near the baggage-reclaim area.

These advertisements reinforce the vision of the future envisaged by people like Ray Anderson and my informant Chet, a future in which responsible business and financial strategies play the main role in sustaining the lives and lifestyles of people as they procreate, grow old, retire, and reunite with their children and grandchildren. They help the financial industry present itself as a force for good, giving capitalism a "caring" veneer and a "human face."[7] It is a sustainable future in which elites can recognize themselves, a sustainable future that does not cost them anything, reminiscent of Miranda's earlier understanding of sustainability as not about sacrifices. These advertisements reinforce the idea that capitalism is something that can evolve into something more "sophisticated" and more "caring" and more "inclusive," an evolution that many theorists of corporate sustainability explicitly try to instigate.

Utility Closet

Shortly after arriving in Geneva in 2015, I attended a networking event for young and aspiring sustainability professionals, where I met Stephen, an undergraduate student who was deeply passionate about sustainable development. As one tends to do at these kinds of events, I gave an overview of my CV—bachelor's degrees in international studies and Chinese from the University of Mississippi, where I had developed an interest in Chinese environmental policy, followed by a master's degree in environmental economics from the London School of Economics, before starting a PhD in environmental studies at Yale, where I quickly switched from the economics track to the anthropology track. Stephen wanted to hear more about my master's program, asking whether I thought it had prepared me for a career in finance or consulting. I responded that it was hard to say, joking that I had never had a real job since I had gone straight from my master's program into the PhD program but that several of my classmates had gone into finance and consulting, and I assumed they were sufficiently prepared for those kinds of careers.

I was a bit confused, though, and I asked him why he would want to pursue a career in one of those fields if he was so passionate about sustainability, as he had claimed just moments before. He responded that he thought it was better to make as much money as you can and then decide which kinds of sustainability solutions you should fund; his goal, essentially, was to become rich enough to start a philanthropic organization that he would manage according to objective cost-benefit analyses in order to generate the highest return on investment, with an expanded definition of "returns" that includes measurable social and environmental impacts. It struck me as a bit self-serving, and I said as much. He laughed and said he thought the same thing at first, but he then invited me to the next meeting of Geneva's "effective altruism" group, which was scheduled for a few weeks later at a beer bar in the Jonction neighborhood, where the Arve flows into the Rhône. I accepted his invitation, and we exchanged phone numbers so he could send me the details later that evening.

When I showed up at the effective altruism (EA) mixer, Stephen was already there. He waved me over to a group of his friends and introduced me, promising that we would have a lot to talk about given our shared interests in sustainability. They asked me what I was researching, so I explained that I was interested in the way people working in corporate sustainability and sustainable finance thought about their impacts, which I was hoping to explore ethnographically through participant observation in different sustainability organizations and through interviews with people working in the city's companies and private banks. They asked if I had been successful setting up interviews with private bankers, and I said that a few had agreed to be interviewed, which I hoped would lead to more interviews through "snowball" sampling. One of Stephen's friends asked if I would be willing to invite one of my informants to the next EA meeting as a guest speaker. Everyone there, he assured me, would be extremely interested in learning about sustainability from a private banker.

At the mixer, I was told that the concept of effective altruism is based on the utilitarian philosophy of Peter Singer.[8] The basic lesson of effective altruism, which transforms the "moral indictment" of Singer's hyperutilitarianism into an "empowering investment opportunity," is that if you have $1,000 to give to a charity, then you should make sure you give that $1,000 to the charity that will have the most impact.[9] Few people will disagree with this kind of statement, but in conversations with effective altruists—who refer to themselves as such and often refer to the movement as "EA"—they often took it a step further. Stephen, for instance, told me that he only had twenty-four hours in a day, and he could only reasonably devote about half of that time to work. Assuming, then, that he had twelve hours a day to make an impact, should he not try to maximize his impact through his work? There were several options available for him to try to achieve this. He could work for an NGO that does boots-on-the-ground-type interventions, but he considered this kind of impact too local and too limited. A better option, according to Stephen, was to work for a consulting or investment firm, where he could influence companies to implement systemic changes, through either advice provided to their executives or stipulations he could attach to corporate financing.

An even better option, though, would be to make as much money as possible and allocate his own capital to what he considered the best causes, but only after doing his research to make sure that his decisions were evidence based and "rational." As it turns out, one of EA's central tenets is that working in, say, investment banking or the oil industry is better than working for some inconsequential little NGO, because you will do more good by donating your money to causes that maximize impact than you would working for an NGO with a smaller impact. "What if I made a few million francs a year?" Stephen asked, before answering his own question: "Think of all the *good* I could do." The problem, of course, is that it can be difficult to have a good sense of what your actual impacts are. Like his hero Peter Singer, whose philosophical project revolves around a specific definition of what it means to be a person (Singer and his acolytes have pondered, for instance, whether a pig has a stronger claim to personhood than a human infant or an adult with severe cognitive disabilities), Stephen is very interested in defining "impact." Not dissimilar from the sustainable financiers we met in chapter 4, he thinks the biggest challenge for sustainability advocates is figuring out how to measure impacts. He personally favors a metric known as "disability-adjusted life years," or DALYs, a concept developed in the mid-1990s as "an indicator of the time lived with a disability and the time lost due to premature mortality."[10] A similar metric is "quality-adjusted life years," or QALYs, the number of which vary for an average life depending on one's socioeconomic situation, which is often used in cost-benefit analyses; whether the government decides to build a bridge, or the stringency of the standards a government requires an engineering firm to adhere to when building that bridge, is a decision that is often based on these kinds of calculations, often referred to as the "value of a statistical life" (VSL). If a *super*-safe bridge costs a billion dollars more than a bridge that's merely *pretty* safe, but the benefits of building the super-safe bridge are only expected to be a handful of QALYs, the government will probably decide to save the money and risk those few statistical lives. For Stephen, these kinds of indicators help guide philanthropic decision-making because they provide an easy answer to the questions posed earlier: If I have $1,000 dollars, where can I donate it in order to maximize aggregate DALYs, qua impact? The problem evolves from figuring out the most effective way to have an impact to figuring out the most rigorous way to measure DALYs.

The Risk of Longtermism

Effective altruists, according to the philosopher Amia Srinivasan, love coming up with provocative counterintuitions through their "number-crunching," such as the claim that a more cost-effective solution to the problem of poor educational outcomes in rural Kenya is to fund childhood deworming programs rather than buying new textbooks or hiring more teachers or the claim that getting a high-paying job that allows you to buy and donate insecticide-treated mosquito nets is a more effective use of your time and money than, for instance, working for an organization that distributes drugs to treat malaria.[11] These kinds of "low-hanging metrics" are fundamental to EA's moral legitimacy, not dissimilar from the kinds of measurements sustainability professionals use to show that their own interventions are working or that they could work.[12] In making these claims, the debate shifts to a discussion of the merits of the measurements on which those claims are based, rather than a discussion of more radical alternatives. Letters sent in response to Srinivasan's essay in the *London Review of Books*, for example, pointed out flaws in the academic studies underlying these claims. William MacAskill, one of EA's luminaries, responded with further nitpicking: only 1 percent of the bed nets were used for other purposes (like fishing), and the epidemiological study that debunked the econometric study of deworming used slightly different statistical parameters, thus failing to invalidate his claim. By the end of this brief back-and-forth, more fundamental questions about the moral legitimacy of utilitarianism or the politics of elite preferences, though raised in Srinivasan's text, were almost completely ignored, not dissimilar to the way technical reports like those discussed earlier preclude more fundamental discussions about rights and responsibilities now and in the future.

If the stark utilitarianism of the effective altruism movement is disconcerting, its extension in the increasingly influential philosophy of longtermism is downright chilling. Consider an article on "existential risk prevention as global priority" by one of the leaders of the longtermist movement, the Oxford University philosopher Nick Bostrom. In it, Bostrom rather appallingly concludes that "even the tiniest reduction of existential risk has an expected value greater than that of the definite provision of any 'ordinary' good, such as the direct benefit of saving 1 billion lives." Using what he refers to as a "conservative" estimate of how many humans might potentially exist over the next billion years, he finds that

> the expected value of reducing existential risk by a mere *one millionth of one percentage point* is at least a hundred times the value of a million human lives. The more technologically comprehensive estimate of 10^{54} human-brain-emulation subjective life-years (or 10^{52} lives of ordinary length) makes the same point even more starkly. Even if we give this allegedly lower bound on the cumulative output potential of a technologically mature civilization a mere 1% chance of being correct, we find that the expected value of reducing existential risk by a mere *one billionth of one billionth of one percentage point* is worth a hundred billion times as much as a billion human lives.[13]

Some of the world's richest men—for example, Peter Thiel (PayPal), Elon Musk (Tesla), and Jaan Tallinn (Skype)—have bought into these extreme claims, often in a literal sense, funneling tens of millions of dollars to Bostrom's Future of Humanity Institute at Oxford and a similar Centre for the Study of Existential Risk at Cambridge. As Émile P. Torres notes in his critique of longtermism, it is easy to cynically suspect that, given these longtermists' vast wealth, "this might be just another case of a super-wealthy tech guy [Tallinn] dismissing or minimizing threats that probably won't directly harm *him personally*. Despite being disproportionately responsible for the climate catastrophe, the super-rich will be the least affected by it." Torres then invites us to consider the unsettling scenario in which longtermists are standing in front of two buttons, one that "would save the lives of 1 million living, breathing, actual people" and another that "would increase the probability that 10^{14} currently unborn people come into existence in the *far future* by a *teeny-tiny* amount."[14] The reason that this is so unsettling is because, after reading a bit of longtermist thinking, it is not at all clear which button they would choose.

Burn It Down

Longtermism's commensuration of the lives of people living today with the lives of the hundreds of billions of people who might live over the coming millennia seems radical. And yet, longtermism is grounded in the same kind of statistical thinking about risk and reward that pervades mainstream policy discussions about climate mitigation and adaptation. In these debates, the probability that different climate scenarios might occur is integrated into models of population growth. One of the liveliest discussions in environmental economics over the past decade, for instance, has focused on the discount rate we should apply to the well-being of future humans. A policy maker with a high discount rate will find less value in the future than a policy maker with a low discount rate, because the former "discounts" the future at a higher rate than the latter, yielding a lower value in the present. In an experimental setting, a person with a high discount rate might choose to have $100 now rather than $110 a year from now, whereas a person with a low discount rate might choose to wait and take the $110 in a year. Discount rates are important in calculating the so-called present value of something we might expect to have or happen in the future. In the context of climate mitigation, a low discount rate, as advocated by the British economist Lord Stern, demands substantial investments in mitigating climate change today, because the welfare of future humans is calculated as relatively valuable; a higher discount rate, as advocated by the Nobel laureate William Nordhaus, justifies spending less on climate change today, because the value of future humans' welfare has been more aggressively discounted. If you heavily discount the welfare of future generations, then the value you ascribe to that future welfare in the present will be lower, and your willingness to pay to protect or improve it will also be lower; vice versa for people whose discount rates are lower.[15]

Even as this debate became increasingly heated—Nordhaus at one point accused Stern of "[taking] the lofty vantage point of the world social planner, perhaps stoking the dying embers of the British Empire, in determining the way the world should combat the dangers of global warming"—Nordhaus applauded Stern's "[selection of] climate change policies with an eye to balancing economic priorities with environmental dangers."[16] Conceptually, at least, the existential risk of longtermism is not so far away from this quantified approach to the commensuration of economic values with climate risks, and yet the former seems radical while the latter seems relatively banal. From both of these perspectives, the future is viewed through the epistemological lens of quantifiable risks and derivable discount rates, populated by statistical lives. The policy implications of this should not be understated. At one end of the spectrum, there are those who argue that our current happiness matters most and that we should not make too many sacrifices today to help people in the future; at the other end of the spectrum, there are those who argue that no cost is too high to avoid existential risks, leading to a characterization of events like the Spanish flu and the Holocaust (and presumably the ongoing COVID-19 pandemic) as "scarcely registering" as existential catastrophes.

In the anthropologist Ann Laura Stoler's work on the politics of colonial archives, she identifies what she calls the vernacular "practicing epistemologies" of powerful actors—"what they imagined they could know and more importantly *what epistemic habits they developed to know it.*"[17] From effective altruists like Stephen to the data analysts,

ESG advisers, and social impact consultants we met in earlier chapters, the practicing epistemology of sustainability professionals is relatively straightforward. They imagine that they can know the impacts of their various sustainability projects in a way that allows these impacts to be compared with the costs of these projects' implementation, whether it is a project geared toward ending world hunger, mitigating the spread of HIV, reducing child slavery, or promoting private-sector innovation in green technology. Sustainability professionals want their interventions to be rational and based on reason, for the positive impacts of these interventions to be maximized relative to their investments, for the costs of sustainability to be offset by its benefits. Their practicing epistemology presupposes that costs and benefits are comparable and thus commensurable and that a common metric exists or can at least be derived. The epistemic habits they develop to know whether an intervention or an investment is having the desired impacts are equally straightforward: they develop and refine the definitions of various social and environmental indicators, and they amass a huge amount of data about those indicators.

Particular epistemologies—that is, particular ways of producing knowledge and particular ways of determining what counts as knowledge in the first place—structure social reality and are thus inseparable from ontology and ethics.[18] This interrelatedness is fundamental to the notion of "Indigenous epistemology," which "assumes all epistemological systems to be socially constructed and (in)formed through sociopolitical, economic, and historical context and processes."[19] Recognizing the entanglements of being, doing, and knowing is crucial to an ethics of worlding that accounts for how various practices matter from perspectives beyond the myopic view of the market and the people whose power it obscures. If the reality is that for-profit companies, "by their very nature," are unsustainable and that the corporate form is inherently ecocidal, then an approach to sustainability that is grounded in producing quantitative data about impacts so the market can manage them is not only a fool's errand but also deeply and irredeemably unethical.[20]

Reflecting on Indigenous practices of pyro-regeneration, in which controlled burns clear undergrowth and allow new plants and animals to flourish, the archaeologist Paulette Steeves coined the term "pyro-epistemology" to describe an important facet of critical Indigenous scholarship: "A practice of Pyro-epistemology through the ceremony of Indigenous ways of knowing, being, and doing is one which cleanses the academic landscape of discussions that misinform worldviews and fuel misunderstanding and racism. Such literary renewal clears the way for new discussions and intellectual growth in academic fields of thought and centers of knowledge production."[21] Steeves's focus on clearing the way for new discussions in centers of knowledge production is relevant to the way sustainability professionals, through the enforcement of their increasingly hegemonic practicing epistemologies, reinforce enduring forms of oppression even as they attempt to improve the lives of others. Tracing the relationship between the practicing epistemology of sustainability professionals and the kind of future we might expect to emerge if that epistemology remains dominant demonstrates the stakes of such a pyro-epistemology. The politics of knowledge extend far beyond stilted academic practitioner debates about what counts as evidence of sustainable; in dismantling the practicing epistemology of neoliberal sustainability, we come a step closer to what David Gegeo and Karen Watson-Gegeo call "dehegemonization" and rejecting the normalization of elite visions of the future.[22]

Dissonant Temporalities

The futures of sustainability rarely line up, and the predominance of one future typically corresponds to a specific temporality, with others obscured or erased. Climate scientists warn us that our only hope for avoiding catastrophic climate change is to immediately implement a radical redesign of our social and economic systems. These warnings are met with tepid commitments from corporations, investors, and Western governments to try to achieve "net zero" emissions over the next several decades. Consider A.P. Moller-Maersk, one of the world's largest shipping companies and, recently, a darling of corporate sustainability reporting.[23] In its 2020 sustainability report, Maersk revisited an earlier commitment to making its fleet of more than seven hundred cargo ships carbon neutral by 2050, part of its efforts toward "decarbonising logistics": "In 2018, a 2050 net zero ambition for shipping was a moonshot goal. Today, we see it as a challenging target, but clearly possible to reach. Customers, investors and authorities are accelerating their ambitions, and their expectations are rising fast for A.P. Moller-Maersk (Maersk) and our industry to deliver more solutions, more visibility and more help in decarbonising supply chains."[24] The kind of "net zero" strategy that the Maersk report goes on to outline has been criticized by researchers and activists on several fronts.[25] Some of these schemes rely on payments for ecosystem services, which are essentially a way for polluters in the West to continue business as usual by paying a small fee that ostensibly prevents carbon-intensive land-use changes in other parts of the world. Others rely on technologies that do not exist yet, as is the case with Maersk: in 2021, the company put in an order for several supposedly carbon-neutral vessels. "The only problem?" mused an article from CNN: "There's not enough carbon neutral methanol to power the vessels."[26]

Problems like this are typical of eco-modernist approaches to sustainability. Technological advances like carbon-neutral fuels for shipping vessels and airplanes are imagined as a kind of obvious solution to the climate crisis, despite the fact they often do not exist yet, at least not on a scale large enough to support these industries and their ambitions of endless growth. More to the point, they often ignore other, more pressing time scales. Even if Maersk were able to achieve its goal of a completely carbon-neutral fleet by 2050, and even if it has successfully placed its first order for carbon-neutral boats several years before its original 2030 deadline, the sixth assessment report (AR6) of the Intergovernmental Panel on Climate Change (IPCC), published in early 2022, made it clear that plans to reduce emissions over the next ten, twenty, and thirty years are insufficient. Without immediate actions to radically reduce the amount of greenhouse gas emissions in the atmosphere in the next two to three years, catastrophic global warming of at least three degrees Celsius becomes essentially guaranteed.

Debates around the start date of the Anthropocene help us understand the politics of time and temporality. Whereas members of the Anthropocene Working Group, a division of the International Commission on Stratigraphy's Subcommission on Quaternary Stratigraphy, have proposed 1964 and the "great acceleration" as a convincing start date of the Anthropocene (and, consequently, the end date of the Holocene), the environmental social scientists Heather Davis and Zoe Todd see this as flattening the responsibilities and experiences of the Anthropocene not only historically but as it continues to unfold into the future. "We are all grouped together under the sign of the ubiquitous hockey stick graphs—the graphs that show the increase of various human activities indicative of the 'great acceleration'—where McDonald's, international tourism, population and ocean acidification bind the whole of humanity together into one horrifying reality." They follow Simon Lewis and Mark Maslin in proposing an alternative Anthropocene start date of 1610, "the beginning of the colonial period." Linking colonialism and the Anthropocene, they argue, "draws attention to the violence at its core, and calls for the consideration of Indigenous philosophies and processes of Indigenous self-governance as a necessary political collective, alongside the self-determination of other communities and societies violently impacted by the white supremacist, colonial, and capitalist logics instantiated in the origins of the Anthropocene."[27]

Davis and Todd draw on Christina Sharpe's notion of "wake work" to think about the relationship between these interconnected logics and how they reverberate across space and time. According to Sharpe, "Racism, the engine that drives the ship of state's national and imperial projects, . . . cuts through all of our lives and deaths inside and outside the nation, in the wake of its purposeful flow."[28] The wake of a boat is only one of the many meanings the word wake can evoke: "wake" as in wakefulness or consciousness, being aware of the processes over time that give texture to lived experience; "wake" as in the vigil held for someone who has died. With these definitions in mind, Sharpe argues that, "rather than seeking a resolution to blackness's ongoing and irresolvable abjection, one might approach Black being in the wake as a form of consciousness." Being "in the wake," she writes, "is to occupy and be occupied by the continuous and changing present of slavery's as yet unresolved unfolding."[29] In light of these intersecting spatial, temporal, and political wakes, the task, according to Tim Edensor, is not to figure out whether the elite narrative of linear time is "right" or "wrong" vis-à-vis the more cyclical rhythms and diverse time scales of everyday life but rather to examine the generative and coconstitutive ways in which these temporalities interact with each other.[30]

Maersk's decision to invest in carbon-neutral boats vanished from the sustainability news cycle almost as quickly as it appeared, a blip on the radar of announcements that corporations make every day about their various social and environmental commitments. And yet, like the company's futuristic methanol-powered ships, its decision leaves something in its wake, a vision of sustainability that imagines the solution to climate change as profitable investment opportunities and business partnerships. This delusional and delusive imaginary of a future in which ten- and twenty-year sustainable investment strategies prove to be a sufficient response to the climate crisis ignores the alternative temporalities that structure the future, the other wakes that intersect and refract the gentle waves of a barge full of shipping containers. Corporations like Maersk, in positioning themselves as harbingers of a more sustainable future, also, perhaps inadvertently, insert themselves in a centuries-long history of social and environmental degradation. At the same time, for many corporations, whose investors expect annual and even quarterly earnings reports, a ten- or twenty-year sustainability plan is already considered "long term." At even more distant ends of the spectrum, the growth of algorithmic trading has reduced the temporal horizon of financial transactions to the span of several milliseconds, while, as debates around the Anthropocene suggest, these same economic processes are now relevant on a planetary, geological time scale.[31] Even in a single company's approach to climate mitigation, these "alternate temporal renderings," as the anthropologist James Maguire refers to them, "invoke competing claims of the future." Efforts to anticipate the future thus become "a form of temporal politics" in which different actors struggle to legitimize or resist these different visions and interventions.[32] It is through the cracks that appear in these otherwise-monolithic neoliberal imaginaries that alternatives start to be visible.

Indigenous Futures

One of the places that these alternatives have been most visible to me is in the speculative fiction of queer and Indigenous authors whose work tends to push back against the linear temporal narratives of white masculinist science fiction and fantasy. In "History of the New World," for instance, Adam Garnet Jones conjures a world in which "most governments had stopped believing in the possibility of saving the planet and moved on to serious exploration of potentially habitable nearby planets," a vision eerily reminiscent of the contemporary billionaire space race and political inaction on climate change. Jones traces an increasingly familiar story intersecting crises in the Global South and the refusal of the Global North to help or even accept responsibility. What started as "indirect murder" via border walls and turned-away refugees evolved into the "visible murder of families torn apart at borders and the mass incarceration and enslavement of the undocumented," shocking at first, "and then commonplace." Soon after a lush, habitable planet is discovered, advertisements start to appear beckoning people on Earth to purchase their spots on space-bound ships. It turns out, however, that this new planet is populated by an underwater species of nonhuman people. A bulletin reported that the "United Governments of the New World were rocked yesterday by an audio communication from an underwater species that bears a striking physical resemblance to Earth's extinct manatees," followed immediately by a radio advertisement for New World condominiums.[33]

The story's protagonist, Em, a "brown-eyed Two-Spirit nehiyow with a homemade haircut and marrow-deep longing for the old things that rumbled under the surface of the world," anticipates the destruction of these New World inhabitants, history repeating itself on a world with "no history at all." Em's girlfriend, Thorah, a descendant of settlers, sees it differently; she is optimistic: "Maybe we'll draft treaties with them, real treaties." Em responds, "Only a white girl could step into a completely unknown universe with the blind faith that everything was going to work out."[34]

In Jones's story, a cultural history of Indigenous genocide prevents Em from acting on Thorah's self-serving settler naïveté, her willful ignorance of the conditions of consequences of what she imagines as "the greatest adventure in human history."[35] Other stories, however, complicate the link between these painful histories and the futures populated by Indigenous peoples, demonstrating the importance of refusing to attribute some inherent righteousness to marginalized groups, which merely reproduces the idea that they lead less complicated and conflicted political and ethical lives. In William Sanders's "When All This World Is on Fire," Cherokee sheriffs come across a family of white squatters on Cherokee land. An altercation ensues, the white father hurling racist insults at the sheriffs. The roles seem reversed, but only partially. Indigenous people police Native lands, protecting their increasingly scant resources for themselves, even as the white squatters and neighbors retain their racist sensibilities. Finally, in Zainab Amadahy's *Moons of Palmares*, a military officer on one of Earth's colonies is tempted to overlook the government-sanctioned torture of mining protestors, and he has to be reminded of his own history from centuries earlier: "Your ancestors were indigenous North Americans," the whistleblower reminds him. "You must have read your history."[36] An important lesson from these stories is the reminder that inequities persist, even in "an ostensibly *post*colonial era."[37]

I have found these stories helpful in orienting myself toward a future that feels increasingly bleak, just like I have found Indigenous theories of knowledge, power, and ethics helpful in making sense of my observations about corporate sustainability and sustainable finance. One of these is the idea that critically reflecting on "culture, history, knowledge, politics, economics, and the sociopolitical contexts in which [people] are living their lives" should lead to acting on these reflections. This "Indigenous critical praxis" is a key aspect of what Gegeo and Watson-Gegeo call "Indigenous epistemology," and it feels like one of the biggest things missing from my informants' own epistemological approach to sustainability.[38] It is not that they fail to critically reflect on the failures of current "solutions" to meaningfully address the climate crisis but rather that they never take the next step of really acting on those reflections, opting instead to double down to their data-driven, market-oriented sustainability strategies. In a situation like this, what options do we have? Steeves's pyro-epistemology was revelatory for me in that sense, because it showed that rather than being stuck with the "hierarchy of evidence" that positivist epistemologies create between quantitative data at the top and qualitative, "anecdotal" data at the bottom, we can actively and intentionally prune one epistemology so that others might be able to flourish.[39]

At the same time, this raises an uncomfortable question: Are the lessons from Indigenous literature and philosophy meant for everyone? "Indigenous lessons about sustainability," according to Kyle Whyte, Chris Caldwell, and Marie Schaefer, "are not just for 'all humanity.'"[40] Non-Indigenous people often seek to appropriate Indigenous lessons as a way of "saving themselves or humankind" without attempting to address the legacy of colonialism that generated the problem in the first place.[41] The growing embrace of agroecology and back-to-the-land movements that encourage settlers to buy relatively large plots of private land and superficially adopt Indigenous farming techniques, rather than contesting the privatization and commodification of land that characterize settler colonialism in the first place, is a good example of this. Especially during the first year of the COVID-19 pandemic, I regularly came across White couples in the United States on social media appropriating Indigenous agricultural practices—particularly the "three sisters" of pumpkin, corn, and beans—as their jobs in fields like finance, consulting, and marketing allowed them to work remotely and buy rural property. Rather than coming up with simple answers or solutions that reinforce the status quo, "Indigenous planning, as a way of reflecting on Indigenous sustainability, is about figuring out the planning processes arising from the contexts that we actually live in today, in which our societies are greatly limited and threatened by settler colonialism and other forms of oppression. Reflecting on sustainability in this way . . . keeps us aware of how oppression endures as one of the largest threats to Indigenous peoples and many other groups."[42] Indigenous pasts, presents, and futures are not there to be mined—exploited—for quick fixes and easy solutions. Rather, through an engagement with these experiences and imaginaries, we find a way to map a path onward, a way of defining problems in ways that do not prioritize technoscientific expertise and the systems of power it tends to reinforce.

While it may be the case that Indigenous lessons are not for everyone, I cannot help but see myself in some of these futures: the "blue-eyed Liberal" who, in Jones's story, tries to justify colonizing a historyless New World; the white squatter who, in Sanders's story, finds it difficult to accept his place in a world patrolled by Cherokee sheriffs.[43] In several of the stories collected in Simon Ortiz's *Men on the Moon*, characters work or have worked in the dangerous and dusty mines and petroleum factories owned by Kerr-McGee, with one comparing the temporal rhythms of working in a mine with the geological times of rocks and mountains that the mine exploits: "It's my time and the mountain's time."[44] Reading this, I cannot help but think of my uncle who died of an aggressive cancer that most people in my family simply assume was a result of his exposure to toxic chemicals working at a Kerr-McGee factory in North Mississippi. What I find instructive in these accounts of the future is the implicit rejection of the idea that there are easy paths forward. They reject the trope of the "ecological Indian," a recognition, as Kyle Whyte observes, that "our ancestors had many flaws," and in doing so, they reject the idea that we, whoever "we" might include, will simply be saved based on some inherent goodness.[45] As Kim TallBear writes in her review of Shepard Krech's book on the myth of the ecological Indian, however, "it isn't only saints that are massacred, dislocated, and systematically oppressed."[46] Indigenous speculative fiction projects this critique onto the future, reminding readers that there is not one solution for the future because there is not one problem in the present, nor is there one history that connects them.

Ends and Beginnings

A key feature of Indigenous science fiction, according to Grace L. Dillon, is that it often forces readers to reckon with the fact that apocalypse is not something to be imagined as a potential, future occurrence but is something that many Indigenous peoples have already lived through. "It is almost commonplace to think that the Native Apocalypse, if contemplated seriously, has already taken place," leading to many forms of Indigenous futurism that imagine "a reversal of circumstances, where Natives win or at least are centered in the narrative." As Dillon argues, "Native apocalyptic storytelling . . . shows the ruptures, the scars, and the trauma in its effort ultimately to provide healing and a return to bimaadiziwin," which refers to "the state of balance, one of difference and possibility, a condition of resistance and survival."[47]

This stands in rather stark contrast to the way apocalyptic storytelling features in corporate sustainability. The market-driven utopianism implicit in my informants' embrace of technological fixes belies the dystopian backdrop against which the future innovation of the private sector is advertised. Recall how Miranda defined sustainable development as "living as well as we can but with a lower impact." What we "should be striving for," according to Miranda, is a world where innovations like Tesla's battery-powered vehicles allow us to reduce our impact without having to make the sacrifices that hippies think we should make. As Gökçe Günel has shown, however, the utopian promise of "innovative" companies like Tesla is often cast against bleak prognoses of apocalyptic futures. Tesla's cars, she tells us, are equipped with a "bioweapons defense mode" that, with the push of a button, filters 99.97 percent of toxins from the air as it is pumped into the car's cabin. She quotes the company's founder, Elon Musk, who described Tesla as "a leader in apocalyptic defense scenarios." In proffering this vision of safety amid danger, Tesla (and other green or sustainable businesses) presume an "apocalyptic future in which some passengers remain protected while others are left exposed, breathing in toxic air. Rather than seeking to resolve toxicity in a collective manner, the bioweapon defense button eliminates toxic air for individuals with enough cash."[48] This is an extreme example, but the sentiment is not so different from more mainstream advertisements. The Danish renewable energy company Ørsted, for example, ran an ad several years ago that encouraged customers to "create a world that runs entirely on green energy." The first half of the ad features snippets of people enjoying lush outdoor spaces and close-up shots of various flora and fauna. "Our home has treated us well," says a soothing female voice, as the video shifts to flashes of severe storms, parched soil, melting ice, and flooded roads. "But as temperatures increase and sea levels rise, it's time to change the way we treat it." The ad ends with an uplifting narrative about Ørsted's transformation from a black energy company to a green energy company, accompanied by swooping footage of its offshore windmills.[49] Implicit in the ad is what happens if companies like Ørsted do not take the lead in the sustainability transition: storms, droughts, floods—all at apocalyptic scales.

Whereas Native apocalyptic storytelling often seeks a return to bimaadiziwin, neoliberal apocalypses tend to be threatening and circumscriptive, a warning of what will happen if we resist business as usual. Neoliberal sustainability conjures dystopian images of famine and drought and storms and fire as a contrast to what the future might look like if the market-driven solutions that it promotes today are resisted or refused. It evokes the grim expectations of climate scientists while at the same time appropriating that same technoscientific language to call for business-friendly, net-zero solutions. "It *could be* worse," these imaginaries imply. "It *could be* apocalyptic." Speculative fiction, as it were, also offers a glimpse into a future in which these kinds of actors get their way: Octavia Butler's eerily prescient parables are a prime example. In the *Parable of the Sower* and the *Parable of the Talents*, we get a firsthand account of the immense difficulty of trying to carve out a better life in a world defined by the increasingly familiar intersection of mass privatization and fascist governments. Within neoliberal sustainability, the end of the world serves a disciplinary function, reorienting subjects toward the future in a way that requires them to accept the maintenance—the sustainability—of the status quo.

However, even against this backdrop of a looming apocalypse that only the private sector can prevent, alternatives tend to break through. Indigenous-led political movements, such as resistance to the Dakota Access Pipeline's traversal of the Standing Rock Indian Reservation and protests against the Trans Mount and Coastal Gaslink pipelines orchestrated by Indigenous activists in Canada, not only suggest but enact a future in which the economizing logic that drives the development of new oil infrastructures is abandoned. These movements expose the entanglements of resistance, responsibility, and sovereignty at the heart of Indigenous futurism. According to a 2021 report by the Indigenous Environmental Network, "Our climate cannot afford new oil, gas, or coal projects of any kind; phasing out existing fossil fuel infrastructure will already be a monumental challenge. Indigenous resistance to carbon is both an opportunity and an offering—now is the time to codify the need to keep fossil fuels in the ground, to safeguard both the climate and Indigenous Rights."[50] As Chief Howihkat of the Unist'ot'en House Group, Freda Hudson, observed after her 2020 arrest alongside other Wet'suwet'en matriarchs protesting the GasLink pipeline, "It's all of our responsibility to protect future generations, . . . to find alternative energy sources that don't destroy the land."[51] These movements are different from corporate-led sustainability initiatives in several ways, but perhaps the most salient is that they start by accepting the reality of the climate crisis rather than downplaying it, denying it, or hoping that it will miraculously go away.

Claims that we are unable to "afford" new hydrocarbon projects and the invocation of future generations in need of protection recall the economizing logic of sustainability professionals and the images of happy grandchildren plastered on the walls of the Geneva airport. And yet, in these actors' rejection of the kinds of comparisons and causal connections that my informants' obsession with measurement and reporting facilitates, they point to a radically different vision of the future, one in which the equivalence of economic priorities and environmental

dangers slips out of the realm of possibility. And although the experiences of Indigenous people, Black people, queer people, working-class
people, and other marginalized groups are different, several critical
traditions have shown us that these groups' distinct experiences of oppression often resonate with each other, intersecting in powerful and
generative ways.[52]

We see this in other movements and political formations. Like Indigenous futurisms, which center the experiences of Natives in stories of
both improvement and decline, recent work at the intersection of anti-
Black racism and socioecological systems has emphasized the agency of
Black people in resisting the dynamics of racial capitalism. The anthropologist Ashanté Reese's *Black Food Geographies*, for example, theorizes
agency through Black people's efforts to cultivate self-reliance within
the neighborhood foodscapes of Washington, DC. Rather than focusing on the systems of oppression that make it difficult for poor people of
color to access affordable and healthy food, however, Reese shows how
residents' creative responses to different forms of oppression generate
"blueprints" for food futures that reflect their own values rather than
those of elite do-gooders. As the geographer J. T. Roane and colleagues
have observed, "The seeds of a different world are already alive in the
everyday practices of ordinary Black and Indigenous people. . . . The future is alive in the everyday acts of survival, refusal, and collectivity in
catastrophe. This contrasts with the people who are currently in power,
where the only horizon is finding new places to take, new resources
to exploit, new populations (human and non-human) to displace and
destroy."[53]

What strikes me about these diverse futurities is that they all prioritize
a kind of localism, a future that is necessarily pluralized as it is cultivated,
at first, between the cracks in the façade of neoliberalism and its lineage
of colonial and capitalist exploitation. The grounding of these futures in
local contexts does not foreclose an engagement with global politics or
even cosmological orientations, but it does demand an attunement to
the ways in which the intersection of histories and events looks different
from different perspectives. This is another reason that these lessons are
not for "all humanity" and why we should approach with skepticism solutions that claim to be flexible enough to be applied anywhere. In trying
to cultivate what Malea Powell has called "alliance as a practice of surviv-

ance," it is important make sure that new approaches to sustainability maintain a connection to their place- and time-specific roots.[54]

This is one thing that distinguishes the future of neoliberal sustainability from alternatives: whereas neoliberal sustainability sees the climate apocalypse as a threat to be managed in the future, Black, Indigenous, and other marginalized futurities are grounded in experiences of apocalypses that have been, and continue to be, survived. In contrast to the politics of survivance instantiated through Indigenous and intersectional praxis, neoliberal sustainability instantiates a politics of discipline and acquiescence, mobilizing apocalypse as a threat rather than a lesson. The future of neoliberal sustainability requires Walter Benjamin's angel of history to spin itself around and ignore the ruin left in its wake. Queer, Black, and Indigenous futures, on the other hand, cultivate what Nishant Shahani has called a "retrospective futurity" that weaves the past into the present as a way of actively orienting ourselves toward—and preparing ourselves for—both the certainties and the uncertainties of what is to come.[55]

Conclusion

This chapter has approached the future from two different angles. First, it asked what kind of future neoliberal sustainability prefigures and what kinds of futures it forecloses. Second, it asked which visions of the future motivate the dominant approach to sustainability today and which visions might inform a more pluralized approach to sustainability instead. As we have seen, neoliberal sustainability posits a very specific future, one in which banks and businesses save the world through profitable investments in new technologies that not only fail to challenge the status quo but actively reinforce it. In this future, the rich stay rich, and the poor are given the opportunity to become rich through a commitment to hard work and an embrace of market forces. Capitalism is tweaked rather than abolished. There is a kind of magical thinking about the role that new technologies will play—things like carbon capture and storage technologies, desalination technologies, food-production technologies, and so on—that is inextricable from another kind of magical thinking about the role that financial markets will play in allocating capital to these world-saving technologies. But this magical thinking is attended by more mundane practices of accounting that reinforce a radical ideology of commensuration across time and space. As we saw in previous chapters, discussions about how to measure and report different dimensions of sustainability, even when they fail to come up with clear methods or guidelines, leave behind durable infrastructures that channel resources into neoliberal solutions and away from more radical alternatives, a kind of lock-in effect similar to those created by physical infrastructures like roads and bridges. In these narratives of corporate sustainable futures, apocalyptic visions of climate collapse loom large in the background, threatening us to fall in line with elite ideas about what kinds of solutions we should pursue.

There are, of course, other ways of worldbuilding and future-making, evident in the histories, politics, and imaginaries of marginalized groups. The stories discussed earlier invite us to reflect not only on the kind of future we stand to inherit if we continue to rely on neoliberal sustainability to evade the end of the world but also on the unavoidable challenges of realizing better futures. Reflecting on Gerald Vizenor's "Custer on the Slipstream," Dillon identifies two key elements of native slipstream writing: first, its provision of a "nonlinear way of thinking through complex cultural tensions" and, second, its conveyance of "the very real psychological experience of slipping into various levels of awareness and consciousness."[56] This notion of slipstreams resonates with Sharpe's wakes, not just in the mechanical sense that slipstreams occur in the wake of a passing object but also in the sense that the slipstream, like wake work, provokes an understanding of time and temporality that rejects the idea of a singular, linear history connecting past, present, and future, as well as an understanding of how our shifting awareness of these histories informs both our experiences and our expectations.

What follows in the wake of a market-oriented obsession with measurement and reporting hurtling its way into the future? What gets dragged along by the slipstream of neoliberal sustainability? In thinking about these questions, I cannot help but return to Paulette Steeves's pyro-epistemology. Surely one of the things that gets reproduced in these debates about defining and measuring social and environmental impacts is a particular way of *knowing* society and the environment as discrete sets of indicators and a strict definition of who counts as a knower and a producer of knowledge. As we have seen, ways of knowing, being, and doing—our epistemologies, ontologies, and ethics—are inseparable. Thinking about social and environmental risks as if they were comparable to the financial risks faced by wealthy investors is a kind of thinking that relies on the development of quantitative social and environmental impacts to facilitate commensuration and comparison, which is inseparable from the radical ideology of longtermism and its attendant ethical claims. In searching for an epistemology to incinerate so that other ways of knowing, being, and doing might flourish in—and contribute to—a more just and sustainable future, the neoliberal approach to accounting for impacts seems like a really good place to start.

Conclusion

Against Sustainability

So they holler on about the end of the world in the hope of
making us give up on our dreams.
—Ailton Krenak, *Ideas to Postpone the End of the World*

In early 2022, I checked on the status of the "Blue Number" initiative
that the International Trade Center's executive director had so proudly
announced almost seven years earlier at the Trade for Sustainable Development conference in Geneva. On Google, my search results for "blue
number" yielded clip art, birthday balloons, and a Delaware-based nonprofit that promotes data sovereignty but seems to be unrelated to the
ITC's initiative. When I searched "ITC blue number," I came across a
blue LED light strip for boats marketed by a company called ITC Marine
before finding a chapter written by the ITC's director in a book about
"African perspectives on trade," in which she repeated much of what she
had said in her opening speech at the T4SD conference in 2015.[1]

This seems to be a fairly typical biography for these kinds of data-
driven sustainability initiatives. They align themselves with lofty, ambitious goals that garner excitement about a market-oriented technological
fix, before gradually disappearing, usually because they failed to attract
private-sector supporters. In fact, the vast majority of the indicators developed to track performance on things like human rights and other sustainable development issues, as Sally Merry observes, ultimately fail to
catch on, quickly fading from public consciousness.[2] But the ebb and flow
of these kinds of initiatives leaves something important behind, bolstering
the idea that these are the *kinds* of solutions we should be pursuing, solutions that rely on rendering the problems of sustainability legible from
the perspective of the market so the market can manage it for us. That is
precisely what the Blue Number offered and was surely part of its appeal.

As we have seen in diverse contexts throughout this book—from efforts to standardize the measurement and reporting of social capital to the prioritization of collecting and disclosing sustainability indicators in certification schemes, from the obsession with ESG ratings in sustainable finance to the disconcerting rise of "longtermist" thinking that is ultimately just an extension of the same ideology of commensuration and commensurability that underlies many of our most popular climate policies—data-driven sustainability initiatives are often fraught and contentious, rarely getting off the ground. The social capital project, for example, never yielded a clear method for measuring and reporting social capital, certainly not one that many companies decided to adopt, and banks still have no clue how to consistently evaluate environmental, social, or governance risks, even for their own internal decision-making. Impact investors hesitate to invest in social or environmental projects without first establishing clear KPIs for their social return on investment, opting instead to leave their money with conventional investors who promise to manage their wealth with ESG considerations in mind. The promise of data-driven sustainable supply chain management still rests on ambiguous ideas about the relationship between information about social and environmental impacts and the market's ability to interpret that information and yield efficient, and therefore sustainable, outcomes through things like consumer demand and producer empowerment. Constricted by the belief that sustainability should be profitable, my informants have a hard time imagining a world in which sustainability can be anything other than large companies and their investors making incremental progress toward some insufficient emissions goal. Consequently, the futures they imagine are rather unsavory, futures in which the environment and those who populate it are seen as sources of data to be exploited and managed by an all-powerful market.

The metrological regimes that my informants try to construct to account for sustainability are exceedingly fragile, and much of their work is devoted to refining and promoting methods for measuring and reporting social and environmental impacts. From NGOs to private banks, sustainability professionals try to develop measurement and reporting guidelines that will attract companies to adopt them. But it is precisely the fragility of specific metrological regimes and my informants' constant attempts to improve and fortify them that renders accounting infrastructures so durable and so pervasive. In focusing so much of their attention on ways to make these measurement and reporting systems less fragile, sustainability professionals reinforce the idea that a metrological regime is something worth pursuing in the first place. Their work reinscribes a definition of sustainability wherein these metrological regimes are seen as necessary, where social, environmental, and economic impacts are seen as commensurable and equivalent, rendered legible to an omniscient and omnipotent market that uses the data they disclose to generate the most sustainable outcomes.

This book has shown how the impulse to define and measure sustainability indicators, which is at the heart of contemporary practices of global sustainability, contributes to the rule of markets. Neoliberal governance is not only facilitated by this kind of commensuration but relies on it. Focusing so explicitly on measurement and reporting allows the ideology of market rule to remain implicit and the power of the most powerful market actors—multinational corporations and their investors—to remain opaque. One goal of the book, then, has been to draw an explicit connection between the obsession with sustainability indicators and the power of large corporations and their shareholders. One of the main ways they exercise their power is by defining sustainability in a way that suits their own interests, a key aspect of which is the unrelenting focus on indicators. This leads to a lot of nitpicking that precludes much meaningful action, with the definition of specific indicators or guidelines for sharing them constantly under debate. The goal posts are constantly shifting. In May 2022, for instance, with the war in Ukraine raging, Citigroup tweeted a video of its CEO, Jane Fraser, speaking at the Milken Institute's Global Conference, where she said that "there's a new S in ESG, which is security . . . and that security can be food security, it's energy security, it's operational resilience, it's cyber, it's defense."[3] The potential new indicators for measuring these kinds of security issues are innumerable, and if organizations take Fraser seriously, it will almost certainly prompt years of conferences and workshops and focus groups on how to integrate security indicators into sustainable investing strategies. The can gets kicked a bit further down the road, all while catastrophic socioecological crises continue hurtling toward us. It is precisely this power—the power to maintain a "business as usual" stance in the face of disaster—that this book has sought to address.

Another goal of the book has been to offer a critical perspective on this increasingly hegemonic approach to sustainability so that other modes of sustainability might find ways to flourish. Neoliberal sustainability reduces the diversity of human and nonhuman experiences and expectations to quantitative indicators of sustainability performance, whose "improvement" is left to the whims of global financial markets. The paradox of corporate sustainability is that the for-profit corporation, which, by definition, is rapaciously exploitative, is also presented as the solution. We are supposed to put our faith in businesses, guided by the market, to fix problems that those same businesses, guided by that same market logic, not only created in the first place but have spent the past half a century ignoring (and, in some cases, actively covering up). Neoliberal sustainability tries to resolve this paradox by changing the terms of sustainability in a way that makes it commensurable with the profit motive of businesses, so that sustainability can be understood in terms of the organizational form—and ultimately the broader capitalist political economy—of the for-profit corporation. It circumscribes our social imaginary, limiting what we think is possible to the realm of what the market says is profitable. This has been most depressingly obvious in a university setting, where, in theory at least, we should be teaching students to "think outside the box." And yet, when students are invited to think about solutions to various social and environmental problems, they are often instructed to think about the business case for their solutions. Several years ago, for instance, I was invited to act as a mentor and judge to a large group of university students participating in a sustainability "hackathon." The students broke up into groups of three or four to come up with solutions to different sustainability challenges, and my role was to mingle with the different groups and give them feedback on their ideas. I was struck by their commitment to making their ideas attractive to investors from the outset. Interesting ideas were dismissed because the students could not come up with a viable business case. For them, an unprofitable solution was dead in the water. Like my informants working in the private sector and even those working for large NGOs, it was difficult, if not impossible, for these students to imagine a noncapitalist world where sustainability did not have to make a lot of money.

But other imaginaries exist, and new imaginaries emerge every day to show that the commensurability of nature, society, and the economy is not only socially produced and fragile but unnecessarily constraining. Within these imaginaries, we find ways of relating to each other and the world that are not governed by the logic of the market. As Kim TallBear and Angela Willey observe, "Our ability to imagine nature and relationality differently are deeply enmeshed, and this imaginative work is vital to the re-worlding before us."[4] Within these imaginaries, we find examples of worlds in which neoliberal sustainability's logic of equivalence, which is reinforced by its commitment to perpetually fortifying its metrological regimes and forcing all of us to see the world like the market does, is actively suppressed. We find examples of worlds in which different, more complete histories provoke different, more just futures. We find speculations about what happens when this logic is allowed to advance unchecked, how it mingles with fascism and racism and settler colonialism to instantiate futures that are becoming disconcertingly familiar. Within these other imaginaries that neoliberal sustainability inhibits, we find different politics and different ethics and different ways of knowing, being, and doing. We find ways to move past the "myth of sustainability," the belief "that we can stimulate economic growth while mitigating the effects of climate change, without any sacrifice."[5]

What these alternative visions of sustainability demonstrate is that sustainability is necessarily plural, and not just in a superficial sense that rests on the purported "flexibility" of an approach that promotes a blinkered focus on metrics and ends up reinforcing the rule of markets. "There are a million paths into the future," writes adrienne maree brown, "and many of them can be transformative for the whole."[6] These sustainabilities emerge dialectically, bringing the local and the global into relation with each other in ways that are constantly evolving. As inherently critical sustainabilities, they are attuned to questions of power, place, and history that determine both our experiences of unsustainability and our imaginaries of more sustainable futures.[7] Organizing against the hegemonic force of the for-profit corporation and its neoliberal agenda is a daunting task, but knowing how that force propels itself is an important step. We know what to push back against, namely, the pervasive idea that sustainability is something that can be expressed through KPIs and left to the market to manage on our behalf. We know where neoliberal sustainability's weak points are, evinced through the efforts of sustainability professionals to constantly reinforce a measured, calculated approach to sustainability.

In the context of this "battle of imaginations," we must first understand the way companies imagine the world in order to find ways to allow other imaginaries to come out on top. That is easier said than done, but by critically embracing principles of sustainability and organization that are rooted in other imaginaries, we can start to find a way forward. Drawing from a theory of change enunciated in Octavia Butler's parables, brown identifies several core principles of what she calls "emergent strategy," including "small is good, small is all" and "change is constant."[8] Emergent strategies for sustainability will be grounded in local experiences that are situated in global histories and challenges, and they will not be bound by the strictures of Western technoscientific epistemologies. In formulating these strategies, it becomes much easier to recognize that a problem like climate change is a global phenomenon with radically different impacts across time and space and to respond to these diverse impacts with diverse solutions that are nevertheless situated in a common, global struggle. What I find particularly attractive about this approach to strategizing and organizing is that it does not preclude other principles. It is easy to see, for example, how emergent sustainability strategies intersect with the model of sustainable development advanced by the College of Menominee Nation's Sustainable Development Institute and how they cut across the model's six facets of land and sovereignty; natural environment; institutions; technology; economics; and human perception, activity, and behavior.[9] Like brown's emergent strategy, the SDI's model of sustainability emphasizes that tensions between the model's different dimensions are constantly shifting and that sustainable development is defined not just by static targets projected years into the future but by a recognition that situations change and an ability to respond to those changes. Embracing the dynamism of the SDI's model allows us to develop sustainability strategies that are premised on constant change, and it offers an antidote to the neoliberal approach to sustainability that forces us to pin down society and the environment so we can slice them up and extract the most profitable components.

So, what about all these measurements and calculations and indicators and data sets? What about markets? What about corporate sustainability? At the end of the day, I believe that metrics are useful tools that can inform more critical approaches to sustainability. The point is not to discard tools that can tell us about our impacts on society and the environment; the point is to refuse to allow these tools to govern us and not to rely on the tools developed by corporations to solve the problems they created. In resisting the seductive power of these metrics, we resist the power of corporations that develop and wield these metrics in their own interests. To suppress the logic of equivalence that these metrics help corporations enact is to suppress the encroachment of the logic of markets across every facet of life. The goal is not to abandon markets completely, which are just one of many ways we relate to each other, or to discard social and environmental indicators, which can be valuable sources of information; the goal, rather, is to figure out how these things can be put to use by diverse communities for diverse ends, without allowing them to rule us. Faced with the end of this world, we have to work hard to make sure the next one is better.

ACKNOWLEDGMENTS

Thanks, first and foremost, to my informants, who were generous with their time and expertise. Writing a book like this is impossible without honest, reflexive participants, and I feel lucky to have met so many people who are passionate about sustainability, even if we rarely agreed on what sustainability means or what it should look like. I also want to thank the people who developed and shared the ideas I have been fortunate enough to engage with in the process of writing this book, even if I have surely neglected many important interventions and conversations.

I abandoned my ambitions of becoming an economist during the first year of my PhD and was lucky to end up across the desk from Karen Hébert, who introduced me to anthropology and human geography and has been a wonderful mentor ever since. At Yale, Michael Dove, Paul Kockelman, Kate Dudley, and Henry Sussman all made a lasting impact on the way I think and write about the world, and I am very grateful for their generosity during and after my PhD. Conversations with members of the Dove Lab, with my writing group (Sayd Randle, Gabriela Morales, Caroline Merrifield, and Nilay Erten), and with Chris Hebdon and Dina Omar in their living room helped me flesh out many of the ideas in this book. At the Graduate Institute in Geneva, where I was based during my dissertation fieldwork and where I worked more recently as postdoctoral researcher, Filipe Calvão was an excellent supervisor who has become a good friend. In Copenhagen, Nanna Bonde Thylstrup, Stefano Ponte, Lisa Richey, Maha Rafi Atal, and Frederik Schade helped carve out a space in the business school where we could be critical and creative. A special shout-out to Hannah Elliott and Dan Souleles, my anthropological coconspirators at CBS.

In the process of writing this book, Ryan Parsons and Sayd Randle were extremely generous with their comments and critiques, as were three anonymous reviewers. I also feel very fortunate to have had the chance to work with Jennifer Hammer at NYU Press. I have heard horror stories about the publication journeys of first books, but this one has been a real pleasure from start to finish. An earlier version of chapter 4 appeared in *Focaal: Journal of Global and Historical Anthropology*, and I am grateful to that journal's publisher, Berghahn, for its early commitment to open access. Notes in the text indicate where other chapters draw from and build on my previously published work.

Research is expensive, and I thank the organizations that funded mine: the Fulbright Association; the Swiss State Secretariat for Education, Research and Innovation (SERI); the Independent Research Fund of Denmark (through a Sapere Aude starting grant: #7023-00115AB); the Yale Institute for Biospheric Studies; and the MacMillan Center at Yale. My parents paid for my bachelor's and master's degrees, and they supplemented my research stipend when I was living in Geneva so I could fly home for Christmas, for which I am very grateful.

Speaking of family, I really have the best. Huge thanks to my parents, Walter and Patricia, and my sister, Anna, to whom this book is dedicated. *En een dikke merci* to my in-laws: Patrik and Marleen; Filip, Ellen, Roan, and Menoa; Tim, Sanne, and Noah; and Isabel and Woody. Friends from many different stages of life have kept me grounded while researching and writing, especially recently during the worst days of the COVID-19 pandemic, and I am very grateful to them. (They know who they are.) Finally, there's Jan, my husband and my best friend, with whom life feels much more sustainable, to whom the book is also dedicated.

NOTES

INTRODUCTION

1 Roy, "Ethical Subjects."
2 See, for example, Calvão and Archer, "Digital Extraction." For a good, general overview of current thinking on the relationship between transparency and sustainability in the context of global supply chains, see Gardner et al., "Transparency and Sustainability."
3 Van Dijck, "Datafication, Dataism and Dataveillance." On traceability, see Thylstrup, Archer, and Ravn, "Traceability." For a good overview of the emerging anthropological approach to data, see Douglas-Jones, Walford, and Seaver, "Introduction."
4 Merry, *Seductions of Quantification*.
5 A sociotechnical imaginary is "a set of ideas, beliefs, and visions about the future" that "is always in the process of becoming—expanding in both scope and reach." Sadowski and Bendor, "Selling Smartness," 542. Throughout the book, I take this notion of imaginaries quite seriously, especially to the extent that particular ways of imagining the future are one window into the politics of determining which futures materialize. See Milkoreit, "Imaginary Politics"; van Lente, "Imaginaries of Innovation"; Archer, "Imagining Impact in Global Supply Chains."
6 Merry, *Seductions of Quantification*, 3.
7 This is based on Solability's Global Sustainable Competitiveness index.
8 Mair et al., "Critical Review of the Role of Indicators."
9 Political ecologists have made this point forcefully in the context of technoscientific approaches to conservation and development. See, for example, Blaikie, *Political Economy of Soil Erosion*; Hobart, "Introduction," 1993.
10 Porter, *Trust in Numbers*.
11 Scott, *Seeing like a State*; Desrosières, *Politics of Large Numbers*; Power, *Audit Society*; Shore and Wright, "Governing by Numbers."
12 Cooper, "Measure for Measure?"
13 Mosse, *Cultivating Development*.
14 Barry, "Anti-Political Economy"; Cooper, "Measure for Measure?"; Freidberg, "Calculating Sustainability in Supply Chain Capitalism."
15 The idea that more information makes markets more efficient is a basic tenet of neoclassical economics, and while that may be true in the narrow context of the neatly defined models of economists, problems start to arise when those technical terms seep into much broader discourses.

16 Fourcade, "Ordinal Citizenship."

17 Cooper, "Measure for Measure?"

18 While it is no doubt true that these trends disproportionately affect communities in developing countries, even people living in Europe and North America are increasingly—and increasingly visibly—vulnerable, especially working-class people and minorities. See, for instance, Sultana, "Unbearable Heaviness of Climate Coloniality"; Taylor, *Toxic Communities*.

19 D. Whyte, *Ecocide*, 20.

20 Bookchin, *Toward an Ecological Society*, 66.

21 The term "sustainability industry" is a nod to Marina Welker's conceptualization of the "CSR industry" in her groundbreaking book *Enacting the Corporation*, a key moment in a longer history of thinking about the emergence of "development" as a very profitable industry in the work of scholars like Arturo Escobar and James Ferguson. In Welker's account, the CSR industry is on the one hand heterogeneous and flexible, while on the other hand unambiguously promoting economic growth and industry profitability through its commitment to the "business case" for social and environmental sustainability. This resonates with the dynamics of the "sustainability industry" I observed during my fieldwork, where CSR had been largely abandoned in favor of corporate sustainability. We can expect these dynamics to persist as other "industries" emerge, such as the ESG industry and the circular economy industry. See also Welker, "Corporate Security Begins in the Community."

22 Harvey, *Brief History of Neoliberalism*, 2–3.

23 A classic example of an externality is a polluting factory whose emissions waft into the homes and yards of nearby residents. From the perspective of many economists, the solution to this problem is to determine the monetary value of clean air from the point of view of neighboring home owners in order to determine the right corrective actions, whether that involves charging the factory a fee that is paid out to residents (maybe to install some kind of air filter on their houses) or forcing the factory to install a scrubber on its smokestacks, so long as the cost of installing the scrubber does not exceed the value that the residents actually place on clean air; otherwise, according to this theory, there remains a market inefficiency.

24 Strange, *Retreat of the State*; Atal, "Janus Faces of Silicon Valley."

25 Freidberg, "Footprint Technopolitics," 185.

26 Hébert, "Chronicle of a Disaster Foretold," 110, 112.

27 Dyke, Knorr, and Watson, "Why Net Zero Policies Do More Harm than Good," 49.

28 Welker, Partridge, and Hardin, "Corporate Lives"; Rajak, *In Good Company*; Welker, *Enacting the Corporation*; Little, *Toxic Town*; Ottinger, *Refining Expertise*.

29 There are of course several notable exception to this characterization. One is Gwen Ottinger's work on how engineers working in an oil refinery in rural Louisiana co-opted local residents' concerns about the health effects of the refinery's

pollution to thwart their efforts to hold the company accountable (*Refining Expertise*). Another is Jesse Goldstein's analysis of cleantech entrepreneurs in New York City and their efforts to navigate the contradictory impulses to both "do well" and "do good" under the aegis of green capitalism (*Planetary Improvement*). I build on their insights throughout the book, especially Ottinger's theorization of expertise and Goldstein's conceptualization of impact, connecting these explicitly to the way sustainability professionals actively promote the quantification of impacts as a specific mode of sustainability governance.

30 Nader, "Up the Anthropologist"; Garsten and Sörbom, "Small Places, Big Stakes."

31 Souleles, "How to Study People"; Souleles, "How to Think about People."

32 Archer, "Navigating the Sustainability Landscape."

33 Randle et al., "Unsustainability in Action."

34 Sen, *Everyday Sustainability*.

35 Sze et al., introduction to *Sustainability*, 3. In pushing a vision of sustainability that relies on markets to achieve its goals, these organizations also encourage the further expansion and entrenchment of the market and its logic.

36 Cavanagh and Benjaminsen, "Political Ecology."

37 Sen, *Everyday Sustainability*; Loftus, *Everyday Environmentalism*; Escobar, *Designs for the Pluriverse*.

38 Martinez-Alier, *Environmentalism of the Poor*; Seymour, *Bad Environmentalism*; Agyeman, Bullard, and Evans, *Just Sustainabilities*.

39 Gabriel Castilloux Calderon, in a story about storytellers at the end of the world, translates the word *andwànikàdjigan* as "record; to set down in writing or the like, as for the purpose of preserving evidence." This resonated with me as I tried to think about different ways we might account for sustainability, for which accounting, in its most basic sense, is also recording for the purpose of preserving evidence. Calderon, "Andwànikàdjigan," 112.

40 Although I discuss this subject in more detail in chapter 6, my use of the phrase "in the wake" here is a reference to Christina Sharpe's notion of "wake work" (*In the Wake*).

41 My informants would certainly agree with the idea that there is no one-size-fits-all approach to sustainability, and they would insist that we need to be flexible in order to meet the diverse challenges of unsustainability. As I argue throughout the book, however, in their attempt to come up with a way of thinking about sustainability that is flexible enough to account for its social, environmental, and economic dimensions, they have paradoxically created a vision of sustainability that *inflexibly* requires us to accept the commensurability of things across these dimensions, leaving little room for approaches to sustainability that do not rely on the market to achieve social and environmental goals.

42 Dockry et al., "Sustainable Development Education, Practice, and Research," 131.

43 Gegeo and Watson-Gegeo, "How We Know"; Rotz, "They Took Our Beads"; Pulido, "Geographies of Race and Ethnicity II"; Pulido, "Geographies of Race and Ethnicity III"; Seymour, *Bad Environmentalism*.

44 Krenak, *Ideas to Postpone the End of the World*.

45 Tsing, "Blasted Landscapes"; Moore, *Capitalism in the Web of Life*.

46 Dunlap, "'Solution' Is Now the 'Problem.'"

47 See, for example, Sène-Harper and Séye, "Community-Based Tourism."

48 MacKenzie, *Engine, Not a Camera*; Callon, "Performativity, Misfires and Politics"; Helgesson and Muniesa, "Valuation Is Work."

49 Pearce and Warford, *World without End*.

50 There are at least two problems with this approach: first, it fails to account for the way power is distributed within the capitalist political economy that this kind of neoliberal utopianism reinforces; second, it leaves little room to imagine relations that are structured by something other than cost-benefit analyses and price considerations, forcing us to see each other as competitors for scarce resources and forcing us to see the rest of the world as the resource for which we are competing.

51 Alfred, "Sovereignty"; Schneider, Kallis, and Martinez-Alier, "Crisis or Opportunity?"; Gilmore, *Abolition Geography*; Ergene, Banerjee, and Hoffman, "(Un) Sustainability and Organization Studies."

52 Bookchin, *Toward an Ecological Society*, 66.

53 Martin-Booran Mirraboopa, "Ways of Knowing, Being and Doing"; Cameron, Mearns, and McGrath, "Translating Climate Change"; Todd, "Indigenous Feminist's Take."

54 Krenak, *Ideas to Postpone the End of the World*, 21; Benson and Kirsch, "Corporate Oxymorons."

55 King, Navarro, and Smith, *Otherwise Worlds*, 19.

CHAPTER 1. THE MEANING OF SUSTAINABILITY

1 Larner and Laurie, "Travelling Technocrats, Embodied Knowledges"; Kockelman, *Chicken and the Quetzal*.

2 Nyqvist, "Corporation Performed"; Garsten and Sörbom, "Values Aligned"; Garsten and Sörbom, "Small Places, Big Stakes."

3 Archer, "Navigating the Sustainability Landscape."

4 Krenak, *Ideas to Postpone the End of the World*, 21.

5 SMEs, according to the World Bank, represent 90 percent of global businesses and employ 50 percent of the world's workforce. Although the definition of an SME changes depending on whom you talk to, it is usually wrong to think of a stereotypical "mom-and-pop store" as a representative SME, even though my informants often lumped them together when talking about companies other than multinational corporations, since a company with hundreds of employees and tens of millions of dollars in annual turnover can be considered an SME.

6 Eisenberg, "Ambiguity as Strategy"; Milne and Gray, "W(h)Ither Ecology?"

7 Archer, "Imagining Impact in Global Supply Chains."

8 This is a bit simplistic, and as I show in chapter 6, many of the most prominent "philanthropists" have adopted a market-driven approach to giving that explicitly

foregrounds ROI, inspired by the "effective altruism" movement and so-called longtermist thinking.

9 These two concepts are fundamental to contemporary notions of sustainability, especially in corporate sustainability but also in sustainable development, especially the stakeholder concept, which is ubiquitous. Major corporations such as Nestlé and Coca-Cola have adopted the CVS approach in their social responsibility and environmental sustainability strategies, and it is difficult to find documents about sustainability that do not mention the word "stakeholder" multiple times. In an interesting back-and-forth in management studies between Porter and a team of critical management scholars, Porter pushed back against critiques of his creating shared value concept as greenwashing, claiming (in my view, quite absurdly) that the strength of the concept was clearly demonstrated by the fact that companies like Nestlé and Coca-Cola had embraced it so enthusiastically.

10 More nuanced accounts at sustainability conferences and in the academic literature frantically repeat the mantra that "correlation is not causation," insisting that it could be possible that more profitable companies have more money to invest in sustainability, thereby reversing the causal relationship. Instances of slippage between these two causal directions are interesting, typically emerging in conversations about start-ups and smaller companies that do not have such a public-facing sustainability strategy. In these conversations, people sometimes told me that companies must grow first and then think about sustainability, and that it is better for a company to be bigger so it is on the public's radar, eliciting pressure from consumers and regulators to be more socially and environmentally responsible. This reverses the causal direction implied in the phrase "doing well by doing good," suggesting instead that companies can only do good once they have done well.

11 Enfield, *Utility of Meaning*.

12 Keane, "Semiotics and the Social Analysis of Material Things."

13 Lévi-Strauss, *Savage Mind*; Douglas, *Purity and Danger*; Rosa, *Looking like a Language, Sounding like a Race*; Medby and Thornton, "More than Words"; Plumwood, "Belonging, Naming and Decolonisation"; Dhillon, "Introduction"; Sinclair, "Righting Names"; Le Guin, *Books of Earthsea*.

14 Blühdorn, "Governance of Unsustainability."

15 Kockelman, "Grading, Gradients, Degradation, Grace."

16 Krenak, *Ideas to Postpone the End of the World*, 21.

17 Espeland and Stevens, "Commensuration as a Social Process," 315–16.

18 Miller, *Reimagining Livelihoods*.

19 Paehlke, *Democracy's Dilemma*, viii.

20 F. Li, "Engineering Responsibility," 62; McElwee, "Metrics of Making Ecosystem Services," 103.

21 F. Li, 63.

22 Sullivan, "What's Ontology Got to Do with It?"; Sullivan, "On 'Natural Capital,' 'Fairy Tales' and Ideology."

23 Pigg, "Languages of Sex and AIDS in Nepal."

24 Gilbert, Gilbertson, and Jakobsen, "Incommensurability and Corporate Social Technologies," 448.

25 Barry, "Anti-Political Economy."

26 Freidberg, "Assembled but Unrehearsed," 396.

27 Ramirez, "Contentious Dynamics"; Dunlap, "'Solution' Is Now the 'Problem.'"

28 Schaltegger and Wagner, *Managing the Business Case for Sustainability*.

29 Chossière et al., "Country- and Manufacturer-Level Attribution of Air Quality Impacts."

30 "Independent" is always an interesting word to see in discussions of corporate sustainability, especially when an "independent" firm is hired to provide a service to a company that is typically mired in some scandalous situation. It evokes the purported independence of financial accounting firms—PwC, EY, Accenture, and so on—that audit companies' annual reports, establishing another layer of equivalence between the social and environmental aspects of sustainability and the financial aspects of corporate performance.

31 Sustainability managers from Nestlé propagated this narrative at several of the sustainable development conferences I attended in 2016. It is important to note, however, that while Nestlé was being lauded for its commitment to transparency (by itself and others), the company was also being sued for its reliance on (child) slavery in multiple US courts, including by a class of pet owners who had inadvertently purchased cat food produced by slave labor and by former child slaves from Côte d'Ivoire. Nestlé's lawyers argued that their client was not obligated to uncover and disclose every instance of slavery in its supply chains and that such a strict expectation of transparency would be too burdensome to monitor and enforce.

32 Maybe she was right. As recently as 2019, the CEO of Volkswagen was in the news again, this time for making a joke about Auschwitz. *Plus ça change . . .*

33 Tim Choy observes that knowledge practices like those that my informants use to determine how sustainable a company or an investment is "rely on and generate scales of comparative analysis—local, global, specific, general, particular, universal, species, ecosystem—in the course of drawing ecological comparisons and relations. . . . Ecologies work through comparisons, and comparisons work through ecologies." Choy, *Ecologies of Comparison*, 12.

34 Ambec and Lanoie, "Does It Pay to Be Green?"

35 Porter and Van der Linde, "Toward a New Conception."

36 Schaltegger and Wagner, "Managing and Measuring the Business Case for Sustainability," 4.

37 Dyllick and Hockerts, "Beyond the Business Case for Corporate Sustainability." This shift from metaphors to measurable objects is one of the key moments in turning something like "social capital" or "natural capital" into something that can be legitimately seen as a source of potential profits. See McElwee, "Metrics of Making Ecosystem Services," 99.

38 Kockelman, "Grading, Gradients, Degradation, Grace," 390.

39 Kockelman, 400.

40 Kockelman, 400.

41 Kockelman, "Semiotic Ontology of the Commodity," 96–97.

42 O'Neill, *Market*; O'Neill, "Markets, Ethics and Environment."

43 See, for example, Stiglitz, "Markets, Market Failures, and Development"; Jaffe, Newell, and Stavins, "Tale of Two Market Failures."

44 In the context of "market-oriented" urban sustainability initiatives, Miriam Greenberg sees the rise of rankings and other metrics as a key aspect of turning sustainability into a profitable competition. See Greenberg, "Situating Sustainability in the Luxury City."

CHAPTER 2. MEASURING SUSTAINABILITY

1 Goldstein, "Appropriate Technocracies?," 26.

2 T. Li, *Will to Improve*.

3 This paints quite a dark picture of the world, where the prioritization of people and planet over profit is seen as merely "bearable," while viability and equitability come at the expense of social welfare and environmental protection, respectively. Implicit in these conceptualizations of viability and equitability are answers to rather uncomfortable questions: Can we consider the planet viable, capable of sustaining life, if those who are socially marginalized do not survive? Does extinction on an unviable planet represent some perverse form of equity? If a fundamental element of contemporary sustainability is to be taken seriously, the answer to both of these questions is a frightening *yes*.

4 Sullivan, "On 'Natural Capital,' 'Fairy Tales' and Ideology," 405.

5 Sullivan, "Making Nature Investable," 65.

6 Sullivan, 65; Mennicken and Miller, "Accounting, Territorialization and Power."

7 Sullivan, "On 'Natural Capital,' 'Fairy Tales' and Ideology," 405.

8 Freeman, *Strategic Management*, v, 212, iv.

9 Porter and Kramer, "Creating Shared Value," 4, 17.

10 Barman, *Caring Capitalism*.

11 Zelizer, *Pricing the Priceless Child*.

12 It was never really clear to me where this pressure came from, but most of my informants gestured to some increasing pressure to measure and report their impacts. Some attributed it to specific regulations or codes of conduct, but most simply seemed to believe it was there. Given that most of my informants worked in sustainability, it is likely that they feel an inflated sense of pressure in this area. The portfolio managers we meet in chapter 4, for example, do not seem particularly concerned with sustainability, even though they also admit that everyone in the industry is hearing more about sustainability than ever before.

13 This followed a brief discussion about a campaign I had seen by a large consulting firm to recruit LGBT employees as part of its diversity and inclusion strategy. I told Amanda that it had rubbed me the wrong way, to see an elite firm targeting

mostly well-off, White gays and lesbians at an elite university, only to then use it as evidence that the firm was committed to diversity and inclusivity. Amanda agreed that hiring a bunch of gay people with Ivy League master's degrees was a concerning appropriation of the notion of diversity.

14 Adler and Kwon, "Social Capital"; Arrow, "Observations on Social Capital"; Coleman, "Social Capital in the Creation of Human Capital"; Halpern, *Social Capital*; Jackman and Miller, "Social Capital and Politics"; Putnam, "Social Capital."

15 Coleman, "Social Capital in the Creation of Human Capital." I say "famously" because Coleman's 1988 article on social capital has been cited nearly sixty thousand times, according to a 2022 Google Scholar search.

16 Coleman, S104.

17 Coleman, S105.

18 Power, "How Accounting Begins," 51–52.

19 Kurunmäki, Mennicken, and Miller, "Quantifying, Economising, and Marketising."

20 Kurunmäki, Mennicken, and Miller, 11.

21 Schwab, *Global Competitiveness Report*.

22 Scrivens and Smith, "Four Interpretations of Social Capital."

23 Scrivens and Smith.

24 Warner, "Corporate Angels Need to Spread Their Wings."

CHAPTER 3. CERTIFYING SUSTAINABILITY

1 These examples are drawn from a box of Lipton Yellow Label tea purchased in late 2021 in Copenhagen, Denmark.

2 I refer here to the Rainforest Alliance's 2020 standard, which was being revised and was eventually published while I was doing fieldwork for the Sustainable Tea Infrastructures (SUSTEIN) project.

3 Although countries like India and China produce more tea, Kenya, which is the fourth biggest producer by volume, is actually the world's largest exporter of tea. Most Kenyan tea is produced through the cut-tear-curl (CTC) method, which yields the inexpensive granules of black tea sold in supermarkets around the world for a few cents per pouch under household brands like Lipton, Tetley's, and PG Tips. After water, tea is the most consumed beverage on the planet, and although there is a huge variety of tea available on the market, its marketed diversity belies its origin, a single species (*Camellia sinensis*) with only a few varieties, including the well-known *assamica* cultivar. Like coffee and chocolate, much of the tea available in Western supermarkets is subject to various sustainability standards, from Fairtrade International's crop-specific standards to the Rainforest Alliance's more general standard, as well as an array of smaller, private and independent standards.

4 ITC, "State of Sustainable Markets 2018."

5 In a 2020 webinar on the contribution of sustainability standards to smallholder livelihoods, one of the participants cited PhD research conducted by Daphne Ska-

lidou to note that, when it comes to the question of who has the power to decide who gets certified, self-selection by farmers themselves is very rare. Instead, as Skalidou persuasively argues, the "rapid growth of [sustainability standards and certification] programmes" must be understood in the context of a "market asymmetry" between a powerful "oligopoly of corporations," on the one hand, and "a fragmented body of mainly unorganised farmers [who are] faced with decreasing productivity and deteriorating supporting structures," on the other. Skalidou, "In or Out?," 47.

6 Ponte, Gibbon, and Vestergaard, *Governing through Standards*.

7 Ponte, *Business, Power and Sustainability*; Jaffee and Howard, "Corporate Cooptation."

8 Graeber, *Toward an Anthropological Theory of Value*; Appadurai, *Social Life of Things*.

9 Kopytoff, "Cultural Biography of Things," 66–67.

10 Kopytoff, 67.

11 Freidberg, *French Beans*; Tsing, *Mushroom at the End of the World*; Osterhoudt et al., "Chains of Meaning."

12 Kopytoff, "Cultural Biography of Things," 67; Sussman, *Task of the Critic*.

13 Appadurai, *Social Life of Things*, 34. Laura and Paul Bohannan's work among the Tiv of Nigeria is the classic example of these different spheres of value and exchange: subsistence goods like chickens and yams belonged in one sphere, prestige items like cattle and brass rods belonged in another sphere, and rights-in-people such as wives and children belonged in another sphere. The exchange of different goods within a sphere (e.g., yams for chickens) is considered normal, but to exchange across spheres, especially downward given that these spheres were ordered hierarchically, there had to be some acceptable moral justification: a man who traded cattle for yams, for instance, could get away with it by claiming that he was doing it for members of his family. Whereas brass rods at one point served as an imperfect way to initiate exchanges across different spheres, the introduction of colonial money (and the radical degree of commensuration it facilitated) into the Tiv economy fundamentally changed the way the relationship between the different spheres was governed. Bohannan and Bohannan, *Tiv Economy*; Bohannan, "Some Principles of Exchange and Investment."

14 This standard, as it were, is provided by the ISEAL Alliance, which has developed widely used "credibility principles" and "codes of good practice" for developing and revising sustainability standards.

15 Over the past few years, standards developers have embraced a "landscape approach" to impacts, and one of their primary concerns is the scalability—the ability to scale up—their standards.

16 Dietz and Grabs, "Additionality and Implementation Gaps."

17 Van Der Ven, "Gatekeeper Power."

18 De Bakker, Rasche, and Ponte, "Multi-Stakeholder Initiatives on Sustainability."

19 A similar observation about big impacts on a small scale versus smaller impacts on a larger scale motivated a different informant's decision to switch jobs from a small, "on-the-ground" NGO to a large international organization in New York City; see Archer, "Navigating the Sustainability Landscape."

20 Archer, "Stakes and Stakeholders."

21 Writing about Roma bottle collectors in Copenhagen, Camilla Ravnbøl has shown how "informal" waste pickers have a profound understanding of both Denmark's physical recycling infrastructures and its exclusionary, digitized financial infrastructures. See Ravnbøl, "Patchwork Economies in Europe."

22 See Ottinger, *Refining Expertise*.

23 Fortin, "Transnational Multi-Stakeholder Sustainability Standards and Biofuels," 579.

24 Fortin, "Repoliticising Multi-Stakeholder Standards Processes."

25 For a seminal account of the role (and production) of legitimacy in the context of private environmental governance, see Cashore, "Legitimacy and the Privatization of Environmental Governance."

26 Rainforest Alliance, "Continuous Improvement and Smart Meters," 1.

27 Rainforest Alliance, "Rainforest Alliance Sustainable Agriculture Standard," 8.

28 Rainforest Alliance, "Continuous Improvement and Smart Meters," 2.

29 Dolan and Humphrey, "Changing Governance Patterns," 502.

30 This draws from Archer, "How to Govern a Sustainable Supply Chain."

31 This section expands on an earlier analysis of my conversation with Emily and Bruno. See Archer, "Imagining Impact in Global Supply Chains."

32 Lafargue-Molina, "Marker Development," 158.

33 Scott, *Seeing like a State*; Foster, Clark, and York, *Ecological Rift*; Marx, *Machine in the Garden*.

34 Günel, *Spaceship in the Desert*.

35 Heede, "Tracing Anthropogenic Carbon Dioxide and Methane Emissions"; Wiedmann et al., "Scientists' Warning on Affluence"; LeBaron and Lister, "Hidden Costs."

36 We are, according to many commentators, in the midst of a fourth industrial revolution, evinced by our growing reliance on automation, digitization, and so on. Tech companies like IBM and SAP are, perhaps unsurprisingly, quite invested in promoting this narrative. Recently, the extractive industry has embraced Industry 4.0 as a way of making claims about its sustainability.

37 Cavale, "Unilever Denies Reports."

38 Unilever, "Unilever to Sell Its Tea Business."

39 Schipani, Evans, and Wiggins, "How Unilever's Tea Business Became a Test."

40 Odhiambo, "Unilever Sale Saga."

41 Schipani, Evans, and Wiggins, "How Unilever's Tea Business Became a Test."

42 Ferguson, *Anti-Politics Machine*; Escobar, *Encountering Development*; T. Li, *Will to Improve*.

43 Mwita, "Boost to Tea Farmers."

44 Loconto, "Sustainably Performed," 216.
45 Bachram, "Climate Fraud and Carbon Colonialism."
46 Fouilleux and Loconto, "Voluntary Standards, Certification, and Accreditation," 10.

CHAPTER 4. MORALIZING SUSTAINABILITY

 1 Hertz, *Trading Crowd*, 134.
 2 Hertz, 133.
 3 Dal Maso, *Risky Expertise in Chinese Financialisation*.
 4 Barman, *Caring Capitalism*.
 5 Roy, "Ethical Subjects," 106–7.
 6 SSF, "What Is Sustainable Finance."
 7 Van Duuren, Plantinga, and Scholtens, "ESG Integration."
 8 Eccles, Lee, and Stroehle, "Social Origins of ESG"; UNGC, "About the UN Global Compact."
 9 UNGC, *Who Cares Wins*, ii, 1.
10 PRI, "Sustainable Markets."
11 Eccles, Lee, and Stroehle, "Social Origins of ESG," 577. Eccles is a well-known management scholar at Oxford Saïd Business School and a prominent voice in discussions about ESG integration. Lee is a managing director and global head of ESG research at MSCI, which is among the most influential providers of ESG research and indices. Stroehle is the research and program lead of the public-facing Initiative on Rethinking Performance at Saïd Business School.
12 Eccles, Lee, and Stroehle, 577. See also Pollman, "Making and Meaning of ESG."
13 Leins, *Stories of Capitalism*; see also Leins, "Narrative Authority."
14 Of course, this is also good for Norebank, which either charges fees based on the profitability of its actively managed funds or attracts more passively managed assets on the basis of the relative performance of its exchange-traded funds.
15 Sullivan, "Making Nature Investable."
16 Bracking, "Financialisation," 714. Bracking follows Foucault in defining a *dispositif* as "a thoroughly heterogeneous set consisting of discourses, institutions, architectural forms, regulatory decisions, laws, administrative measures, scientific statements, philosophical, moral, and philanthropic propositions . . . [and] the network that can be established between these elements" (714).
17 See, for instance, Bracking; Christophers, "Environmental Beta"; Sullivan, "Making Nature Investable"; Tripathy, "Translating to Risk."
18 Tripathy, "Translating to Risk," 246.
19 H. Ortiz, "Financial Value."
20 Graeber, "It Is Value."
21 Berndt and Wirth, "Market, Metrics, Morals," 28.
22 Roy, "Ethical Subjects," 106–7.
23 Berndt and Wirth, "Market, Metrics, Morals," 30.
24 Fourcade and Healy, "Seeing like a Market," 16, 13.
25 Zigon, "Narratives," 214.

26 Duranti, "Husserl, Intersubjectivity and Anthropology," 24.

27 Paulson, "We Need a New Asset Class."

28 Duranti, "Husserl, Intersubjectivity and Anthropology," 27, 17 (emphasis added); Kockelman, *Agent, Person, Subject, Self,* 90.

29 Pigg, "Languages of Sex and AIDS in Nepal"; F. Li, "Engineering Responsibility."

30 McKinsey, "Why ESG Scores Are Here to Stay"; EY, "Why Sustainability and ESG Are as Important as Ever."

31 O'Leary and Valdmanis, "ESG Reckoning Is Coming"; Pucker, "Overselling Sustainability Reporting."

32 Walter and Suina, "Indigenous Data."

CHAPTER 5. SUSTAINABLE LIVES

1 Krenak, *Ideas to Postpone the End of the World,* 32. This sounds harsh, but the fact remains that Geneva hosts dozens of conferences every day that are devoted to improving the lives of people in some other part of the world and is home to numerous international and nongovernmental organizations that, at least implicitly, share that mission.

2 T. Li, *Will to Improve.*

3 Malkki, *Need to Help,* 22.

4 Sultana, "Emotional Political Ecology," 633–34.

5 An exception to this is Melissa Checker's notion of "sustainaphrenia," which theorizes the way green capitalism transforms our climate anxieties into sustainable consumption (*Sustainability Myth*).

6 Fletcher, "Neoliberal Environmentality."

7 There are exceptions to this, of course. Someone's idea of the good life might be to hoard as much wealth as possible no matter the socioecological effects of their actions, something we refer to as psychopathic on an individual level but seem to evaluate as entrepreneurial and successful when it operates at a planetary scale.

8 Dove, "Theories of Swidden Agriculture"; Noe, "Spatiality and 'Borderlessness'"; Bluwstein et al., "Between Dependence and Deprivation."

9 Lezaun and Muniesa, "Twilight in the Leadership Playground."

10 Orta, "Commentary," 38.

11 Orta, "Managing the Margins," 691.

12 The irony, of course, is that many of the problems "there" are due to extraction and exploitation that benefits people "here."

13 Ahmed, *Cultural Politics of Emotion,* 8, 52.

14 Reinert, "Requiem for a Junk-Bird," 30.

15 John Bodley argued almost fifty years ago that "progress" leaves many victims in its wake, especially when modernist development programs intersect with Indigenous communities (*Victims of Progress*). Since then, we have learned to remain more attuned to the agency of development's target populations, seeing them not as passive victims of Western interference but as actors who often successfully negotiate and contest powerful outside forces.

16   Ticktin, *Casualties of Care*, 6; Bocci, "Tangles of Care."

17   Butler, *Precarious Life*, xiv–xv.

18   Butler, 34.

19   Butler, *Frames of War*, 15.

20   One immediately thinks of colonial governments' treatment of Indigenous populations or of contemporary efforts by organizations like the World Bank to incentivize the descendants of some of those same populations to abandon traditional livelihoods in favor of more "modern" lifestyles.

21   T. Li, *Will to Improve*.

22   I discuss this in Archer, "Stakes and Stakeholders in the Climate Casino."

23   Goldstein, *Planetary Improvement*.

24   See Jacka, *Alchemy in the Rain Forest*.

25   Le Guin, "Ones Who Walk Away from Omelas," 157.

26   Tsing, "Supply Chains and the Human Condition."

27   For an eye-opening history of the Swiss financial industry, see Bauer and Blackman, *Swiss Banking*.

28   Espeland and Stevens, "Commensuration as a Social Process," 315.

29   It is worth reading Jemisin's interview with Abigail Bereola in the *Paris Review*, which includes an extended discussion of the former's profound respect for Le Guin's fiction and her politics and situates her own writing in relation to it. Essentially, what Jemisin wanted to contemplate in "The Ones Who Stay and Fight" is what she refers to as the "flawed ideology" that happiness for one (group) depends on another's suffering. Bereola, "True Utopia."

30   Jemisin, "Ones Who Stay and Fight."

31   Jemisin.

32   Kockelman, "Semiotic Ontology of the Commodity."

33   Archer, "Stakes and Stakeholders in the Climate Casino," 182.

34   Rocheleau and Roth, "Rooted Networks."

35   See, for example, Pigg, "Inventing Social Categories."

CHAPTER 6. SUSTAINABLE FUTURES

1   Sultana, "Unbearable Heaviness of Climate Coloniality"; Nyambura, "In Between Rhetoric and the UNFCCC's Detachment"; Nakate and Sirleaf, "Climate Crisis Is Already Here."

2   Mathews and Barnes, "Prognosis," 11.

3   Dean, "Executive on a Mission."

4   This story diverges a bit from the *New York Times'* account of Anderson's entrepreneurship, which claims that his idea for carpet tiles was a response to the needs of the "modern office" of the 1970s, which had lots of wires under the floor that needed to be moved around fairly regularly (Dean). His approach to sustainability focused on the materials used in the production of carpet tiles, especially the development of recyclable nylon, rather than the invention of carpet tiles themselves. Like most myths, of course, these details are less important than moral of the story.

5   Hellman, "Feeling Good and Financing Impact," 103.
6   Anderson, "Business Logic of Sustainability."
7   Barman, *Caring Capitalism*; Brittan, *Capitalism with a Human Face*; Shiller, *Finance and the Good Society*.
8   I later learned that Peter Singer once told the disability rights activist Harriet Johnson—to her face, apparently—that, as a disabled person, there was an argument for killing her as a baby. See Johnson, "Unspeakable Conversations."
9   Srinivasan, review of *Stop the Robot Apocalypse*.
10 Murray, "Quantifying the Burden of Disease," 429.
11 Srinivasan, review of *Stop the Robot Apocalypse*.
12 McGoey and Thiel, "Charismatic Violence."
13 Bostrom, "Existential Risk Prevention," 19.
14 Torres, "Dangerous Ideas."
15 Thanks to Leela Raina, Lin Yang, and Paul Hudson for giving this paragraph the economists' seal of approval.
16 Nordhaus, "Review of the Stern Review," 691. In general, I find Nordhaus's probabilistic approach to climate mitigation quite troubling. See Archer, "Stakes and Stakeholders in the Climate Casino."
17 Stoler, "Epistemic Politics," 350.
18 Karen Barad uses the term "onto-ethico-epistemology" to highlight the inseparability of ontology, ethics, and epistemology (*Meeting the Universe Halfway*).
19 Gegeo and Watson-Gegeo, "How We Know," 59.
20 Krenak, *Ideas to Postpone the End of the World*, 21.
21 Steeves, "Decolonizing the Past and Present," 62.
22 Gegeo and Watson-Gegeo, "How We Know."
23 Over the years, Maersk has won several awards for its corporate sustainability reporting.
24 Maersk, *2020 Sustainability Report*, 16.
25 Dyke, Knorr, and Watson, "Why Net Zero Policies Do More Harm than Good."
26 Horowitz, "Maersk Just Ordered 8 Carbon Neutral Ships."
27 Davis and Todd, "On the Importance of a Date," 766, 763; Lewis and Maslin, "Defining the Anthropocene."
28 Sharpe, *In the Wake*, 3.
29 Sharpe, 13–14.
30 Edensor, "Reconsidering National Temporalities."
31 For reference, a few milliseconds is about the same speed that human neurons process visual stimuli, according to Tovée, "Neuronal Processing." At ten milliseconds per trade, an investor could execute around eight trades every time a hummingbird flaps its wings.
32 Maguire, "Temporal Politics of Anthropogenic Earthquakes," 706.
33 Jones, "History of the New World," 40–43.
34 Jones, 38–40, 46.
35 Jones, 46.

36 Amadahy, *Moons of Palmares*, 140.
37 Leggatt, "Critiquing Economic and Environmental Colonization," 128.
38 Gegeo and Watson-Gegeo, "How We Know," 59.
39 Steeves, "Decolonizing the Past and Present"; Asokan, Yarime, and Onuki, "Review of Data-Intensive Approaches for Sustainability," 966.
40 Whyte, Caldwell, and Schaefer, "Indigenous Lessons about Sustainability."
41 Sène, "Against Wildlife Republics."
42 Whyte, Caldwell, and Schaefer, "Indigenous Lessons about Sustainability," 174–75.
43 Jones, "History of the New World," 40; Sanders, "When All This World Is on Fire."
44 S. Ortiz, *Men on the Moon*, 192.
45 K. Whyte, "Indigenous Science (Fiction) for the Anthropocene," 230–31; Krech, *Ecological Indian*; Seymour, *Bad Environmentalism*.
46 TallBear, "Shepard Krech's *The Ecological Indian*," 2.
47 Dillon, "Imagining Indigenous Futurisms," 8–9.
48 Günel, "Business," 61.
49 Ørsted, "Let's Create a World."
50 Indigenous Environmental Network, "Indigenous Resistance against Carbon."
51 Renner, "How Indigenous Pipeline Resistance."
52 Driskill, "Doubleweaving Two-Spirit Critiques"; Seymour, *Bad Environmentalism*; Crenshaw, "Demarginalizing the Intersection"; Gaard, "Toward a Queer Ecofeminism."
53 Roane et al., "Seeds of a Different World," 136.
54 Powell, "Down by the River," 38; Driskill, "Doubleweaving Two-Spirit Critiques"; Powell, "Rhetorics of Survivance"; Vizenor, *Survivance*.
55 Shahani, "If Not This, What?," 83.
56 Dillon, introduction to "Custer on the Slipstream," in *Walking the Clouds*, 16–17.

CONCLUSION

1 González, "Building Capacity in Africa."
2 Merry, *Seductions of Quantification*.
3 Citi, "There's a New 'S' in ESG. Security."
4 TallBear and Willey, "Critical Relationality," 5.
5 Checker, *Sustainability Myth*, 7.
6 brown, *Emergent Strategy*, 8. I am grateful to Alice Grandoit-Sutka for introducing me to brown's work.
7 Greenberg, "Situating Sustainability in the Luxury City."
8 brown, *Emergent Strategy*, 41.
9 Dockry et al., "Sustainable Development Education, Practice, and Research."

BIBLIOGRAPHY

Adler, Paul S., and Seok-Woo Kwon. "Social Capital: Prospects for a New Concept." *Academy of Management Review* 27, no. 1 (2002): 17–40.

Agyeman, Julian, Robert Doyle Bullard, and Bob Evans. *Just Sustainabilities: Development in an Unequal World.* Cambridge, MA: MIT Press, 2003.

Ahmed, Sara. *The Cultural Politics of Emotion.* New York: Routledge, 2013.

Alfred, Taiaiake. "Sovereignty." In *A Companion to American Indian History*, edited by Philip J. Deloria and Neal Salisbury, 460–74. Malden, MA: Wiley-Blackwell, 2002.

Amadahy, Zainab. *Moons of Palmares.* N.p.: Future History Press, 2013.

Ambec, Stefan, and Paul Lanoie. "Does It Pay to Be Green? A Systematic Overview." *Academy of Management Perspectives* 22, no. 2 (2008): 45–62.

Anderson, Ray. "The Business Logic of Sustainability." TED Talk, YouTube, May 18, 2009. www.youtube.com/watch?v=iP9QF_lBOyA.

Appadurai, Arjun, ed. *The Social Life of Things: Commodities in Cultural Perspective.* Cambridge: Cambridge University Press, 1986.

Archer, Matthew. "How to Govern a Sustainable Supply Chain: Standards, Standardizers, and the Political Ecology of (In)advertence." *Environment and Planning E: Nature and Space* 5, no. 2 (2022): 881–900.

———. "Imagining Impact in Global Supply Chains: Data-Driven Sustainability and the Production of Surveillable Space." *Surveillance & Society* 19, no. 3 (2021): 282–98. https://doi.org/10.24908/ss.v19i3.14256.

———. "Navigating the Sustainability Landscape: Impact Pathways and the Sustainability Ethic as Moral Compass." *Focaal* 91 (2021): 85–99.

———. "Stakes and Stakeholders in the Climate Casino." *GeoHumanities* 6, no. 1 (2020): 171–87.

Arrow, Kenneth J. "Observations on Social Capital." *Social Capital: A Multifaceted Perspective* 6 (2000): 3–5.

Asokan, Vivek Anand, Masaru Yarime, and Motoharu Onuki. "A Review of Data-Intensive Approaches for Sustainability: Methodology, Epistemology, Normativity, and Ontology." *Sustainability Science* 15, no. 3 (May 1, 2020): 955–74. https://doi.org/10.1007/s11625-019-00759-9.

Atal, Maha Rafi. "The Janus Faces of Silicon Valley." *Review of International Political Economy* 28, no. 2 (2020): 336–50.

Bachram, Heidi. "Climate Fraud and Carbon Colonialism: The New Trade in Greenhouse Gases." *Capitalism Nature Socialism*, May 23, 2006. https://doi.org/10.1080/10455750420000287299.

Barad, Karen. *Meeting the Universe Halfway: Quantum Physics and the Entanglement of Matter and Meaning*. Durham, NC: Duke University Press, 2007.

Barman, Emily. *Caring Capitalism: The Meaning and Measure of Social Value*. Cambridge: Cambridge University Press, 2016.

Barry, Andrew. "The Anti-Political Economy." *Economy and Society* 31, no. 2 (2002): 268–84.

Bauer, Hans, and Warren J. Blackman. *Swiss Banking: An Analytical History*. New York: St. Martin's, 1998.

Benson, Peter, and Stuart Kirsch. "Corporate Oxymorons." *Dialectical Anthropology* 34, no. 1 (2010): 45–48.

Bereola, Abigail. "A True Utopia: An Interview with N.K. Jemisin." *Paris Review*, December 3, 2018. www.theparisreview.org.

Berndt, Christian, and Manuel Wirth. "Market, Metrics, Morals: The Social Impact Bond as an Emerging Social Policy Instrument." *Geoforum* 90 (2018): 27–35.

Blaikie, Piers. *The Political Economy of Soil Erosion in Developing Countries*. New York: Routledge, 2016.

Blühdorn, Ingolfur. "The Governance of Unsustainability: Ecology and Democracy after the Post-Democratic Turn." *Environmental Politics* 22, no. 1 (2013): 16–36.

Bluwstein, Jevgeniy, Jens Friis Lund, Kelly Askew, Howard Stein, Christine Noe, Rie Odgaard, Faustin Maganga, and Linda Engström. "Between Dependence and Deprivation: The Interlocking Nature of Land Alienation in Tanzania." *Journal of Agrarian Change* 18, no. 4 (2018): 806–30.

Bocci, Paolo. "Tangles of Care: Killing Goats to Save Tortoises on the Galápagos Islands." *Cultural Anthropology* 32, no. 3 (2017): 424–49.

Bodley, John. *Victims of Progress*. San Francisco: Cummings, 1975.

Bohannan, Paul. "Some Principles of Exchange and Investment among the Tiv." *American Anthropologist* 57, no. 1 (1955): 60–70.

Bohannan, Paul, and Laura Bohannan. *Tiv Economy*. Evanston, IL: Northwestern University Press, 1968.

Bookchin, Murray. *Toward an Ecological Society*. Montreal: Black Rose Books, 1980.

Bostrom, Nick. "Existential Risk Prevention as Global Priority." *Global Policy* 4, no. 1 (2013): 15–31.

Bracking, Sarah. "Financialisation, Climate Finance, and the Calculative Challenges of Managing Environmental Change." *Antipode* 51, no. 3 (2019): 709–29.

Brittan, Samuel. *Capitalism with a Human Face*. Cambridge, MA: Harvard University Press, 1996.

brown, adrienne maree. *Emergent Strategy: Shaping Change, Changing Worlds*. Chico, CA: AK Press, 2017.

Butler, Judith. *Frames of War: When Is Life Grievable?* New York: Verso, 2016.

———. *Precarious Life: The Powers of Mourning and Violence*. New York: Verso, 2004.

Butler, Octavia. *Parable of the Sower*. New York: Warner Books, 2000.

———. *Parable of the Talents*. New York: Seven Stories, 2000.

Calderon, Gabriel Castilloux. "Andwànikàdjigan." In *Love after the End: An Anthology of Two-Spirit and Indigiqueer Speculative Fiction*, edited by Joshua Whitehead, 95–112. Vancouver: Arsenal Pulp, 2020.

Callon, Michel. "Performativity, Misfires and Politics." *Journal of Cultural Economy* 3, no. 2 (2010): 163–69.

Calvão, Filipe, and Matthew Archer. "Digital Extraction: Blockchain Traceability in Mineral Supply Chains." *Political Geography* 87 (2021): 102381.

Cameron, Emilie, Rebecca Mearns, and Janet Tamalik McGrath. "Translating Climate Change: Adaptation, Resilience, and Climate Politics in Nunavut, Canada." *Annals of the Association of American Geographers* 105, no. 2 (2015): 274–83.

Cashore, Benjamin. "Legitimacy and the Privatization of Environmental Governance: How Non-State Market-Driven (NSMD) Governance Systems Gain Rule-Making Authority." *Governance: An International Journal of Policy, Administration, and Institutions* 15, no. 4 (2002): 503–29.

Cavale, Siddharth. "Unilever Denies Reports That Its Tea Business Is Up for Sale." Reuters, November 25, 2019, sec. Deals. www.reuters.com.

Cavanagh, Connor Joseph, and Tor A. Benjaminsen. "Political Ecology, Variegated Green Economies, and the Foreclosure of Alternative Sustainabilities." *Journal of Political Ecology* 24, no. 1 (September 27, 2017). https://doi.org/10.2458/v24i1.20800.

Checker, Melissa. *The Sustainability Myth: Environmental Gentrification and the Politics of Justice.* New York: New York University Press, 2020.

Chossière, Guillaume P., Robert Malina, Florian Allroggen, Sebastian D. Eastham, Raymond L. Speth, and Steven R. H. Barrett. "Country- and Manufacturer-Level Attribution of Air Quality Impacts Due to Excess NOx Emissions from Diesel Passenger Vehicles in Europe." *Atmospheric Environment* 189 (2018): 89–97.

Choy, Tim. *Ecologies of Comparison: An Ethnography of Endangerment in Hong Kong.* Durham, NC: Duke University Press, 2011.

Christophers, Brett. "Environmental Beta or How Institutional Investors Think about Climate Change and Fossil Fuel Risk." *Annals of the American Association of Geographers* 109, no. 3 (2019): 754–74.

Citi [@Citi]. "'There's a New "S" in ESG. Security.' CEO Jane Fraser Shares Her Views on the Global Outlook at @MilkenInstitute #MIGlobal. Learn More: https://T.Co/QstXRmOppb." Twitter, May 6, 2022. https://twitter.com/Citi/status/1522578192741064710.

Coleman, James S. "Social Capital in the Creation of Human Capital." *American Journal of Sociology* 94 (1988): S95–120.

Cooper, Mark H. "Measure for Measure? Commensuration, Commodification, and Metrology in Emissions Markets and Beyond." *Environment and Planning A* 47, no. 9 (2015): 1787–1804.

Crenshaw, Kimberlé. "Demarginalizing the Intersection of Race and Sex: A Black Feminist Critique of Antidiscrimination Doctrine, Feminist Theory and Antiracist Politics." *University of Chicago Legal Forum*, 1989, 139–68.

Dal Maso, Giulia. *Risky Expertise in Chinese Financialisation: Returned Labour and the State-Finance Nexus*. Singapore: Springer, 2020.

Davis, Heather, and Zoe Todd. "On the Importance of a Date, or Decolonizing the Anthropocene. *ACME: An International Journal for Critical Geographies* 16, no. 4 (2017): 761–80.

Dean, Cornelia. "Executive on a Mission: Saving the Planet." *New York Times*, May 22, 2007, sec. Science. www.nytimes.com.

De Bakker, Frank G. A., Andreas Rasche, and Stefano Ponte. "Multi-Stakeholder Initiatives on Sustainability: A Cross-Disciplinary Review and Research Agenda for Business Ethics." *Business Ethics Quarterly* 29, no. 3 (2019): 343–83.

Desrosières, Alain. *The Politics of Large Numbers: A History of Statistical Reasoning*. Cambridge, MA: Harvard University Press, 1998.

Dhillon, Jaskiran. "Introduction: Indigenous Resurgence, Decolonization, and Movements for Environmental Justice." *Environment and Society* 9, no. 1 (2018): 1–5.

Dietz, Thomas, and Janina Grabs. "Additionality and Implementation Gaps in Voluntary Sustainability Standards." *New Political Economy* 27, no. 2 (2022): 203–24.

Dillon, Grace L. "Imagining Indigenous Futurisms." In *Walking the Clouds: An Anthology of Indigenous Science Fiction*, edited by Grace L. Dillon, 1–12. Tucson: University of Arizona Press, 2012.

———, ed. *Walking the Clouds: An Anthology of Indigenous Science Fiction*. Tucson: University of Arizona Press, 2012.

Dockry, Michael J., Katherine Hall, William Van Lopik, and Christopher M. Caldwell. "Sustainable Development Education, Practice, and Research: An Indigenous Model of Sustainable Development at the College of Menominee Nation, Keshena, WI, USA." *Sustainability Science* 11, no. 1 (2016): 127–38.

Dolan, Catherine, and John Humphrey. "Changing Governance Patterns in the Trade in Fresh Vegetables between Africa and the United Kingdom." *Environment and Planning A* 36, no. 3 (2004): 491–509.

Douglas, Mary. *Purity and Danger: An Analysis of Concepts of Pollution and Taboo*. New York: Routledge, 2003.

Douglas-Jones, Rachel, Antonia Walford, and Nick Seaver. "Introduction: Towards an Anthropology of Data." *Journal of the Royal Anthropological Institute* 27 (2021): 9–25.

Dove, Michael R. "Theories of Swidden Agriculture, and the Political Economy of Ignorance." *Agroforestry Systems* 1, no. 2 (1983): 85–99.

Driskill, Qwo-Li. "Doubleweaving Two-Spirit Critiques: Building Alliances between Native and Queer Studies." *GLQ: A Journal of Lesbian and Gay Studies* 16, nos. 1–2 (2010): 69–92.

Dunlap, Alexander. "The 'Solution' Is Now the 'Problem:' Wind Energy, Colonisation and the 'Genocide-Ecocide Nexus' in the Isthmus of Tehuantepec, Oaxaca." *International Journal of Human Rights* 22, no. 4 (2018): 550–73.

Duranti, Alessandro. "Husserl, Intersubjectivity and Anthropology." *Anthropological Theory* 10, nos. 1–2 (2010): 16–35.

Dyke, James G., Wolfgang Knorr, and Robert Watson. "Why Net Zero Policies Do More Harm than Good." In *Negotiating Climate Change in Crisis*, edited by Steffen Böhm and Sian Sullivan, 39–52. Cambridge, UK: Open Book, 2021.

Dyllick, Thomas, and Kai Hockerts. "Beyond the Business Case for Corporate Sustainability." *Business Strategy and the Environment* 11, no. 2 (2002): 130–41.

Eccles, Robert G., Linda-Eling Lee, and Judith C. Stroehle. "The Social Origins of ESG: An Analysis of Innovest and KLD." *Organization & Environment* 33, no. 4 (2020): 575–96.

Edensor, Tim. "Reconsidering National Temporalities: Institutional Times, Everyday Routines, Serial Spaces and Synchronicities." *European Journal of Social Theory* 9, no. 4 (2006): 525–45.

Eisenberg, Eric M. "Ambiguity as Strategy in Organizational Communication." *Communication Monographs* 51, no. 3 (1984): 227–42.

Enfield, N. J. *The Utility of Meaning: What Words Mean and Why*. Oxford: Oxford University Press, 2015.

Ergene, Seray, Subhabrata Bobby Banerjee, and Andrew J. Hoffman. "(Un)Sustainability and Organization Studies: Towards a Radical Engagement." *Organization Studies* 42, no. 8 (2021): 1319–35.

Escobar, Arturo. *Designs for the Pluriverse*. Durham, NC: Duke University Press, 2018.

———. *Encountering Development: The Making and Unmaking of the Third World*. Princeton, NJ: Princeton University Press, 1995.

Espeland, Wendy Nelson, and Mitchell L. Stevens. "Commensuration as a Social Process." *Annual Review of Sociology* 24, no. 1 (1998): 313–43.

EY. "Why Sustainability and ESG Are as Important as Ever." June 12, 2020. www.ey.com.

Ferguson, James. *The Anti-Politics Machine: "Development," Depoliticization, and Bureaucratic Power in Lesotho*. Minneapolis: University of Minnesota Press, 1994.

Fletcher, Robert. "Neoliberal Environmentality: Towards a Poststructuralist Political Ecology of the Conservation Debate." *Conservation and Society* 8, no. 3 (2010): 171–81.

Fortin, Elizabeth. "Repoliticising Multi-Stakeholder Standards Processes: The Roundtable on Sustainable Biomaterials' Standards and Certification Scheme." *Journal of Peasant Studies* 45, no. 4 (2018): 805–24.

———. "Transnational Multi-Stakeholder Sustainability Standards and Biofuels: Understanding Standards Processes." *Journal of Peasant Studies* 40, no. 3 (2013): 563–87.

Foster, John Bellamy, Brett Clark, and Richard York. *The Ecological Rift: Capitalism's War on the Earth*. New York: Monthly Review Press, 2010.

Fouilleux, Eve, and Allison Loconto. "Voluntary Standards, Certification, and Accreditation in the Global Organic Agriculture Field: A Tripartite Model of Techno-Politics." *Agriculture and Human Values* 34, no. 1 (2017): 1–14.

Fourcade, Marion. "Ordinal Citizenship." *British Journal of Sociology* 72, no. 2 (2021): 154–73.

Fourcade, Marion, and Kieran Healy. "Seeing like a Market." *Socio-Economic Review* 15, no. 1 (2017): 9–29.

Freeman, R. Edward. *Strategic Management: A Stakeholder Approach*. Cambridge: Cambridge University Press, 2010.

Freidberg, Susanne. "Assembled but Unrehearsed: Corporate Food Power and the 'Dance' of Supply Chain Sustainability." *Journal of Peasant Studies* 47, no. 2 (2020): 383–400.

———. "Calculating Sustainability in Supply Chain Capitalism." *Economy and Society* 42, no. 4 (2013): 571–96.

———. "Footprint Technopolitics." *Geoforum* 55 (2014): 178–89.

———. *French Beans and Food Scares: Culture and Commerce in an Anxious Age*. Oxford: Oxford University Press, 2004.

Gaard, Greta. "Toward a Queer Ecofeminism." *Hypatia* 12, no. 1 (1997): 114–37.

Gardner, Toby A., Magnus Benzie, Jan Börner, Elena Dawkins, Stephen Fick, Rachael Garrett, Javier Godar, A. Grimard, Sarah Lake, and Rasmus K. Larsen. "Transparency and Sustainability in Global Commodity Supply Chains." *World Development* 121 (2019): 163–77.

Garsten, Christina, and Adrienne Sörbom. "Small Places, Big Stakes: Meetings as Moments of Ethnographic Momentum." In *Meeting Ethnography: Meetings as Key Technologies of Ethnographic Momentum*, edited by Jen Sandler and Renita Thedvall, 126–42. New York: Routledge, 2017.

———. "Values Aligned: The Organization of Conflicting Values within the World Economic Forum." In *Configuring Value Conflicts in Markets*, edited by Susanna Alexius and Kristina Tamm Hallström, 159–77. Cheltenham, UK: Edward Elgar, 2014.

Gegeo, David Welchman, and Karen Ann Watson-Gegeo. "'How We Know': Kwara'ae Rural Villagers Doing Indigenous Epistemology." *Contemporary Pacific* 13, no. 1 (2001): 55–88.

Gilbert, Jacqueline Elyse, Tamra Gilbertson, and Line J. Jakobsen. "Incommensurability and Corporate Social Technologies: A Critique of Corporate Compensations in Colombia's Coal Mining Region of La Guajira." *Journal of Political Ecology* 28, no. 1 (2021): 434–52.

Gilmore, Ruth Wilson. *Abolition Geography: Essays towards Liberation*. New York: Verso, 2022.

Goldstein, Jesse. "Appropriate Technocracies? Green Capitalist Discourses and Post Capitalist Desires." *Capitalism Nature Socialism* 24, no. 1 (2013): 26–34.

———. *Planetary Improvement: Cleantech Entrepreneurship and the Contradictions of Green Capitalism*. Cambridge, MA: MIT Press, 2018.

González, Arancha. "Building Capacity in Africa to Facilitate Integration into Global Value Chains: Contributions from the ITC." In *African Perspectives on Trade and the WTO: Domestic Reforms, Structural Transformation and Global Economic Integration*, edited by Chiedu Osakwe, Maika Oshikawa, and Patrick Low, 43–51. Cambridge: Cambridge University Press, 2016.

Graeber, David. "It Is Value That Brings Universes into Being." *HAU: Journal of Ethnographic Theory* 3, no. 2 (2013): 219–43.

———. *Toward an Anthropological Theory of Value: The False Coin of Our Own Dreams*. New York: Palgrave, 2001.

Greenberg, Miriam. "Situating Sustainability in the Luxury City." In *Sustainability: Approaches to Environmental Justice and Social Power*, edited by Julie Sze, 180–95. New York: New York University Press, 2018.

Günel, Gökçe. "Business." In *Anthropocene Unseen: A Lexicon*, edited by Cymene Howe and Anand Pandian, 59–62. Santa Barbara, CA: Punctum Books, 2020.

———. *Spaceship in the Desert: Energy, Climate Change, and Urban Design in Abu Dhabi*. Durham, NC: Duke University Press, 2019.

Halpern, David. *Social Capital*. Cambridge, UK: Polity, 2005.

Harvey, David. *A Brief History of Neoliberalism*. New York: Oxford University Press, 2007.

Hébert, Karen. "Chronicle of a Disaster Foretold: Scientific Risk Assessment, Public Participation, and the Politics of Imperilment in Bristol Bay, Alaska." *Journal of the Royal Anthropological Institute* 22, no. S1 (2016): 108–26.

Heede, Richard. "Tracing Anthropogenic Carbon Dioxide and Methane Emissions to Fossil Fuel and Cement Producers, 1854–2010." *Climatic Change* 122, no. 1 (2014): 229–41.

Helgesson, Claes-Fredrik, and Fabian Muniesa. "Valuation Is Work." *Valuation Studies* 2, no. 1 (May 26, 2014): 1–4. https://doi.org/10.3384/vs.2001-5992.14211.

Hellman, Jacob. "Feeling Good and Financing Impact." *Historical Social Research / Historische Sozialforschung* 45, no. 3 (2020): 95–116.

Hertz, Ellen. *The Trading Crowd: An Ethnography of the Shanghai Stock Market*. Cambridge: Cambridge University Press, 1998.

Hobart, Mark. "Introduction: The Growth of Ignorance?" In *An Anthropological Critique of Development: The Growth of Ignorance*, edited by Mark Hobart, 1–30. London: Routledge, 1993.

Horowitz, Julia. "Maersk Just Ordered 8 Carbon Neutral Ships. Now It Needs Green Fuel." CNN, August 24, 2021. www.cnn.com.

Indigenous Environmental Network. "Indigenous Resistance against Carbon." Washington, DC: Oil Change International, August 2021.

ITC. "The State of Sustainable Markets 2018: Statistics and Emerging Trends." Geneva: International Trade Center, September 30, 2018.

Jacka, Jerry K. *Alchemy in the Rain Forest: Politics, Ecology, and Resilience in a New Guinea Mining Area*. Durham, NC: Duke University Press, 2015.

Jackman, Robert W., and Ross A. Miller. "Social Capital and Politics." *Annual Review of Political Science* 1, no. 1 (1998): 47–73.

Jaffe, Adam B., Richard G. Newell, and Robert N. Stavins. "A Tale of Two Market Failures: Technology and Environmental Policy." *Ecological Economics* 54, nos. 2–3 (2005): 164–74.

Jaffee, Daniel, and Philip H. Howard. "Corporate Cooptation of Organic and Fair Trade Standards." *Agriculture and Human Values* 27, no. 4 (2010): 387–99.

Jemisin, N. K. "The Ones Who Stay and Fight." In *How Long 'til Black Future Month?* New York: Orbit, 2018. ebook.

Johnson, Harriet McBryde. "Unspeakable Conversations." *New York Times*, February 16, 2003, sec. Magazine. www.nytimes.com.

Jones, Adam Garnet. "History of the New World." In *Love after the End: An Anthology of Two-Spirit and Indigiqueer Speculative Fiction*, edited by Joshua Whitehead, 35–60. Vancouver: Arsenal Pulp, 2020.

Keane, Webb. "Semiotics and the Social Analysis of Material Things." *Language & Communication* 23, nos. 3–4 (2003): 409–25.

King, Tiffany Lethabo, Jenell Navarro, and Andrea Smith. *Otherwise Worlds: Against Settler Colonialism and Anti-Blackness*. Durham, NC: Duke University Press, 2020.

Kockelman, Paul. *Agent, Person, Subject, Self: A Theory of Ontology, Interaction, and Infrastructure*. Oxford: Oxford University Press, 2012.

———. *The Chicken and the Quetzal: Incommensurate Ontologies and Portable Values in Guatemala's Cloud Forest*. Durham, NC: Duke University Press, 2016.

———. "Grading, Gradients, Degradation, Grace: Part 1: Intensity and Causality." *HAU: Journal of Ethnographic Theory* 6, no. 2 (2016): 389–423.

———. "A Semiotic Ontology of the Commodity." *Journal of Linguistic Anthropology* 16, no. 1 (2006): 76–102.

Kopytoff, Igor. "The Cultural Biography of Things: Commoditization as Process." In *The Social Life of Things: Commodities in Cultural Perspective*, edited by Arjun Appadurai, 64–91. Cambridge: Cambridge University Press, 1986.

Krech, Shepard. *The Ecological Indian: Myth and History*. New York: Norton, 1999.

Krenak, Ailton. *Ideas to Postpone the End of the World*. Toronto: House of Anansi Press, 2020.

Kurunmäki, Liisa, Andrea Mennicken, and Peter Miller. "Quantifying, Economising, and Marketising: Democratising the Social Sphere?" *Sociologie du Travail* 58, no. 4 (2016): 390–402. Page numbers cited in notes refer to preprint version accessed at LSE Research Online, https://eprints.lse.ac.uk.

Lafargue-Molina, Pedro. "Marker Development for the Traceability of Certified Sustainably Produced Cacao." University of the West of England, 2021. https://uwe-repository.worktribe.com.

Larner, Wendy, and Nina Laurie. "Travelling Technocrats, Embodied Knowledges: Globalising Privatisation in Telecoms and Water." *Geoforum* 41, no. 2 (2010): 218–26.

LeBaron, Genevieve, and Jane Lister. "The Hidden Costs of Global Supply Chain Solutions." *Review of International Political Economy* 29, no. 3 (2021): 669–95.

Leggatt, Judith. "Critiquing Economic and Environmental Colonization: Globalization and Science Fiction in *The Moons of Palmares*." In *Science Fiction, Imperialism, and the Third World: Essays on Postcolonial Literature and Film*, edited by Ericka Hoagland and Reema Sarwal, 127–40. Jefferson, NC: McFarland, 2010.

Le Guin, Ursula K. *The Books of Earthsea: The Complete Illustrated Edition*. New York: Hachette, 2018.

———. "The Ones Who Walk Away from Omelas." In *The Wind's Twelve Quarters*, 151–59. New York: Bantam Books, 1976.

Leins, Stefan. "Narrative Authority: Rethinking Speculation and the Construction of Economic Expertise." *Ethnos* 87, no. 2 (2022): 347–64.

———. *Stories of Capitalism: Inside the Role of Financial Analysts.* Chicago: University of Chicago Press, 2018.

Lévi-Strauss, Claude. *The Savage Mind.* Chicago: University of Chicago Press, 1966.

Lewis, Simon, and Mark Maslin. "Defining the Anthropocene." *Nature* 519 (2015): 171–80.

Lezaun, Javier, and Fabian Muniesa. "Twilight in the Leadership Playground: Subrealism and the Training of the Business Self." *Journal of Cultural Economy* 10, no. 3 (2017): 265–79.

Li, Fabiana. "Engineering Responsibility: Environmental Mitigation and the Limits of Commensuration in a Chilean Mining Project." *Focaal* 60 (2011): 61–73.

Li, Tania Murray. *The Will to Improve: Governmentality, Development, and the Practice of Politics.* Durham, NC: Duke University Press, 2007.

Little, Peter C. *Toxic Town: IBM, Pollution, and Industrial Risks.* New York: New York University Press, 2014.

Loconto, Allison. "Sustainably Performed: Reconciling Global Value Chain Governance and Performativity." *Journal of Rural Social Sciences* 25, no. 3 (2010): 193–225.

Loftus, Alex. *Everyday Environmentalism: Creating an Urban Political Ecology.* Minneapolis: University of Minnesota Press, 2012.

MacKenzie, Donald. *An Engine, Not a Camera: How Financial Models Shape Markets.* Cambridge, MA: MIT Press, 2008.

Maersk. *2020 Sustainability Report.* Copenhagen: A.P. Moller-Maersk A/S, 2021.

Maguire, James. "The Temporal Politics of Anthropogenic Earthquakes: Acceleration, Anticipation, and Energy Extraction in Iceland." *Time & Society* 29, no. 3 (2020): 704–26.

Mair, Simon, Aled Jones, Jonathan Ward, Ian Christie, Angela Druckman, and Fergus Lyon. "A Critical Review of the Role of Indicators in Implementing the Sustainable Development Goals." In *Handbook of Sustainability Science and Research*, edited by Walter Leal Filho, 41–56. Cham, Switzerland: Springer, 2018.

Malkki, Liisa H. *The Need to Help: The Domestic Arts of International Humanitarianism.* Durham, NC: Duke University Press, 2015.

Martin-Booran Mirraboopa, Karen. "Ways of Knowing, Being and Doing: A Theoretical Framework and Methods for Indigenous and Indigenist Re-Search." *Journal of Australian Studies* 27, no. 76 (2003): 203–14.

Martinez-Alier, Joan. *The Environmentalism of the Poor: A Study of Ecological Conflicts and Valuation.* Cheltenham, UK: Edward Elgar, 2003.

Marx, Leo. *The Machine in the Garden: Technology and the Pastoral Ideal in America.* Oxford: Oxford University Press, 1964.

Mathews, Andrew S., and Jessica Barnes. "Prognosis: Visions of Environmental Futures." *Journal of the Royal Anthropological Institute* 22, no. S1 (2016): 9–26.

McElwee, Pamela. "The Metrics of Making Ecosystem Services." *Environment and Society* 8 (2017): 96–121.

McGoey, Linsey, and Darren Thiel. "Charismatic Violence and the Sanctification of the Super-Rich." *Economy and Society* 47, no. 1 (2018): 111–34.

McKinsey. "Why ESG Scores Are Here to Stay." May 26, 2020. www.mckinsey.com.

Medby, Ingrid A., and Pip Thornton. "More than Words: Geopolitics and Language." *Area* 55, no. 1 (2023): 2–9.

Mennicken, Andrea, and Peter Miller. "Accounting, Territorialization and Power." *Foucault Studies* 13 (2012): 4–24.

Merry, Sally Engle. *The Seductions of Quantification: Measuring Human Rights, Gender Violence, and Sex Trafficking.* Chicago: University of Chicago Press, 2016.

Milkoreit, Manjana. "Imaginary Politics: Climate Change and Making the Future." *Elementa: Science of the Anthropocene* 5, no. 62 (2017): 1–18. https://doi.org/10.1525/elementa.249.

Miller, Ethan. *Reimagining Livelihoods: Life beyond Economy, Society, and Environment.* Minneapolis: University of Minnesota Press, 2019.

Milne, Markus J., and Rob Gray. "W(h)ither Ecology? The Triple Bottom Line, the Global Reporting Initiative, and Corporate Sustainability Reporting." *Journal of Business Ethics* 118, no. 1 (2013): 13–29.

Moore, Jason. *Capitalism in the Web of Life: Ecology and the Accumulation of Capital.* New York: Verso, 2015.

Mosse, David. *Cultivating Development: An Ethnography of Aid Policy and Practice.* London: Pluto, 2005.

Murray, Christopher J. "Quantifying the Burden of Disease: The Technical Basis for Disability-Adjusted Life Years." *Bulletin of the World Health Organization* 72, no. 3 (1994): 429–45.

Mwita, Martin. "Boost to Tea Farmers as KTDA Increases Producer Prices." *The Star,* August 23, 2021. www.the-star.co.ke.

Nader, Laura. "Up the Anthropologist: Perspectives Gained from Studying Up." Washington, DC: ERIC Clearinghouse, 1972.

Nakate, Vanessa, and Ellen Johnson Sirleaf. "The Climate Crisis Is Already Here: Why We Must Listen to Voices in the Global South." The Elders, May 1, 2020. https://theelders.org.

Noe, Christine. "Spatiality and 'Borderlessness' in Transfrontier Conservation Areas." *South African Geographical Journal = Suid-Afrikaanse Geografiese Tydskrif* 92, no. 2 (2010): 144–59.

Nordhaus, William D. "A Review of the Stern Review on the Economics of Climate Change." *Journal of Economic Literature* 45, no. 3 (2007): 686–702.

Nyambura, Ruth. "In Between Rhetoric and the UNFCCC's Detachment from the Lived Realities of the People on the Frontlines of the Climate Crisis." *Development* 59, no. 3 (2016): 205–10.

Nyqvist, Anette. "The Corporation Performed: Minutes from the Rituals of Annual General Meetings." *Journal of Organizational Ethnography* 4 (2015): 341–55.

Odhiambo, Allan. "Unilever Sale Saga Stirs Kenya Tea Sector Ghosts." *Nation.Africa,* November 30, 2021, sec. Business Prime. https://nation.africa.

O'Leary, Michael, and Warren Valdmanis. "An ESG Reckoning Is Coming." *Harvard Business Review*, March 4, 2021.

O'Neill, John. *The Market: Ethics, Knowledge and Politics*. New York: Routledge, 1998.

———. "Markets, Ethics and Environment." In *The Oxford Handbook of Environmental Ethics*, edited by Stephen M. Gardiner and Allen Thompson, 40–50. Oxford: Oxford University Press, 2016.

Ørsted. "Let's Create a World That Runs Entirely on Green Energy." YouTube, November 9, 2017. www.youtube.com/watch?v=56MhjXTcSCg.

Orta, Andrew. "Commentary: Response to Karen Ho on Cultures of Capitalism, Contexts of Capitalism." *American Ethnologist* 41, no. 1 (2014): 38–39.

———. "Managing the Margins: MBA Training, International Business, and" the Value Chain of Culture." *American Ethnologist* 40, no. 4 (2013): 689–703.

Ortiz, Horacio. "Financial Value: Economic, Moral, Political, Global." *HAU: Journal of Ethnographic Theory* 3, no. 1 (2013): 64–79.

Ortiz, Simon. *Men on the Moon*. Tucson: University of Arizona Press, 1999.

Osterhoudt, Sarah, Shaila Seshia Galvin, Dana J. Graef, Alder Keleman Saxena, and Michael R. Dove. "Chains of Meaning: Crops, Commodities, and the 'In-Between' Spaces of Trade." *World Development* 135 (2020): 105070.

Ottinger, Gwen. *Refining Expertise: How Responsible Engineers Subvert Environmental Justice Challenges*. New York: New York University Press, 2013.

Paehlke, Robert C. *Democracy's Dilemma: Environment, Social Equity, and the Global Economy*. Cambridge, MA: MIT Press, 2004.

Paulson, Henry. "We Need a New Asset Class of Healthy Soils and Pollinators." *Financial Times*, September 8, 2020. www.ft.com.

Pearce, David William, and Jeremy J. Warford. *World without End: Economics, Environment, and Sustainable Development*. Oxford: Oxford University Press, 1993.

Pigg, Stacy Leigh. "Inventing Social Categories through Place: Social Representations and Development in Nepal." *Comparative Studies in Society and History* 34, no. 3 (1992): 491–513.

———. "Languages of Sex and AIDS in Nepal: Notes on the Social Production of Commensurability." *Cultural Anthropology* 16, no. 4 (2001): 481–541.

Plumwood, Val. "Belonging, Naming and Decolonisation." In *Habitus: A Sense of Place*, 2nd ed., edited by Jean Hiller and Emma Rooksby, 387–408. New York: Routledge, 2017.

Pollman, Elizabeth. "The Making and Meaning of ESG." University of Pennsylvania, Institute for Law & Economics Research Paper no. 22–23, 2022.

Ponte, Stefano. *Business, Power and Sustainability in a World of Global Value Chains*. London: Zed Books, 2019.

Ponte, Stefano, Peter Gibbon, and Jakob Vestergaard. *Governing through Standards: Origins, Drivers and Limitations*. Basingstoke, UK: Palgrave Macmillan, 2011.

Porter, Michael E., and Mark R. Kramer. "Creating Shared Value." *Harvard Business Review*, January–February 2011, 2–17.

Porter, Michael E., and Claas Van der Linde. "Toward a New Conception of the Environment-Competitiveness Relationship." *Journal of Economic Perspectives* 9, no. 4 (1995): 97–118.

Porter, Theodore M. *Trust in Numbers: The Pursuit of Objectivity in Science and Public Life*. Princeton, NJ: Princeton University Press, 1995.

Powell, Malea. "Down by the River, or How Susan La Flesche Picotte Can Teach Us about Alliance as a Practice of Survivance." *College English* 67, no. 1 (2004): 38–60.

———. "Rhetorics of Survivance: How American Indians Use Writing." *College Composition and Communication* 53, no. 3 (2002): 396–434.

Power, Michael. *The Audit Society: Rituals of Verification*. Oxford: Oxford University Press, 1997.

———. "How Accounting Begins: Object Formation and the Accretion of Infrastructure." *Accounting, Organizations and Society* 47 (2015): 43–55.

PRI. "Sustainable Markets." Accessed October 29, 2022. www.unpri.org.

Pucker, Kenneth P. "Overselling Sustainability Reporting." *Harvard Business Review* 99, no. 3 (2021): 134–43.

Pulido, Laura. "Geographies of Race and Ethnicity II: Environmental Racism, Racial Capitalism and State-Sanctioned Violence." *Progress in Human Geography* 41, no. 4 (2017): 524–33.

———. "Geographies of Race and Ethnicity III: Settler Colonialism and Nonnative People of Color." *Progress in Human Geography* 42, no. 2 (2018): 309–18.

Putnam, Robert. "Social Capital: Measurement and Consequences." *Canadian Journal of Policy Research* 2, no. 1 (2001): 41–51.

Rainforest Alliance. "Continuous Improvement and Smart Meters: Empowering Farmers to Be the Drivers of Their Success." New York and Amsterdam: Rainforest Alliance, July 2020. www.rainforest-alliance.org.

———. "Rainforest Alliance Sustainable Agriculture Standard: Supply Chain Requirements." New York and Amsterdam: Rainforest Alliance, January 31, 2022.

Rajak, Dinah. *In Good Company: An Anatomy of Corporate Social Responsibility*. Stanford, CA: Stanford University Press, 2011.

Ramirez, Jacobo. "Contentious Dynamics within the Social Turbulence of Environmental (in) Justice Surrounding Wind Energy Farms in Oaxaca, Mexico." *Journal of Business Ethics* 169, no. 3 (2021): 387–404.

Randle, Sayd, Lauren Baker, C. Anne Claus, Chris Hebdon, Alder Keleman, and Michael R. Dove. "Unsustainability in Action: An Ethnographic Examination." In *Routledge Handbook of Environmental Anthropology*, edited by Helen Kopnina and Eleanor Shoreman-Ouimet, 170–81. New York: Routledge, 2016.

Ravnbøl, Camilla Ida. "Patchwork Economies in Europe: Economic Strategies among Homeless Romanian Roma in Copenhagen." In *Constructing Roma Migrants: European Narratives and Local Governance*, edited by Tina Magazzini and Stefano Piemontese, 209–26. Cham, Switzerland: Springer, 2019.

Reese, Ashanté M. *Black Food Geographies: Race, Self-Reliance, and Food Access in Washington, DC*. Chapel Hill: University of North Carolina Press, 2019.

Reinert, Hugo. "Requiem for a Junk-Bird: Violence, Purity and the Wild." *Cultural Studies Review* 25, no. 1 (2019): 29–40. https://doi.org/10.5130/csr.v25i1.6387.

Renner, Serena. "How Indigenous Pipeline Resistance Keeps Emissions in the Ground." *CBC News*, December 2, 2021. www.cbc.ca.

Roane, J. T., Megan Femi-Cole, Preeti Nayak, and Eve Tuck. "'The Seeds of a Different World Are Already Alive in the Everyday Practices of Ordinary Black and Indigenous People': An Interview with JT Roane." *Curriculum Inquiry* 52, no. 2 (2022): 129–38.

Rocheleau, Dianne, and Robin Roth. "Rooted Networks, Relational Webs and Powers of Connection: Rethinking Human and Political Ecologies." *Geoforum* 3, no. 38 (2007): 433–37.

Rosa, Jonathan. *Looking like a Language, Sounding like a Race: Raciolinguistic Ideologies and the Learning of Latinidad*. Oxford: Oxford University Press, 2019.

Rotz, Sarah. "'They Took Our Beads, It Was a Fair Trade, Get over It': Settler Colonial Logics, Racial Hierarchies and Material Dominance in Canadian Agriculture." *Geoforum* 82 (2017): 158–69.

Roy, Ananya. "Ethical Subjects: Market Rule in an Age of Poverty." *Public Culture* 24, no. 1 (2012): 105–8.

Sadowski, Jathan, and Roy Bendor. "Selling Smartness: Corporate Narratives and the Smart City as a Sociotechnical Imaginary." *Science, Technology, & Human Values* 44, no. 3 (2019): 540–63.

Sanders, William. "When All This World Is on Fire." In *Walking the Clouds: An Anthology of Indigenous Science Fiction*, edited by Grace L. Dillon, 149–70. Tucson: University of Arizona Press, 2012.

Schaltegger, Stefan, and Marcus Wagner. "Managing and Measuring the Business Case for Sustainability: Capturing the Relationship between Sustainability Performance, Business Competitiveness and Economic Performance." In *Managing the Business Case for Sustainability: The Integration of Social, Environmental and Economic Performance*, edited by Stefan Schaltegger and Marcus Wagner, 1–27. New York: Routledge, 2017.

———, eds. *Managing the Business Case for Sustainability: The Integration of Social, Environmental and Economic Performance*. New York: Routledge, 2017.

Schipani, Andres, Judith Evans, and Kaye Wiggins. "How Unilever's Tea Business Became a Test of Private Equity's Conscience." *Financial Times*, February 16, 2022. www.ft.com.

Schneider, François, Giorgos Kallis, and Joan Martinez-Alier. "Crisis or Opportunity? Economic Degrowth for Social Equity and Ecological Sustainability: Introduction to This Special Issue." *Journal of Cleaner Production* 18, no. 6 (2010): 511–18.

Schwab, Klaus. *The Global Competitiveness Report 2019*. Geneva: World Economic Forum, 2019.

Scott, James C. *Seeing like a State: How Certain Schemes to Improve the Human Condition Have Failed*. New Haven, CT: Yale University Press, 1998.

Scrivens, Katherine, and Conal Smith. "Four Interpretations of Social Capital: An Agenda for Measurement." OECD, December 10, 2013. https://doi.org/10.1787/5jzbcx010wmt-en.

Sen, Debarati. *Everyday Sustainability: Gender Justice and Fair Trade Tea in Darjeeling.* Albany: SUNY Press, 2017.

Sène, Aby L. "Against Wildlife Republics." *The Republic* (blog), November 13, 2022. https://republic.com.ng.

Sène-Harper, Aby, and Moustapha Séye. "Community-Based Tourism around National Parks in Senegal: The Implications of Colonial Legacies in Current Management Policies." *Tourism Planning & Development* 16, no. 2 (March 4, 2019): 217–34. https://doi.org/10.1080/21568316.2018.1563804.

Seymour, Nicole. *Bad Environmentalism: Irony and Irreverence in the Ecological Age.* Minneapolis: University of Minnesota Press, 2018.

Shahani, Nishant. "'If Not This, What?': Time out of Joint and the Politics of Queer Utopia." *Extrapolation* 53, no. 1 (2012): 83–108.

Sharpe, Christina. *In the Wake: On Blackness and Being.* Durham, NC: Duke University Press, 2016.

Shiller, Robert J. *Finance and the Good Society.* Princeton, NJ: Princeton University Press, 2013.

Shore, Cris, and Susan Wright. "Governing by Numbers: Audit Culture, Rankings and the New World Order." *Social Anthropology* 23, no. 1 (2015): 22–28.

Sinclair, Rebekah. "Righting Names: The Importance of Native American Philosophies of Naming for Environmental Justice." *Environment and Society* 9, no. 1 (2018): 91–106.

Skalidou, Dafni. "In or Out? Exploring Selection Processes of Farmers in Cocoa Sustainability Standards and Certification Programmes in Ghana." PhD diss., University of East Anglia, 2018.

Souleles, Daniel. "How to Study People Who Do Not Want to Be Studied: Practical Reflections on Studying Up." *PoLAR: Political and Legal Anthropology Review* 41, no. S1 (2018): 51–68.

———. "How to Think about People Who Don't Want to Be Studied: Further Reflections on Studying Up." *Critique of Anthropology* 41, no. 3 (2021): 206–26.

Srinivasan, Amia. Review of *Stop the Robot Apocalypse*, by William MacAskill. *London Review of Books*, September 23, 2015. www.lrb.co.uk.

SSF (Swiss Sustainable Finance). "What Is Sustainable Finance." Accessed April 17, 2023. www.sustainablefinance.ch.

Steeves, Paulette F. "Decolonizing the Past and Present of the Western Hemisphere (the Americas)." *Archaeologies* 11, no. 1 (2015): 42–69.

Stiglitz, Joseph E. "Markets, Market Failures, and Development." *American Economic Review* 79, no. 2 (1989): 197–203.

Stoler, Ann Laura. "Epistemic Politics: Ontologies of Colonial Common Sense." *Philosophical Forum* 39, no. 3 (2008): 349–61.

Strange, Susan. *The Retreat of the State: The Diffusion of Power in the World Economy.* Cambridge: Cambridge University Press, 1996.

Sullivan, Sian. "Making Nature Investable: From Legibility to Leverageability in Fabricating 'Nature' as 'Natural Capital.'" *Science and Technology Studies* 31, no. 3 (2018): 47–76.

———. "On 'Natural Capital,' 'Fairy Tales' and Ideology." *Development and Change* 48, no. 2 (2017): 397–423.

———. "What's Ontology Got to Do with It? On Nature and Knowledge in a Political Ecology of the 'Green Economy.'" *Journal of Political Ecology* 24, no. 1 (2017): 217–42.

Sultana, Farhana. "Emotional Political Ecology." In *The International Handbook of Political Ecology*, edited by Raymond L. Bryant, 633–58. Cheltenham, UK: Edward Elgar, 2015.

———. "The Unbearable Heaviness of Climate Coloniality." *Political Geography* 99 (2022): 102638.

Sussman, Henry. *The Task of the Critic: Poetics, Philosophy, Religion*. New York: Fordham University Press, 2005.

Sze, Julie, Anne Rademacher, Tom Beamish, Liza Grandia, Jonathan London, Louis Warren, Beth Rose Middleton, and Mike Ziser. Introduction to *Sustainability: Approaches to Environmental Justice and Social Power*, edited by Julie Sze, 1–25. New York: New York University Press, 2018.

TallBear, Kim. "Shepard Krech's *The Ecological Indian*: One Indian's Perspective." *International Institute for Indigenous Resource Management [IIIRM] Publications* 30 (2000): 1–5.

TallBear, Kim, and Angela Willey. "Critical Relationality: Queer, Indigenous, and Multispecies Belonging beyond Settler Sex & Nature." *Imaginations: Journal of Cross-Cultural Image Studies* 10, no. 1 (2019): 5–15.

Taylor, Dorceta. *Toxic Communities: Environmental Racism, Industrial Pollution, and Residential Mobility*. New York: New York University Press, 2014.

Thylstrup, Nanna Bonde, Matthew Archer, and Louis Ravn. "Traceability." *Internet Policy Review* 11, no. 1 (2022): 1–12.

Ticktin, Miriam. *Casualties of Care: Immigration and the Politics of Humanitarianism in France*. Berkeley: University of California Press, 2011.

Todd, Zoe. "An Indigenous Feminist's Take on the Ontological Turn: 'Ontology' Is Just Another Word for Colonialism." *Journal of Historical Sociology* 29, no. 1 (2016): 4–22.

Torres, Émile P. "The Dangerous Ideas of 'Longtermism' and 'Existential Risk.'" *Current Affairs*, July 28, 2021. www.currentaffairs.org.

Tovée, Martin J. "Neuronal Processing: How Fast Is the Speed of Thought?" *Current Biology* 4, no. 12 (1994): 1125–27.

Tripathy, Aneil. "Translating to Risk: The Legibility of Climate Change and Nature in the Green Bond Market." *Economic Anthropology* 4, no. 2 (2017): 239–50.

Tsing, Anna. "Blasted Landscapes (and the Gentle Arts of Mushroom Picking)." In *The Multispecies Salon*, edited by Eben Kirksey, 87–110. Durham, NC: Duke University Press, 2014.

———. *The Mushroom at the End of the World: On the Possibility of Life in Capitalist Ruins*. Princeton, NJ: Princeton University Press.

———. "Supply Chains and the Human Condition." *Rethinking Marxism* 21, no. 2 (2009): 148–76.

Unilever. "Unilever to Sell Its Tea Business, Ekaterra, to CVC Capital Partners Fund VIII." November 18, 2021. www.unilever.com.

United Nations Global Compact (UNGC). "About the UN Global Compact." Accessed April 17, 2023. www.unglobalcompact.org.

———. *Who Cares Wins: Connecting Financial Markets to a Changing World*. Washington, DC: World Bank Group, 2004.

Van Der Ven, Hamish. "Gatekeeper Power: Understanding the Influence of Lead Firms over Transnational Sustainability Standards." *Review of International Political Economy* 25, no. 5 (2018): 624–46.

Van Dijck, José. "Datafication, Dataism and Dataveillance: Big Data between Scientific Paradigm and Ideology." *Surveillance & Society* 12, no. 2 (2014): 197–208.

Van Duuren, Emiel, Auke Plantinga, and Bert Scholtens. "ESG Integration and the Investment Management Process: Fundamental Investing Reinvented." *Journal of Business Ethics* 138, no. 3 (2016): 525–33.

Van Lente, Harro. "Imaginaries of Innovation." In *Handbook on Alternative Theories of Innovation*, edited by Benoît Godin, Gérald Gaglio, and Dominique Vinck, 23–36. Cheltenham, UK: Edward Elgar, 2021.

Vizenor, Gerald, ed. *Survivance: Narratives of Native Presence*. Lincoln: University of Nebraska Press, 2008.

Walter, Maggie, and Michele Suina. "Indigenous Data, Indigenous Methodologies and Indigenous Data Sovereignty." *International Journal of Social Research Methodology* 22, no. 3 (2019): 233–43.

Warner, Edmond. "Corporate Angels Need to Spread Their Wings." *The Guardian*, March 15, 2003, sec. Business. www.theguardian.com.

Welker, Marina A. "'Corporate Security Begins in the Community': Mining, the Corporate Social Responsibility Industry, and Environmental Advocacy in Indonesia." *Cultural Anthropology* 24, no. 1 (2009): 142–79.

———. *Enacting the Corporation: An American Mining Firm in Post-Authoritarian Indonesia*. Berkeley: University of California Press, 2014.

Welker, Marina A., Damani J. Partridge, and Rebecca Hardin. "Corporate Lives: New Perspectives on the Social Life of the Corporate Form: An Introduction to Supplement 3." *Current Anthropology* 52, no. S3 (2011): S3–16.

Whyte, David. *Ecocide: Kill the Corporation before It Kills Us*. Manchester: Manchester University Press, 2020.

Whyte, Kyle P. "Indigenous Science (Fiction) for the Anthropocene: Ancestral Dystopias and Fantasies of Climate Change Crises." *Environment and Planning E: Nature and Space* 1, nos. 1–2 (2018): 224–42.

Whyte, Kyle P., Chris Caldwell, and Marie Schaefer. "Indigenous Lessons about Sustainability Are Not Just for 'All Humanity.'" In *Sustainability: Approaches to*

Environmental Justice and Social Power, edited by Julie Sze, 149–79. New York: New York University Press, 2018.

Wiedmann, Thomas, Manfred Lenzen, Lorenz T. Keyßer, and Julia K. Steinberger. "Scientists' Warning on Affluence." *Nature Communications* 11, no. 1 (2020): 1–10.

Zelizer, Viviana A. *Pricing the Priceless Child: The Changing Social Value of Children.* Princeton, NJ: Princeton University Press, 1994.

Zigon, Jarrett. "Narratives." In *A Blackwell Companion to Moral Anthropology*, edited by Didier Fassin, 204–20. Malden, MA: Wiley-Blackwell, 2012.

INDEX

accountability, 15; through accounting, 4, 26–27; market-driven, 15, 109

accounting infrastructures, 72, 74, 80; accretion of, 74; and power, 7–8

accounting objects, 71–72

advertisements, 171–72, 188

Anderson, Ray, 170–72

Anthropocene: capitalocene, 23; start date, 181–83

apocalyptic storytelling, 187–92

automation, 87–88

bad environmentalism, 21, 147–50

benchmarking, 45, 59

biographical approach, 84–88, 99, 112–13, 195

Brundtland Report, 40, 171

bullshit, 75, 81, 94

business case for sustainability, 3, 36, 47–48, 50–53, 69–70, 80, 170, 198

Coleman, James, 68–71

commensuration/commensurability, 39–40, 43, 135–38; banality of, 178; and causality, 51–52; and comparison, 45–48, 51–52; of different values, 127; and neoliberalism, 51–55, 197; of social and environmental impacts, 41, 127; social production of, 43; "The ones who walk away from Omelas" as a critique of, 161; work of commensuration, 135. *See also* measurement and reporting; quantification

commensurative impulse, 43, 51, 126, 139, 145

corporate oxymoron, 25

corporate sustainability, 12–13, 21, 25, 27–28, 45–46, 54, 60, 170–172; and apocalypse, 187, 191–92; and corporate social responsibility (CSR), 65; and gender, 65–68; paradox of, 12, 33, 198; and political ecology, 12–13, 25, 38, 44, 165–67; research on, 50–51; as weak sustainability, 40, 66

creating shared value, 36, 60

cultural biography, 85

data, 6, 75, 121; data-driven sustainability, 24–26, 44, 75, 83, 101–3, 108–9, 196; dataism, 6; importance of high quality data, 122; and neoliberal sustainability, 77–78; and sustainable finance, 121–25, 133; and transparency/traceability, 108–9

data imperative, 133

degrowth, 147; as alternative, 24, 60

discount rates, 177–78

ecocide, 12, 27, 131, 179

ecological modernism, 40, 108

economics, 24, 36, 41, 77, 139, 177, 205n15

effective altruism, 115–16, 172–75

efficiency: as moral, economic, and political value, 127

emergent strategy, 200

emotional political ecology, 144, 153

end of the world, 23–26, 192, 195, 201; in neoliberal sustainability, 189

ABOUT THE AUTHOR

MATTHEW ARCHER is Assistant Professor of Sustainability in the Department of Environment and Geography at the University of York and coeditor of *Culture, Agriculture, Food and Environment*.

www.ingramcontent.com/pod-product-compliance
Lightning Source LLC
Chambersburg PA
CBHW020536030426
42337CB00013B/870